Prosody Intervention for
High-Functioning Adolescents and
Adults with Autism Spectrum Disorder

of related interest

Building Language Using LEGO® Bricks
A Practical Guide
Dawn Ralph and Jacqui Rochester
Foreword by Gina Gómez De La Cuesta
ISBN 978 1 78592 061 5
eISBN 978 1 78450 317 8

**Developmental Speech-Language Training through Music
for Children with Autism Spectrum Disorders**
Theory and Clinical Application
Hayoung A. Lim
ISBN 978 1 84905 849 0
eISBN 978 0 85700 415 4

Speech in Action
Interactive Activities Combining Speech Language
Pathology and Adaptive Physical Education
America X Gonzalez, Lois Jean Brady and Jim Elliott
ISBN 978 1 84905 846 9
eISBN 978 0 85700 500 7

**Developing Workplace Skills for Young Adults
with Autism Spectrum Disorder**
The BASICS College Curriculum
Michelle Rigler, Amy Rutherford and Emily Quinn
ISBN 978 1 84905 799 8
eISBN 978 1 78450 097 9
Part of the BASICS College Curriculum series

Helping Adults with Asperger's Syndrome Get & Stay Hired
Career Coaching Strategies for Professionals and
Parents of Adults on the Autism Spectrum
Barbara Bissonnette
ISBN 978 1 84905 754 7
eISBN 978 1 78450 052 8

Prosody Intervention for High-Functioning Adolescents and Adults with Autism Spectrum Disorder

Enhancing communication and social engagement through voice, rhythm, and pitch

———

Michelle Dunn and Larry Harris

———

Illustrations by Julia Dunn

———

Jessica Kingsley *Publishers*
London and Philadelphia

First published in 2017
by Jessica Kingsley Publishers
73 Collier Street
London N1 9BE, UK
and
400 Market Street, Suite 400
Philadelphia, PA 19106, USA

www.jkp.com

Library of Congress Cataloging in Publication Data
Names: Dunn, Michelle A., 1959- author. | Harris, Larry (Baritone), author.
Title: Prosody intervention for high-functioning adolescents and adults with
    autism spectrum disorder / Michelle Dunn and Larry Harris ; illustrations
    by Julia Dunn.
Description: London ; Philadelphia : Jessica Kingsley Publishers, [2017] |
    Includes bibliographical references and index.
Identifiers: LCCN 2016020543 | ISBN 9781785920226 (alk. paper)
Subjects: | MESH: Speech Disorders--therapy | Autism Spectrum
    Disorder--therapy | Speech Therapy--methods | Adolescent | Young Adult
Classification: LCC RC428.8 | NLM WM 475.3 | DDC 616.85/506-
-dc23 LC record available at https://lccn.loc.gov/2016020543

British Library Cataloguing in Publication Data
A CIP catalogue record for this book is available from the British Library

ISBN 978 1 78592 022 6
eISBN 978 1 78450 268 3

Printed and bound in Great Britain

For N.C.

Acknowledgement

The development of this curriculum was made possible by the generous support of the John H. and Ethel G. Noble Charitable Trust.

Contents

Introduction **13**
Prosody deficits in ASD 14
The association of prosody deficits with communication and
    socialization 16
Discussion: Implications for clinical practice 17
Chapter content 19
Structure of the lessons 24
Note 25

1. Assessment **26**
The future of prosody assessment 29
The screening instrument 29
Appendix: Qualitative Screening Assessment 31

2. Emotional and Behavioral Modulation **34**
Introduction: Finding calm 34
Lesson 1. Self-calming 36
Lesson 2. Having a calm baseline: Mindfulness of breathing and
    internal triggers 42
Lesson 3. Maintaining calm through mindfulness of emotions,
    thoughts, and behaviors 47
Lesson 4. The importance of being calm: Understanding the
    consequences for your thinking 54
Lesson 5. Communicating emotions and the need for help . . . 57

3. Voice: Creating a More Oral Timbre **63**
Introduction: The concept of the balanced mix 63
Lesson 1. Learning about timbre 68
Lesson 2. Oral timbre: Tongue position – vowels 1 77
Lesson 3. Oral timbre: Tongue position – vowels 2 83

Lesson 4. Oral timbre: Tongue position, vowels, consonants, and words. 89

Lesson 5. Oral timbre: Words and pre-formulated sentences . . 92

Lesson 6. Oral timbre: Consonants in spontaneous speech . . . 95

Lesson 7. Oral timbre: Consonants P, T, and K in consonant–vowel syllables and words 97

Lesson 8. Oral timbre: Consonants P, T, and K in pre-formulated sentences 100

Lesson 9. Oral timbre: Consonants P, T, and K in spontaneously formulated sentences 105

Lesson 10. Oral timbre: Consonants B, D, and G in consonant–vowel syllables and words 106

Lesson 11. Oral timbre: Consonants B, D, and G in pre-formulated sentences 109

Lesson 12. Oral timbre: Consonants B, D, and G in spontaneously formulated sentences 114

Lesson 13. Oral timbre: Consonants M and N in consonant–vowel syllables and words 115

Lesson 14. Oral timbre: Consonants M and N in pre-formulated sentences 118

Lesson 15. Oral timbre: Consonants M and N in spontaneously formulated sentences 122

Lesson 16. Oral timbre: Consonants J and ch in consonant–vowel syllables and words 123

Lesson 17. Oral timbre: Consonants J and ch in pre-formulated sentences 126

Lesson 18. Oral timbre: Consonants J and ch in spontaneously formulated sentences 131

Lesson 19. Oral timbre: Consonants W, L, and R in consonant–vowel syllables and words 132

Lesson 20. Oral timbre: Consonants W, L, and R in pre-formulated sentences 135

Lesson 21. Oral timbre: Consonants W, L, and R in spontaneously formulated sentences 140

Lesson 22. Oral timbre: Persistent problems 141

Lesson 23. Oral timbre: Connected speech 1 144

Lesson 24. Oral timbre: Connected speech 2 146

4. Voice: Volume **147**

Introduction: Increasing volume 147

Lesson 1. Nasal timbre: Introduction to discrimination, production, and anatomy 163

Lesson 2.   Nasal timbre: Tongue position for vowels   172

Lesson 3.   Nasal timbre: Tongue position – nasal and oral vowels   177

Lesson 4.   Nasal timbre: Tongue position for vowels, consonants, and words   183

Lesson 5.   Nasal timbre: Learning the sensations associated with directing airflow and sound through the nasal pharynx: "ah," "uh," and "awh"   185

Lesson 6.   Nasal timbre: Learning the sensations associated with directing airflow and sound through the nasal pharynx: "oh," "ow," and "ooh"   189

Lesson 7.   Breath support: Posture and expansion   194

Lesson 8.   Breath support: Optimal expansion and maintaining expansion.   198

Lesson 9.   Modulating breath release: Learning the relationship between the speed of airflow and volume.   204

Lesson 10.   Modulating breath release: Maintaining an expanded chest   207

Lesson 11.   Modulating breath release: Using the vocal cords as a valve   210

Lesson 12.   Modulating breath release: Regulating the volume of sustained sounds   213

Lesson 13.   Modulating release and increasing volume: Combining the Breath–Pause technique with nasal timbre   219

Lesson 14.   Regulating breath release: Mindfulness of sensations associated with Breath–Pause.   224

Lesson 15.   Modulating breath release: Learn the Breath–Pause notation to practice management of breath release . .   227

Lesson 16.   Modulating breath release: Using the Breath–Pause technique and arc phrasing to increase volume in spontaneous connected speech   233

Lesson 17.   Open passage: Releasing tension in the jaw.   236

Lesson 18.   Open passage: Releasing tension in the jaw and tongue   239

Lesson 19.   Putting it all together: Sound production with an open passage, in combination with nasal timbre and appropriate breath support 1   245

Lesson 20.   Putting it all together: Sound production with an open passage, in combination with nasal timbre and appropriate breath support 2   249

Lesson 21.   Modulation of volume: Adjusting to situation   253

5. Rhythm of Speech **258**

Introduction: Fluency and rate 258

Lesson 1.   Introducing the Breath–Pause technique for improving fluency and rate 264

Lesson 2.   Breath control associated with the Breath–Pause technique. 274

Lesson 3.   Using the Breath–Pause technique with spontaneous single words and pre-formulated connected speech . 276

Lesson 4.   How calming positively influences fluency and rate of speech 280

Lesson 5.   Staying calm and mindful to promote effective fluency through the Breath–Pause technique 282

Lesson 6.   Using the Breath–Pause technique with spontaneous questions and sentences. 284

Lesson 7.   Using the Breath–Pause technique to speak spontaneous sentences fluently and at an appropriate rate 286

Lesson 8.   Shadow Vowel technique: Addressing misarticulation produced by muscle tension resulting from overly rapid speech or anxiety/overexcitement 289

Lesson 9.   Rules for answering others' questions about you . . . 293

Lesson 10. Graphic Organizer: Formulating a description of a person 297

Lesson 11. Graphic Organizer: Using a book, periodical, or article 302

Lesson 12. Sequential Graphic Organizer: Giving step-by-step instructions 1. 307

Lesson 13. Sequential Graphic Organizer: Giving step-by-step instructions 2. 310

Lesson 14. Web Graphic Organizer: My best day ever 313

Lesson 15. Web Graphic Organizer: Description of a vacation . . 316

Lesson 16. Plot Contour Graphic Organizer: Telling a good story 319

Lesson 17. Web Graphic Organizer: Recounting what I learned from an article 322

Lesson 18. Web Graphic Organizer: Recounting a fable and its significance. 326

Lesson 19. Learning to play the Conversation Game to develop fluency in conversation 330

Lesson 20. Achieving fluency in spontaneously generated small talk 333

Lesson 21. Using small talk to get to know someone. 337

Lesson 22. Learning the red card technique to monitor use of the Rules for Fluency. 341

Lesson 23. Fluently relating information and making a point about something you learned 343

Lesson 24. Applying the Rules for Fluency to spontaneous conversation 351

6. Pitch 353

Introduction: Pitch modulation to convey meaning. 353

Lesson 1. Assessment/learning pitch modulation 355

Lesson 2. Pitch modulation: Tones 359

Lesson 3. Pitch stress and word meaning 363

Lesson 4. Pitch stress in sentences 365

Lesson 5. Pitch stress in poetry 1 369

Lesson 6. Pitch stress in poetry 2 372

Lesson 7. Pitch stress in narrative 374

Lesson 8. Pitch stress in written text 377

Lesson 9. Applying pitch notation to spontaneous speech. . . . 379

Lesson 10. Talking about a topic using pitch inflection. 380

7. Stress 383

Introduction: Using stress to convey meaning 383

Lesson 1. Introduction to stress in spoken language 386

Lesson 2. Grammatical stress in single words 389

Lesson 3. Stressing words in sentences 392

Lesson 4. Stressing words in sentences with a louder volume, using volume stress notation 401

Lesson 5. Stressing words in sentences with a change in pitch . 407

Lesson 6. Stressing words in sentences with a change in rhythm, specifically an increase in duration 414

Lesson 7. Stressing words in poetry to inform and share feelings 420

Lesson 8. Stress notation on a famous speech to inform and share feelings 422

Lesson 9. Telling a story from memory, applying all types of stress: Volume, pitch, rhythm (duration). 425

Lesson 10. Telling a personal experience story, placing stress on important words 428

Lesson 11. Talking about a topic, using appropriate stress 432

Lesson 12. Planned discussion of a topic from memory, using all stress forms to inform and share feelings 435

Lesson 13. PowerPoint presentation to inform: Part 1 – Deciding what to include 436

Lesson 14. PowerPoint presentation to inform:
Part 2 – Deciding which words to stress   439

Lesson 15. Spontaneous speech in conversation, employing word
stress to inform and share feelings   441

Conclusion **442**

References **445**

Subject Index **449**

Author Index **455**

Introduction

Prosody is the music of speech. It is the nonverbal aspect of oral communication, which occurs through the modulation of loudness, pitch, and rhythm (including duration, pausing, and tempo). It is necessary for conveying emotion and meaning, through stress on what is important, and through resolution of ambiguity in words and sentences (Diehl *et al.* 2008). It provides signals in discourse which regulate conversational interaction.

Prosody deficits are well documented in people with Autism Spectrum Disorder (ASD) (Provonost, Wakstein, and Wakstein 1966; Fay and Schuler 1980; Tager-Flusberg 1981; Scott 1985; Baltaxe and Simmons 1992; Ghaziuddin and Gerstein 1996; Shriberg *et al.* 2001; Tager-Flusberg 2001; McPartland and Klin 2006; Peppé *et al.* 2007). One in 68 individuals is diagnosed with an ASD (CDC 2014) based on core deficits in social communication and rigid repetitive behaviors (American Psychiatric Association 2013). It is estimated that between 47 percent and 57 percent of high-functioning adolescents with ASD have impaired prosody (Simmons and Baltaxe 1975; Shriberg *et al.* 2001). Deficits in prosody tend to persist even when other aspects of communication improve (Kanner 1971; McCann *et al.* 2007). Prosodic deficits in individuals with ASD are thought to be among the greatest detriments to integration into society, because they profoundly affect social communication (Mesibov 1992) and produce a first impression of oddness (Van Bourgondien and Woods 1992). Specifically, these deficits can prohibit individuals from developing social relationships or from gaining employment. These deficits are also among the most resistant to intervention.

There are many aspects to prosody. The four main categories are: **timbre**, **volume**, **pitch**, and **rhythm**. **Timbre** involves both voice quality and resonance. Voice quality is influenced by the manipulation (voluntary or involuntary) of the larynx and can be influenced by the positioning of the surrounding muscle tissue. Resonance is a quality of sound produced by the shape of the vocal tract (e.g., nasal or oral). **Volume** or loudness is the intensity of the sound, measured in decibels. The **pitch** of an utterance is its highness or lowness, measured by frequency. *Intonation* is pitch contour, used to express meaning (e.g., statement, question). **Rhythm** involves rate, stress, and phrasing. The flow and fluency of spoken utterances are directly affected by the rate or speed of those utterances. Stress involves emphasis on syllables and words for the purpose of conveying a specific meaning and emotion. Stress in language is produced by increasing the volume, pitch, or length of a sound. Phrasing describes the way speech flows, pauses, and ends, and it helps to direct the listener's focus and comprehension. Prosody not only involves the voice but the body as well. Expressive and receptive nonverbal prosody include: gesturing, body posture, eye movement, and facial expression (in both static and transient situations). Prosody communicates important aspects of meaning and intention, including word form, sentence type, and emotion. Through appropriate timbre, volume, pitch, rhythm, and gesture, concepts are communicated effectively and efficiently.

Understanding and addressing the prosody deficits in high-functioning individuals with ASD is necessary in helping these intelligent individuals so that they may have productive adult lives. Atypical prosody can compromise meaning, distract the listener, and cause the listener to become disconnected from the speaker, thus producing further social isolation for the speaker.

Prosody deficits in ASD

What are the specific deficits in prosody observed in high-functioning adolescents and young adults with ASD? How powerfully do they predict social and communication impairment? What efforts have been made to remediate them?

A number of investigators identify specific prosody deficits in individuals with ASD. Wiklund (2016) observed that prosodic features, such as large pitch excursions, stretched syllables, dysfluent rhythm, low volume, and creaky voice quality, in young adolescents with ASD, disrupt comprehension and reciprocal communication. In a group of high-functioning (average IQ) young adults with ASD, Shriberg *et al.* (2001) assessed a range of aspects of prosody including: phrasing, rate, stress, loudness, pitch, voice quality, and resonance. They found significant impairment in phrasing, stress, and resonance. The subjects in their study demonstrated hyper-nasal timbre, connected speech that was dysfluent, and a failure to appropriately stress the focus words in sentences. Individuals with ASD have difficulty imitating stress even on nonsense syllables (Paul *et al.* 2008) and prosodic pattern (Diehl and Paul 2012), suggesting issues with perception and/or motoric production of stress.

Paul, Augustyn *et al.* (2005) examined perception and production of grammatical and pragmatic/affective stress, intonation, and phrasing in people with ASD, ages 14 to 21. Grammatical stress conveys syntactic information in sentences (Warren 1996) and is the term used to describe how emphasis on one syllable or another, within a particular word, determines whether that word is a noun or a verb (e.g., **re**cord *versus* re**cord**). The emphasis placed on a particular word within a sentence is called *pragmatic stress*. Pragmatic stress placed on a different word in the exact same sentence changes the intent of the sentence (e.g., I want **chocolate** ice cream *versus* I want chocolate **ice cream**) (Bates and MacWhinney 1979). Grammatical intonation signifies whether a sentence is a statement or a question through pitch inflection. *Pragmatic intonation* is the term used to describe the change in pitch when speaking to different listeners (e.g., speaking to an adult versus a child). Grammatical phrasing involves pauses in sentences, which determine meaning (e.g., Ellen, the dentist, is here *versus* Ellen, the dentist is here) (Gerken and McGregor 1998). Pragmatic phrasing involves a change in rate (faster) within a sentence to express affect (e.g., excitement, anxiety). Unfortunately, Paul, Augustyn *et al.*'s (2005) findings revealed ceiling effects for some of their measures of prosody, indicating that the tests were too easy for the subjects. However, these investigators did find abnormalities in perception and production of grammatical stress and perception and production of pragmatic/affective stress. These findings are inconsistent with those of Paul, Shriberg *et al.* (2005) in that the two studies were discrepant with regard to whether phrasing is impaired in individuals with ASD.

What are possible reasons for the discrepancies? In the prosody literature to date there are many reasons for discrepancies in the findings. These are methodological differences, including age of the sample studied, limited sample size, lack of normative data and other contrast groups, poor definition of the various aspects of prosody, and much of the data being subjective rather than objective (Paul, Augustyn *et al.* 2005). In the studies by Paul, Shriberg *et al.* (2005) and Paul, Augustyn *et al.* (2005), subjects included similar groups of individuals with ASD, who had normal range verbal and nonverbal IQ scores, similar language scores, and similar Vineland Communication and Socialization scores. However, individuals in the Paul, Shriberg *et al.* (2005) study were older, with an average age of 21.15, whereas subjects in Paul, Augustyn *et al.* (2005) had an average age of 16.8. While this is one possible reason for the discrepancy in findings regarding phrasing/fluency between the studies, a more likely explanation is the difference in the way prosody was assessed. In Paul, Shriberg *et al.* (2005), prosody was assessed with the Prosody Voice Screening Profile (PVSP) (Shriberg, Kwiatkowski, and Rasmussen 1990), in which a spontaneous, conversational language sample is collected and scored. In the Paul, Augustyn *et al.* (2005) study, subjects were seen individually for a direct test of prosody. Subjects were trained, where the examiner gave a typical item and told the subject the correct response and then allowed the subject to try a test item. If the subject responded incorrectly, the examiner corrected the subject and explained why the response was incorrect. There was reinforcement by praise for correct answers. So in comparing these studies it is not surprising that the individuals with ASD demonstrated more deficits in spontaneous conversation than on direct testing where correct responses are modeled. Spontaneous dialogue is more difficult for the individual with ASD, due to language formulation issues. When using the PVSP to assess prosody, conversation was never corrected or prompted. Therefore, the PVSP likely gave a truer (more ecologically valid) assessment of prosody dysfunction.

The association of prosody deficits with communication and socialization

There are data demonstrating that prosody deficits in individuals with ASD are significantly associated with ratings of overall communication, socialization, and independent living skills.

McCann *et al.* (2007) showed an association between expressive and receptive language and prosody. Paul, Shriberg *et al.* (2005) examined the relationship between prosodic deficits in phrasing, stress, and resonance, and ratings of socialization and communication, in high-functioning adolescents and adults with ASD. They found significant correlations between resonance and Vineland Socialization score (Sparrow, Balla, and Cicchetti 1984) and between both stress and resonance and the communication score on the Autism Diagnostic Observational Scale – G (ADOS-G) (Lord *et al.* 2000). The correlation between resonance and Vineland Socialization indicates that when an individual possesses a significantly better vocal resonance, he is judged as having better socialization. The correlations between stress and resonance and communication score on the ADOS-G indicate that when an individual possesses a significantly better vocal resonance and uses stress appropriately, he is judged as having better communication. It is important to note that verbal IQ was not correlated with any of the prosody ratings in this study.

Some researchers have noted a relationship between language level and prosodic use of pitch and duration by adults with ASD. Relative to typical controls, those with higher language ability had greater pitch excursions and weaker ability to emphasize new information in a conversation relative to information that was already given, while those with moderate language impairment used a smaller pitch range and did differentially mark information (DePape *et al.* 2012). Shriberg and Widder (1990) demonstrated an association between prosody and level of independent living in adults with mental deficiency.

Discussion: Implications for clinical practice

In sum, a number of abnormalities in prosody have been identified in the research literature. The most consistently reported of these are nasal timbre and atypical rhythm – specifically, dysfluency and failure to use appropriate grammatical and pragmatic stress. Strong associations are documented between prosody impairment and social and communication impairment, making prosody an important target for intervention. Yet, there are very few intervention programs available.

Prosody intervention

There has been little progress with the development of intervention for prosody deficits in individuals with ASD. The fact that we know little about the sequence of prosody development makes this particularly difficult (Diehl and Paul 2009). However, since prosody deficits present a serious roadblock to a productive adult life for high-functioning people with autism, the field cannot wait for this information before attempting to develop intervention methods. Most recently Rothstein (2013) published his *Prosody Treatment Program*, which appears to be comprehensive. It seeks to develop receptive and expressive prosody in children (including those with ASD) ages 3 through 17. The program addresses loudness, pitch, rhythm, stress, intelligibility, vocal tone, respiration, and phonation. It teaches about intonation contour for statements, questions, commands, and sarcasm, as well as rate and chunking. The author indicates that his intervention uses dynamic temporal and tactile cuing (DTTC) (Strand, Stoeckel, and Baas 2006) as a basis for many of the activities. In this approach, visual, tactile, and gestural cues are used in combination with modeling speech to promote appropriate prosody. This is a method that was developed for children with apraxia; however, it is unclear if this is an appropriate theoretical foundation for treating children with ASD. The biggest problem is that the effectiveness of prosody intervention methods for individuals with ASD has not been established through research.

Our approach

Based on our review of the prosody and neuropsychology literature in ASD and our clinical and professional experiences, we have developed an intervention model and methods. The neuropsychological profile of the majority of individuals with ASD indicates relative strengths in concrete, visual processing and rote memory. Weaknesses are found in auditory processing (Dunn *et al.* 1999; Rapin and Dunn 2003; Dunn, Gomes, and Gravel 2008) and in the understanding of abstract material, as well as in organization and planning (Minshew, Johnson, and Luna 2001). It is generally easier for people with ASD to memorize rules than to extract concepts. Therefore, our approach is rule-based and takes advantage of visual strengths, in that it employs a great deal of visual cuing. Our technique also provides a systematic physical approach to prosody intervention for those with ASD. The rules teach awareness and use of physical sensations associated with breath support, stopping and initiating airflow for phonation, shaping of the vocal tract, and the process of moving air through resonators within the vocal tract. The rules also teach motor sequencing for the muscle groups involved in vocal production. The efficacy of this method has been tested, with positive results seen in as little as five months (Dunn and Harris, in preparation).

Chapter content
Chapter 1: Assessment

The first step in treating prosody impairment is to identify the specific atypical aspects of prosody in any individual. While impaired timbre, fluency, and pragmatic stress are the aspects most often impaired according to the research literature, there can also be issues with volume (too loud or too quiet), pitch, rhythm (rate, duration, pauses), and nonverbal prosody that interfere with effective communication. Clearly, prosody can be impacted in a variety of ways. Careful assessment is instrumental in designing and applying the appropriate prosodic intervention technique for the individual student. The degree of prosodic disruption may vary in its intensity. Interference with communication by one's prosodic challenges may be determined based on evaluation by a speech/language pathologist, vocal pathologist, teacher, psychologist, or other involved/trained professional. Chapter 1 addresses assessment and provides a qualitative assessment tool for determining which aspects of prosody are affected. The rest of this book is divided into chapters of lessons addressing each type of prosodic deficit. After specific deficits in prosody are identified, the clinician administers lessons from the appropriate chapters in the sequence provided. For example, if a child has a hyper-nasal voice and is dysfluent, then lessons from Chapters 3 and 5 would be used. They can be combined in any way that seems to make sense, at the clinician's discretion.

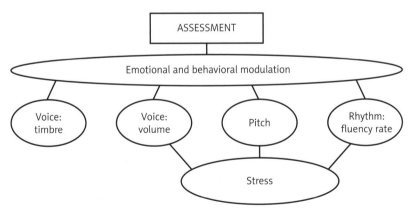

Figure I.1 Organization of the curriculum

Chapter 2: Emotional and Behavioral Modulation

In combination with the lessons from any chapter, it is essential that each student receives all five lessons in the Emotional and Behavioral Modulation chapter. In order for any person to (1) learn and use new rules/strategies (including for effective expression), (2) engage in interaction with others (initiate, monitor, respond), or (3) cope in an effective way, he must first be able to stop an inappropriate behavior or calm an emotional reaction. He must then learn to replace ineffective behaviors with more effective ones. Modulation is of particular importance for developing appropriate prosody, because the quality of prosody depends on the state of one's body. Emotional stress produces physical tension in areas of the upper body and head (chest, neck, jaw, throat, tongue, lips) and affects respiration. Muscular tightness will restrict the flow of air. Irregular fluency patterns, which involve abnormal rhythm and rate, are exacerbated by this same physical tension and by emotional anxiety. Physical tension and anxiety also increase the likelihood of abnormal pitch inflection and volume. This reduces the speaker's ability to effectively communicate his message. The listener will, perhaps, be confused and unable to follow the speaker's intellectual focus. Anxiety will also reduce the ability to monitor the prosodic cues of a conversational partner. A person can only monitor himself and others if he is settled. It is also less distracting for a conversational partner if the speaker appears to be calm. In sum, the ability to modulate emotion and behavior is essential for developing appropriate prosody, because: (1) a calm state allows the musculature involved in vocal production to be relaxed enough to produce appropriate timbre, volume, and pitch; and (2) in addition to calm, the attentional focus gained through effective modulation allows for greater comprehension, resulting in successful implementation of the strategies taught in the lessons.

Chapter 3: Voice: Creating a More Oral Timbre

Timbre is the color or tone quality of the sound of the voice, which is independent of pitch or loudness/volume. Timbre can be described by such contrasting terms as bright or dark, and warm or harsh. We describe the extremes of timbre as either nasal or oral. It is relatively common for individuals on the spectrum to have a hyper-nasal vocal timbre. This tone quality is harsh, too bright, overly resonant, and abrasive. Atypical timbre comes across as odd but actually does not affect the content of the message. So, why work on making timbre more typical? By identifying the atypical qualities of timbre, and then teaching techniques to correct them, the speaker can become a more effective communicator. The technique eliminates many distracting atypical colors or tones for the listener. A speaker's ideas are attended to and taken more seriously if he has a more typical balanced timbre. Improved timbre is also associated with improved confidence.

In Chapter 3, the student learns about the anatomy involved in various aspects of the vocal production of timbre and how it functions, as well as about the flow of air and sound. The flow of one's tone through the nasal pharynx creates a more nasal timbre, because more of the nasal resonators are involved in the manufacturing of this particular tone. When the flow of air and tone is primarily through the oral pharynx, a more oral timbre is created. The position of the velum (soft palate), as well as the uvula and the tongue, directs the flow of air and sound.

As part of this curriculum there are exercises designed for the manipulation of the velum, tongue, and fleshy tissue which encase the entire pharyngeal cavity (the filter), all of which are key in directing the flow of air and sound and in producing resonance. The lessons are instrumental in helping the student shape acoustic surfaces, throughout the vocal tract, to assist with developing a projected sound which is less nasal. For example, if an individual has too nasal a timbre, he is taught to relax the tongue and rest its tip (in neutral position) behind the lower row of front teeth. He is taught to relax his lips and maintain a vertical position of his mouth as he speaks. The person is also taught to raise the velum (soft palate) by forming his natural position for a yawn, which, in turn, produces an acoustically useful tighter/smoother tissue, using the back walls of the mouth. During the execution of the yawn position, the epiglottis naturally extends, to a position out and over the windpipe, partially covering it, thereby directing the flow of air for resonance. The aim in focusing on developing a more oral sound in a student with a hyper-nasal voice is to help the student move towards a more balanced mix between oral and nasal resonances.

Chapter 4: Voice: Volume

Learning to speak with an appropriate volume is necessary for effective communication. Some individuals on the autism spectrum fail to understand the appropriate volume for various situations. Some speak loudly all the time or have trouble modulating their loudness. This is most often associated with a nasal timbre and emotional dysregulation, and can be addressed by remediating those issues.

Some individuals on the spectrum have difficulty actually producing a sufficiently loud sound. People need to hear you no matter the situation, no matter the ambient sound. It can even be dangerous to go unheard. In addition, adequate volume is necessary to communicate emotion, to be more emphatic, to express importance, or to demonstrate concern.

Through the lessons in Chapter 4 students learn breathing technique, how to modulate timbre to project the voice, and why and when it is important to control the loudness of their voice based on location, proximity to a conversational partner, and the nature of the conversation (e.g., public versus private; the need to be assertive).

Chapter 5: Rhythm of Speech

Individuals with ASD frequently show abnormalities in the rhythm of speech. Phrasing is often abnormal. They may make errors with regard to grammatical phrasing (e.g., The panda eats, shoots, and leaves *versus* The panda eats shoots and leaves). For some with ASD, speech is highly dysfluent and faltering (marked by false starts and hesitations). These individuals have an impaired ability to formulate ideas into words, sentences, and paragraphs. For others with ASD, the rate of speech is very fast, without breaks. Pragmatic phrasing (expression of affect) can be disrupted because rate of speech does not vary. In either case there is a failure by the individual to breathe, pause, and think prior to speaking, at the ends of sentences, and at clause boundaries. The dysfluent individual does not give himself time to formulate his thoughts before he speaks. This produces a significant impediment to communication. In addition, any person who does not pause during oral expression does not allow the listener enough time to consolidate the meaning of what he has heard.

Through the lessons in Chapter 5, the individual learns the Breath–Pause technique. The Breath–Pause technique involves a conscious pause in the flow of air and sound before the speaker's next vocal onset (where his next utterance will begin). In this technique the student is taught the physical sensation for breathing in and then immediately stopping the flow of air out by closing the vocal cords, as well as the rules for when to do so. Students learn to recognize units of meaning in language (chunking according to sentence and clause boundaries). This serves to introduce rhythmic patterns into spoken language, making speech more fluent and easier for a listener to process. The Breath–Pause technique gives a speaker adequate time to formulate his ideas into words. Developing rhythm develops fluency. The technique is just this: (1) show the student how to close the vocal cords after breathing in, immediately stopping and holding his breath, as he applies a small amount of pressure from the air in the lungs (the feeling is as if you are lifting something heavy, like the chair you are sitting in); (2) a very small amount of this air pressure is released as speech begins. In addition to the Breath–Pause technique, in Chapter 5 the student is taught to use Graphic Organizers to assist in organizing complex ideas prior to expressing them, and thereby improve the fluency of connected speech.

Chapter 6: Pitch

Pitch is the highness or lowness of a sound. If one speaks using a pitch which is consistently too high or low, "sing-song," or monotone, it distracts from the message. Modulation of pitch is necessary to produce intonation/melodic contours that signify, at the simplest level, whether an utterance is a statement or a question. Higher pitch is often used for emphasis (stress). Pragmatic intonation involves using a higher overall pitch when talking to a child than to an adult and functions such as marking who has the floor in a conversation. The lessons in Chapter 6 teach students to identify and produce a range of pitches. Students learn to modulate pitch to signify a question, a comment, or a command. They learn how pitch gives listeners clues about a speaker's emotions and how changes in pitch are used to stress important words in connected speech and convey meaning.

Chapter 7: Stress

Stress, in spoken language, is the emphasis placed on certain syllables in words or words in sentences. Stress is conveyed by volume, pitch, and rhythm (duration). Stress conveys meaning and emotion and engages the listener. Individuals with ASD have demonstrated deficits in comprehension and production of both grammatical stress and pragmatic stress. Individuals with ASD may fail to stress syllables/words, may use stress inappropriately (McCann and Peppé 2003; Peppé *et al.* 2006), or may overuse stress (Shriberg *et al.* 2001). In Chapter 7, the student learns about specific meanings communicated by different patterns of stress in single words and sentences. He is taught to make decisions about which words to stress in presentations and conversation.

Structure of the lessons

Each lesson in this book begins with a description of the goal of the lesson and specific materials needed. Next, a detailed description of the steps for teaching each prosody skill are included, along with a homework assignment to reinforce each skill between lessons. All prescribed handouts/visual cuing materials are provided as well.

Hierarchy of language presentation within lessons

Within each set of lessons, in each of Chapters 2 through 7, techniques are taught by presenting non-speech and speech stimuli in the following specific sequence (Table I.1):

- *Level 1:* The work begins by teaching basic techniques for correcting timbre, volume, rhythm, and pitch, at the single sound and single word level, first by reading written sounds and words and then by repeating them after they are said by the therapist. The student then formulates single words in response to prompts and applies the techniques to those words as he does this.

- *Level 2:* As the student's proficiency improves, he applies the techniques to phrases and sentences. Again, first in reading written text out loud, then by repeating after the therapist, and then by giving spoken answers to questions. Therefore, in addition to working on the voice, the client is working on developing spontaneous fluency, beginning at the level of single phrases and sentences.

- *Level 3:* The student then applies the techniques to reading lengthy text. This allows the student to practice the learned techniques without having to simultaneously formulate extensive connected speech. We start with pre-formulated text so that the student is not required to multitask, so that he can concentrate on the correct application of techniques. The therapist continues to model the use of the techniques in his own speech, but there is no demand for repetition by the student.

- *Level 4:* At Level 4 the student applies learned techniques to his spontaneous, self-generated language to relate information, express emotion, tell a story, give a presentation, or engage in conversation.

It is preferable to progress as quickly as possible, from single words to the paragraph level, so that the student is able to take on connected speech, and thus use his improved prosody, to convey and express intention and meaning more effectively in his spontaneous speech. Note that repetition and practice are built into the lessons, through homework practice and sometimes within the lessons themselves. This is because it is not enough for the student to learn and know the concepts. The motor patterns must become automatic. This can only be accomplished through repetitive practice.

Table I.1 Hierarchy of difficulty for activities within each chapter of lessons

		Scripted		Spontaneous formulation
		Written	*Oral*	
1	Single sound Single word	X	X	X
2	Phrases and sentences	X	X	X
3	Paragraphs	X	_____	X
4	Conversation	X	_____	X

Note

Throughout the book the pronoun "he" is used in preference to "he or she" or "s/he." In all cases both genders are considered to be included equally.

CHAPTER 1

Assessment

Although prosody has great importance for everyday communication, there are very few assessment tools available and little is known about its typical course of development. Therefore, our ability to diagnose and accurately characterize prosodic disorders for remedial purposes is limited. Yet a high proportion of individuals on the autism spectrum have impairments in prosody, which significantly and negatively impacts their opportunities for employment or social success. Though the predominant expressive deficits appear to be in resonance, stress, and phrasing, many other prosodic issues have been identified in people with ASD. These include large pitch excursions, monotone speech, stretched syllables, dropped syllables, rapid rate, dysfluent rhythm, low volume, and creaky voice. When communication or social acceptance is compromised by unusual vocal quality and/or impairments in the use of volume, pitch, or rhythm, it is clear that the individual has a prosody impairment and is in need of intervention.

In order to determine where to intervene, we must characterize the specific constellation of prosodic impairment. The very few standardized assessment instruments which exist for people of this age are described in this chapter. They are either limited in scope or are cumbersome, requiring too much time to realistically administer as part of a clinical communication assessment. Therefore, we provide a brief screening instrument to assess the quality of specific impairments in prosody. This instrument is not intended to assess degree of impairment but rather alert the clinician to prosody issues. Awareness of the specific issues in the areas of laryngeal quality and resonance (nasality and loudness), pitch, rhythm (rate, fluency, phrasing), and stress is necessary in determining which intervention techniques are indicated. Rating your student on this scale will allow you to determine which chapters of lessons in this book are appropriate for your student. More specific, detailed baseline and outcome assessments are embedded in each chapter of lessons.

There are few formal tests of prosody available, and standardization is limited. While most language tests have stratified, normative samples in the thousands, tests of prosody have standardization samples ranging from less than 100 to, at most, 800. There are not different forms or test items for different ages. Each test assesses different aspects of prosody in a very different way. Some tests model the correct responses while others involve scoring spontaneous language samples.

Kalathottukaren, Purdy, and Ballard (2015) did a thorough review and identified nine tests of prosody. If one eliminates tests with normative samples of less than 100 or those that are not representative of the age range for whom this curriculum is intended, four tests remain. Two of these assess multiple aspects of prosody and two assess affective prosody only. Of the two that assess multiple aspects, only one covers both children and adults.

The two tests that assess multiple aspects of prosody are the Profiling Elements of Prosodic Systems – Children (PEPS-C) (Peppé and McCann 2003) and the Prosody Voice Screening Profile (PVSP) (Shriberg *et al.* 1990). These are the most well-known and widely used assessments, primarily for research purposes.

The PVSP assesses prosody production and is the most ecologically valid of the assessments. For the PVSP, there are 200 language samples from typically developing individuals, used as a comparison sample, to establish a cut-off for what is considered typical versus atypical. The PVSP is said to be appropriate for ages 3 to 81, though the comparison sample includes people only between the ages of 3 and 19. To administer the PVSP one collects a spontaneous language sample, which is transcribed and scored by hand, in order to assess prosody and vocal characteristics, including vocal quality, loudness, pitch, rate, phrasing, and stress.

The PEPS-C represents the best effort to date to formally assess prosody in a standardized way. It assesses children ages 5 to 14 and has a normative comparison group of 120 children and young adolescents. It takes about an hour to administer. This test assesses both comprehension and expression in a number of subcategories of prosody, including affect, chunking, turn-end type, focus, and intonation and prosody. "Intonation and prosody" assessment involves pitch/melody discrimination and imitation. The other four categories (affect, chunking, turn-end type, and focus) measure comprehension and production of meaning through prosody. This test does not assess stress. There is no cumbersome transcription and scoring of a spontaneous language sample required in administering the PEPS-C and it is far easier to administer than the PVSP.

However, the PEPS-C is not as ecologically valid as the PVSP. The PEPS-C may underestimate the degree of impairment in that it has a forced choice format, where the individual being evaluated chooses between two alternatives. It also provides corrective feedback. This is in an effort to make certain the person being tested understands the task, but it brings up the question of whether the test is assessing the ability to meet the demands of the test, or the actual skill in the areas being assessed. This is certainly a problem for any test which attempts to assess a spontaneous behavior (e.g., social interaction, conversation, ability to generate a narrative) in a contrived setting. In the real world, one's attention is not specifically drawn to prosody. Since we know so little, as a field, about the development of prosody, the PEPS-C does not have different items for different ages. In the PEPS-C, adolescents receive the same items as children. This produces ceiling and floor effects.

Of the two tests which assess affective prosody and which have adequate norms, the Social Cognition portion of the Advanced Clinical Solutions (ACS) (Pearson 2009) assesses the widest range of aspects of affective prosody and has the most comprehensive norms. The emotions expressed through prosody which are evaluated include happiness, sadness, anger, surprise, fear, disgust, sarcasm, and neutrality. These are assessed through Prosody-Face matching and Prosody-Pair matching. The normative sample for this test is 800 individuals, ages 16 to 90.11, who have no history of medical, developmental, neurologic, or psychiatric impairment. The sample mirrors the ethnic and educational representation in the 2005 United States census. The test has strong reliability with regard to internal consistency for the prosody subtests (alpha of 0.64 to 0.85). The entire test takes 30 to 40 minutes to administer. The great weakness of this test is that it only assesses receptive abilities and does not look at expressive affective prosody.

The other test with reasonable norms is the Florida Affect Battery (FAB) (Bowers, Blonder, and Heilman 1999). It seems to do a good job of assessing understanding of affective prosody (happiness, sadness, anger, fear, neutrality) in individuals aged 18 to 84, through prosody discrimination, affect naming, and matching emotional faces with affective prosody. Again, this test does not assess expressive affective prosody.

The future of prosody assessment

There is certainly a need for the development of new and improved assessments of prosody. Of course, we need instruments that are comprehensive yet reasonable to administer in a clinical setting. They must capture the behavior in a way that has ecological validity, in that they assess prosody in real-life situations (and not in a way where the individual's attention is drawn to the target behavior being assessed, or where the individual is taught how to respond to the test items). The test must be normed on a large, representative sample, stratified for age, and have strong psychometric properties.

The most difficult aspect of developing a test of prosody has to do with how prosody is conceptualized in general and in specific populations. Our models are limited by lack of data: there is little empirical evidence concerning the typical development of prosody and what prosodic abilities a person should possess at any given age. We have little information based on development or neurologic underpinnings to guide classification of the subtypes of prosody. We only have information about how prosody breaks down to rely on for that.

Building a more complete model of prosody will be an iterative process. It will require behavioral and neurophysiologic research and empirical evaluation of the efficacy of attempts made to remediate prosody deficits. Response to therapy can be instructive about what is going wrong.

The screening instrument

In sum, there are very few standardized instruments available to assess prosody in individuals with developmental disabilities. The instruments that are available are either limited in scope or generally too labor-intensive to easily employ in clinical settings. It is assumed that you are reading this book because you know someone whom you have already identified as having deficient prosody. It is also likely that these prosody deficits are having a significant impact on that person's ability to communicate effectively and on the social impression he makes as well as his interaction with others. The goal of your initial evaluation, then, is to identify the specific aspects of prosody which are impaired and compromise the individual's communication. As stated in the introduction to this book, not all lessons are appropriate for all individuals with prosody impairment. The lessons chosen must be tailored to the individual's pattern of weaknesses. You know your student has deficient prosody; what remains is to characterize the quality of his deficits. To that end we provide a checklist below, as an Appendix to this chapter.

To use the checklist, record a language sample from your student. This sample should include him relating a narrative and engaging in conversation. The checklist will allow you to characterize the language sample you record with respect to vocal quality (nasality and loudness), pitch, rhythm (rate, fluency, phrasing), and stress. The screening provided qualitatively assesses impairment in expressive prosody. Much of this curriculum focuses on developing expressive prosody. Comprehension of timbre, volume, and meaning produced by phrasing and pitch variation are monitored and addressed as they arise. Comprehension of meaning produced by stress is directly addressed. In the Stress chapter (Chapter 7), there is an emphasis on understanding how meaning changes given changes in stress. For example, the student is required to articulate the different meanings or senses of meaning of a sentence based on a change in the words that are stressed. While the screening instrument assesses for impairment in expressive prosody, more detailed and specific baseline and outcome assessments contained in each chapter evaluate comprehension as well.

Once you have identified the specific areas of prosodic deficit, you will know which chapters of lessons to implement with your student. You will begin intervention with the five lessons in the Emotional and Behavioral Modulation chapter (Chapter 2). This is necessary because stress interferes significantly with the ability to use the strategies presented. Stress disrupts cognitive processing, which impacts comprehension of language and formulation, and creates tension in the body that can interfere with timbre and volume. Once the student has learned strategies for self-calming, you will move on to the lessons from the chapters which directly address your student's deficits. Reminders to employ self-calming strategies should be interspersed throughout lessons as needed. If a student needs work in more than one chapter, you may alternate delivery of lessons from each. For example, your student may have a hyper-nasal voice and be dysfluent. It is likely that you will hear that he also has difficulty appropriately stressing important words in connected speech. For that student, after you have completed the Emotional and Behavioral Modulation lessons, you would then go on to a combination of lessons from the Voice: Creating a More Oral Timbre chapter (Chapter 3) and the Rhythm of Speech chapter (Chapter 5). Once those are completed you would move on to the Stress chapter (Chapter 7).

Appendix: Qualitative Screening Assessment

Aspect of prosody	Impairment observed in expression	Check items which apply
Vocal quality (laryngeal quality and resonance)		
Nasality	Displays excessively nasal quality	
	Speaks too loudly most of the time	
	Voice has an abrasive quality	
	Unable to decrease volume of voice for specific environments, surroundings	
	Difficulty whispering	
Loudness	Displays almost inaudible quality (very low volume)	
	Speaks too quietly all of the time	
	Has a breathy voice	
	Has a creaky, low quality voice	
	Vocal quality is excessively throaty	
	Unable to produce clear, pure, unobstructed tone	
	Mouth and tongue are tense	
	Muscles involved in breathing are tight	
	Tightly holds back projection of any tone	
	Difficulty projecting voice over a distance	
	Unable to increase volume of voice for specific environments, surroundings	
	Does not match volume level to that of others in the social situation	

Rhythm (rate, fluency, phrasing)	Speaks too quickly	
	Produces unintelligible words, due to eliding	
	Mispronunciation/slurring of speech sounds	
	Deletes non-stressed syllables in longer words (e.g., "ferchly" for "fortunately")	
	Chunks words with little attention to ends of sentences or clause boundaries or does not chunk them at all	
	Runs together phrases and sentences without beginnings or endings	
	Pauses in the wrong places in sentences	
	Pauses are too short	
	Sounds jerky	
	Words and sentences are cut off mid-utterance	
	Phrases are restarted or repeated	
	Repeated syllables	
	Excessive hesitations (e.g., um, uh)	
	Excessive revisions (qualifiers)	

Pitch	Unable to regulate and control pitch – produce higher and lower sounds	
	Overall pitch is too high	
	Overall pitch is too low	
	Speech is largely monotone	
	Speech has a large range ("sing-song")	
	Pitch is not adjusted based on audience (e.g., higher for little children than for adults)	
	Has difficulty using pitch to express statements versus questions	
	Pitch is not used to express affect	
	Pitch is not used to match another's affect	

Stress	Fails to stress one syllable over another in words to discriminate nouns from verbs	
	Impaired use of volume to stress important words	
	Impaired use of changes in pitch to stress important words	
	Impaired use of increased duration to stress important words	
	Equally stresses each spoken word in a sentence	
	Stresses the unimportant words in a sentence	
	Stresses only the most important words in a sentence, not those of secondary importance	
	Stresses words in brief utterances (single sentences) but not in connected speech	
	Impairment in using voice to reflect emotions	
	Stress is not used to express affect	
	Stress is not used to match another's affect	

CHAPTER 2

Emotional and Behavioral Modulation

Introduction: Finding calm

It may seem strange that the first lessons in a curriculum to remediate prosody deficits would address the modulation of emotions, thoughts, and behaviors. However, it is necessary for a person to be calm in order to: (1) focus on, and then implement, strategies taught; and (2) work on voice and prosody techniques and to relax the muscles involved in vocal production.

In this section of the curriculum, the student is taught mindfulness techniques, which will allow him to focus his attention exquisitely on one thing, while at the same time maintain awareness of all else that is happening around him yet hold those other things outside of the spotlight of attention. The ability to be mindful is necessary for successful focus on work and awareness of one's own body and emotional state. This awareness gives the student the opportunity to modulate his emotions, so that he can start from a calm place and work to remain calm.

The student is taught self-calming techniques so that he can bring himself back to a calm place if he loses control. He learns to communicate his thoughts and feelings to others who can help him remain or regain calm. He also learns to predict events that typically stress him, so that he can plan a way, in advance, to effectively cope and remain calmer and more in control of his behavior when these triggers occur. For individuals on the spectrum, in addition to anxious thoughts, stressful events often precipitate increased engagement in preoccupations and perseverative behavior. It is important, therefore, that the student learn to actively self-calm and reorient his attention through mindfulness, to resist preoccupations, so that he can make use of the strategies he will learn in the other chapters in this book.

The student is taught about the importance and positive consequences of being calm. He learns that it is extremely difficult to regulate his attention when he is not calm. He can become overwhelmed when he is not calm and have difficulty processing information. The student is taught about the concept of short-term memory. He learns that short-term memory contains what a person is attending to and processing; and that it is limited in capacity. If short-term memory is filled with anxious thoughts, or thoughts of a preoccupation, it is impossible to process other information. There is not enough room. Therefore, remembering and implementing brand new strategies also becomes impossible.

Figure 2.1 Emotional and behavioral modulation goals

Self-calming

Materials

Handout A: Personal Story Graphic Organizer

Handout B: The Thermometer

Handout C: Riding the Wave until Calm

One file folder of any color

One red file folder

Scissors

Markers

Pencils

Stapler

Goal

To teach methods of self-calming.

Procedures

1. **Begin by explaining the prosody intervention you will do with your student and the purpose of the following five lessons, which address emotional and behavioral modulation.** Tell the student that he will be developing particular prosody and language skills with you. Be specific with the student about precisely which prosody skills you will address, based on the evaluation you did. Tell the student that it is essential for him to be calm and settled in order to: (1) focus on and then implement the strategies he will be taught; and (2) work on voice and prosody techniques while relaxing the muscles involved in vocal production.

2. **Explain the purpose of the lesson:** To develop strategies for self-calming when feeling strong emotions. Being able to self-calm is extremely important. It is essential to be calm in order to think clearly.

3. **Discuss the fact that it is completely normal for people to have strong feelings.** Have the student make a list of emotions. Ask him to talk about what each emotion feels like and what kinds of things make him feel that way.

4. **Discuss the fact that people can lose control with anxiety, anger, fear, sadness, frustration, silliness, excitement, perseverative thinking or**

behaviors, and so on. Talk about what people do when they are out of control with each of these feelings (e.g., act out, hurt others, regain control, communicate the emotion). Please be sure that the student understands that it is normal to feel these emotions and sometimes in a very strong way.

5. **Talk about the negative consequences of getting out of control with one of these emotions or thinking patterns.** Use the Personal Story Graphic Organizer (Handout A) to write about a situation where your student lost control of his emotions and behavior. Write out the consequences of getting out of control and the alternate ways to express a strong, interfering emotion. The issue is that the student must learn to express those strong emotions in a calm and effective way.

6. **Talk about the positive consequences of having the ability to self-calm.** Use the Personal Story Graphic Organizer (Handout A) to write about a situation where your student started to lose control of his emotions and behavior, but then quickly regained control. Write out the consequences of being able to regain control of oneself. These include being able to: (1) express one's thoughts effectively (fluently); (2) express strong emotions/needs in an effective way; (3) think clearly to control behavioral choices and solve problems; (4) stop an ineffective behavior. If a person can stop an ineffective or inappropriate behavior, then he can replace it with an effective/appropriate behavior. If one *cannot* stop an ineffective behavior, then there is no room for a more effective behavior.

7. **Explain that there are two ways to regain calm:**

   a. One way is to *actively* calm down. This method is used when one must calm down quickly.

   b. The other method is to "ride the wave" of emotion until it is over. This method can be used only when there is enough time.

   Note for the student that sometimes it may be necessary to walk away from a situation that is triggering an out-of-control emotion, in order to regain calm. Sometimes it will be possible to remain in the situation where the strong emotion was triggered, and regain calm right then and there (this is preferable, if possible).

8. **Teach your student a method for *actively* calming down.** Sometimes it is necessary to work to restore calm. The following are the Rules for Self-Calming:

   • STOP

   • DEEP BREATH

   • COUNT SILENTLY TO TEN

   • SAY, "I CAN STOP _____. I CAN THINK INSTEAD."

Practice this script for self-calming. Have the student write this in his notebook.

9. **Give the student Handout B: The Thermometer.** The image of a thermometer can be helpful in learning to self-calm. As a person loses control of behaviors or emotions, he can think of the image of the mercury in a thermometer rising.

   a. Mark "out of control" on the top of the thermometer and "calm and in control" on the bottom.

   b. Practice the Rules for Self-Calming, visualizing a thermometer. Role-play going out of control and calming, using the script for self-calming. As he calms, he should visualize bringing the mercury in the thermometer down to a low level. (*Note:* You can make a "working" thermometer to help your student visualize bringing the mercury down. See Handout B.)

   c. Discuss and mark the "point of no return" on the thermometer. What is meant by the "point of no return" is the point at which the student can no longer calm himself on his own, because the feeling has become too strong. He needs to get help from someone else.

10. **Explain to your student that sometimes he has time to regain calm, and could just stop and do nothing, and ride out the wave of emotion until it is over, before he acts.** Give the student Handout C: Riding the Wave until Calm. Tell the student he can think of a strong emotion as being like a wave. It comes, it rises, and it goes. Sometimes all that is necessary to regain calm is to do *nothing* until the wave subsides. One needs simply to feel the wave come and go, knowing that calm will return on its own, in time.

    Note: Be clear that this strategy is not to be used if there is imminent danger or the student cannot leave the people and situation about which he feels upset. Under those circumstances he *must* actively calm.

11. **Homework:** Write a personal social story (using Handout A). Write about a situation where you became upset and then calmed yourself down or just "rode the wave" until the upset feeling was gone.

Personal Story Graphic Organizer

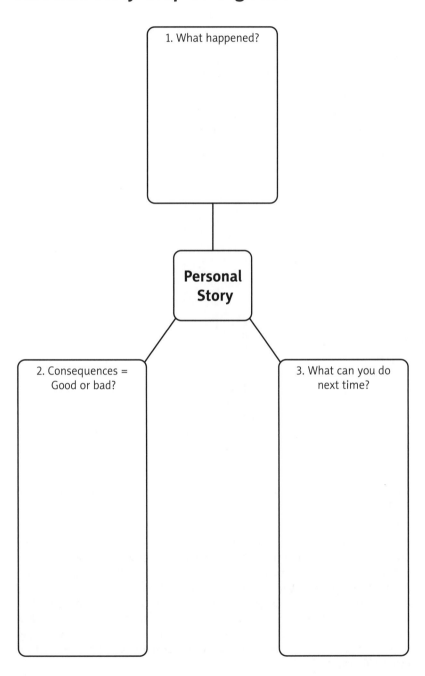

The Thermometer

Note: If you want, you can make a "working" thermometer to illustrate your points:

Take a letter size file folder and hold it vertically so it can open like a book. Cut out a thermometer shape in the top half of the front of the folder. Staple the top edge and the bottom edge closed. Leave the long side open. Cut a piece of red oak-tag paper so that it measures 10.5" by 6.5". Hold it horizontally and insert it into the open side of the folder. You should see a little red in the "bulb" of your thermometer. You can slide this paper up and down to make the mercury in your thermometer go up and down. Now put a mark at the lowest point on the thermometer and write CALM next to it. Put a mark at the highest point on the thermometer and write OUT OF CONTROL next to it.

Riding the Wave until Calm

Having a calm baseline: Mindfulness of breathing and internal triggers

Materials

Handout A: Cue for a Calming Breath

Handout B: Calm Baseline: Addressing Internal Triggers

Flashlight

An array of small objects

Goal

To develop the ability to have a calm baseline through: (1) mindfulness of one's own physical state for a relaxed body; (2) recognition of internal triggers (including negative self-regard) and minimizing their effect by taking care of oneself; and (3) exercise.

Procedures

1. **Explain the purpose of the lesson:** To develop the ability to have a calm baseline through: (1) mindfulness of one's own physical state for a relaxed body; and (2) recognition of internal triggers (including negative self-regard) and minimizing their effect by taking care of oneself.

2. **Explain the concept of "mindfulness" to the student** – specifically, that it involves the "dialectic" that (1) he needs to be completely focused on the specific experience while (2) at the same time aware what is happening outside of the focus of his attention, including any other thoughts that pass through his head. He should notice these outside, potentially distracting thoughts and things in the environment, but continually set them aside and bring his attention back to the object of his focus.

3. **Use a flashlight to demonstrate the concept.** Spread a number of objects out on a table in front of the students. Turn off the lights in the room and shine a flashlight on the central object. Tell the students that the object with the light on it is in the spotlight of attention (the focus). Have them notice that they can still see the objects on the periphery and that they are still there, but they should be set aside in their minds and attention should be maintained on the chosen focus.

4. **Explain the two major purposes of mindfulness:** (1) To be mindful of one's own body and emotions to remain or gain calm (that's what

you are teaching the student in this lesson); and (2) to focus attention exquisitely on the task one is doing (e.g., homework, a chore), without being distracted by external events, preoccupations with preferred topics or activities (e.g., video games, mobile phone, internet), or emotions and thoughts of stress. Have the students write down both purposes for mindfulness in their notebooks. Tell them that the purpose of today's lesson is to use mindfulness for remaining or regaining calm.

5. **Do the following mindfulness exercises for gaining a relaxed baseline.** Allocate two minutes for each activity, for the student and you to each silently observe yourselves. Following each activity ask the student to describe his observations. Be sure to remind the student to observe the movement of his attention and describe where it goes if he is distracted. Also remind him that his job is to bring his attention back to the task at hand if it deviates:

   a. Mindfulness of body as a whole (ask him to note how every part of his body feels as he sits in his chair).

   b. Monitoring breathing (ask him to simply monitor his breathing, how fast/slow, loud/quiet, how it feels).

   c. Breathing slower and deeper (now give him the task of slowing his breathing and making it deeper than what he just noted in b.).

   d. Relax face muscles (now give him the task of relaxing his face muscles; tell him to drop his jaw, teeth apart, keeping his lips lightly touching).

6. **Review the purposes of mindfulness (from step 2 above).** Review that one major way to achieve a calm baseline is to monitor one's breathing and make sure to take long, slow breaths. Tell the student that throughout all lessons in this book, a long, slow, deep, calming breath will be symbolized and cued by a diamond. Do an exercise where you hold up the diamond in Handout A and have the student take a long, deep breath each time you hold it up (in through the nose and out through the mouth).

7. **Managing internal triggers to gain a relaxed baseline.** Now explain that another way to achieve a calm baseline is to understand and reduce triggers that stress a person. Discuss that there are internal and external triggers. Define them. Internal triggers are those such as tiredness, hunger, sickness, and feeling bad about yourself (concentrating on your weaknesses/negative self-regard). External triggers may be related to difficult work or failure, for example. External triggers will be addressed in later lessons. Explain that starting from a calm place requires that internal triggers be kept to a minimum. Give the student Handout B. Emphasize the need for positive self-regard. Have him write in his notebook what it means to sleep well and eat well, and how he can take care of his health. Have him make a list of some of his strengths.

8. **Exercising to gain a relaxed baseline.** Explain that a third way to gain a calm baseline is to exercise on a regular basis. (This reduces stress by expending nervous energy, increasing endorphins and oxygen in the brain.)

9. **Homework:** Fill out the table on Handout B for each day this week. This will help you keep track of how you limited your internal triggers.

Cue for a Calming Breath

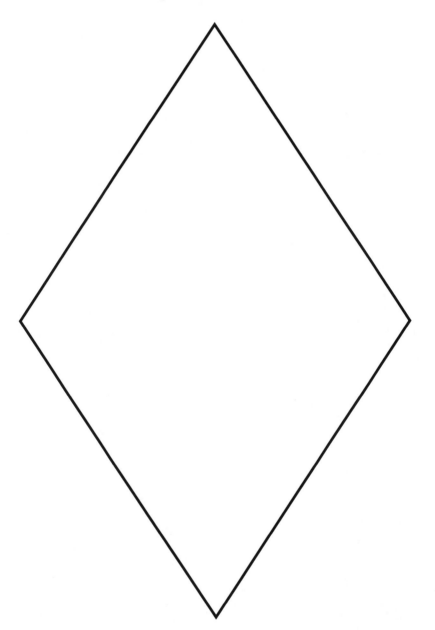

✓

Calm Baseline: Addressing Internal Triggers

Strategy	Think about your strengths and feel good about yourself (write in what strength you thought about or better yet demonstrated that day)	Exercise (write in the exercise you did)	Eat well (3 meals – well balanced) (make a check mark if you succeeded)	Sleep well (hours) (make a check mark if you succeeded and write hours)
Mon				
Tue				
Wed				
Thu				
Fri				
Sat				
Sun				

LESSON 3

Maintaining calm through mindfulness of emotions, thoughts, and behaviors

Materials

Handout A: External Triggers

Handout B: Plans for Dealing with External Triggers

Handout C: Pitfalls and Planks

Modeling clay, for example Play-Doh

Picture of a painting

Stored photos on a smart phone

Goal

To learn to maintain calm through mindfulness of thoughts, activities, body, and emotions, by learning to focus attention exquisitely without being distracted by external events.

Procedures

1. **Explain the purpose of the lesson:** Start with a review of mindfulness for gaining a calm baseline. The purpose of the lesson is to learn to maintain calm through mindfulness of body, emotions, thoughts, and behaviors.

2. **Practice mindful breathing.** Have the student sit in a chair in a relaxed position. Tell him to relax. This will include a relaxed jaw (mouth dropped open, lips lightly touching). Tell the student that for three minutes both of you will concentrate only on breathing. Feel the sensations of the breath going in and out; feel the expansion and contraction of the abdominal cavity and so on. After the three minutes, describe what each of you observed about your breathing and the focus of your attention.

3. **Maintaining calm.** Explain to the student that even though he can try to be calm all the time, sometimes things will happen that make him feel stressed or over-excited, and they may move him away from a calm baseline. He needs to be aware of what is happening to him so that he can quickly regain calm. Explain to the student that being able to be aware of bodily sensations, emotions, and thoughts will allow him to focus his attention on what he needs to process, and not become overwhelmed.

4. **Remind the student of the concept of "mindfulness."** That is, it involves the dialectic that (1) he needs to completely attend to the chosen focus, and (2) at the same time he needs to be aware of what is happening outside of the focus of his attention, including any other thoughts or emotions. He should notice and acknowledge these outside thoughts (including perseverative preoccupations), emotions, and things in the environment, but continually set them aside and bring his attention back to the object of his focus (unless it is important to shift the attentional spotlight to someone who needs your attention or something dangerous). Use the stored photos on your phone to visually demonstrate the concept in the following way. First, choose one picture as the focus of mindfulness. Then scroll through other pictures on your phone, which you will label "distracters." Say, "OK, I see those other pictures but they are not my focus. I need to go back to this one."

5. **Do the following mindfulness exercises where you and your student attend to an object or experience for three minutes.** When the three minutes are up, each of you should describe your mindfulness experience, including your detailed observations of the object of your focus, and the movement of your attention. Explain not only what you observed about the object of your focus, but also potentially interfering thoughts outside the focus of attention, and how each of you set them aside to maintain focus.

   a. **Mindfulness of thoughts.** Show the student the picture of a painting (it can be any painting). Give the student a list of features you will pay attention to, including color, form, line, composition, and meaning. You and the student should then look at the work of art for three minutes. Again, the instructions are for you both to try to focus on the painting but also notice other thoughts and distractions. Be aware, watch them come, and then set them aside.

   b. **Mindfulness of an activity.** You and the student should hold, manipulate, and make something with the modeling clay. He should again focus on the physical sensations and what he is doing with the clay for three minutes. Again, tell him that if his mind wanders to anything that is not the clay, he must acknowledge the movement of his attention and monitor those thoughts, but then bring quickly his focus back to the clay.

   c. **Mindfulness of body.** Sitting quietly for three minutes, have him concentrate on physical sensations (e.g., how his body feels in the chair; the temperature, his breathing). He should monitor thoughts that come into his head but then push them out and focus his attention on the physical sensations only.

6. **Mindfulness of emotions.** It is important that the student not only be mindful of the environment, his thoughts, and activities, but also of his emotions. Being aware of his emotions can help him anticipate when an emotion, especially a negative one, is growing and may

become overwhelming. If he is mindful of the building emotion he may be able to calm himself before he loses control and does something inappropriate or ineffective.

a. **Review the concept of internal triggers.** Discuss how hunger, thirst, fatigue, poor self-regard, etc. can promote negative emotions and make people more reactive to external triggers.

b. **Discuss external triggers.** Define these as events in the environment, rather than within the student, that trigger strong emotions and possibly out-of-control behaviors (and, in the case of students on the autism spectrum, may also trigger repetitive/perseverative behaviors).

   Have the student write a list of situations where he usually feels a strong emotion, the external triggers for that emotion, his associated emotions, and his behavioral reactions in Handout A. For example, a given student may feel a great deal of stress and anger when he has to independently do homework (especially when a parent is continually monitoring or pushing); another may feel stress when asked to tell about his day or explain something (due to his difficulty with expressive formulation); another may feel great stress when having to initiate a social interaction with another person. (Some other examples of external triggers are: future demands and responsibility, trouble understanding something, new situations, crowded places with lots of noise, being disorganized and losing things, events beyond one's control.)

7. **Choose one known external trigger on the list and practice mindfulness and self-calming.** Tell the student that he will practice being mindful of his emotions and any repetitive thoughts, as you help him to envision himself in that situation which triggers him.

a. Have your student envision the specific situation he chooses, and his emotions and thoughts in that situation, for three minutes. Then, while he is feeling that stress, have him try to do the following task. Have him outline an oral discussion concerning how his current education will contribute to his future success. He should then tell you his thoughts on the topic. Record him when he does this. Spend five to seven minutes on this activity.

b. Then have him stop and just be mindful of his emotions in the chosen situation and of regulating his breathing to self-calm, for at least two minutes. He should acknowledge that when he is stressed, his breathing is more rapid than when he is calm and his body is tense. He must be mindful of slowing his breathing, taking long, slow breaths, and of relaxing his muscles.

c. Then he should try again the oral discussion concerning how his current education will contribute to his future success, while in a calm state. He can outline a bit more if he wants and then tell you his thoughts (over the next five to seven minutes), while being mindful of remaining calm. Record him as he does this.

d. Have the student describe his experience of doing the task while stressed and then while calm. Describe your observations of his behavior when he is stressed and calm. Play the recordings of his speech while stressed and while calm. Discuss the comparison.

8. **Unexpected triggers.** Sometimes an unexpected trigger will occur. (For example: There is suddenly a lot of traffic due to an accident and you will be late for an appointment. You drop the report that is due today in a puddle. You leave a book you need in a classroom at school and you cannot get back in to get it.) Ask your student to think of other possible, unanticipated triggers. These unexpected triggers can make us panic. There are a number of things to do when an unanticipated trigger occurs. Have your student write these on Handout C.

a. STOP. Take a deep breath; if you are calm you will think more clearly.

b. THINK. "Don't panic. Problem solve." We can think of those unanticipated triggers as "pitfalls" which simply need to be crossed. We need to find the plank to get over the pitfall (Handout C). We need to solve the problem. Try to think of a solution.

c. GO. Try your solution; or if you cannot think of one, ask a trusted friend or adult.

9. **Explain that, in general life, the student needs to be aware/mindful of his emotional reactions so that he is able to maintain control of his interfering reactions.** If he gets stressed or angry, he should spend at least one minute being mindful only of slowing his breathing and relaxing his muscles, to quickly regain control. He will be more effective in his activities and in his communication when he is calm. Explain to him that if he is in danger of losing control, he can assertively communicate how he feels and ask for help (see Modulation in Lesson 4).

10. **Tell the student that everyone does sometimes lose control of emotional reactions, behaviors, or thoughts.** He will, too. Under those circumstances he will have to invest more energy and time in self-calming. Briefly review the strategies for self-calming in Lesson 1.

11. **Homework:**

a. Fill out Handout B from Lesson 2 each day this week to keep track of how you limit internal triggers.

b. While it is not possible to be ready for all external triggers, identifying known external triggers not only allows one to calm more quickly but it may even help one avoid negative emotions when the trigger occurs. Fill in Handout B from this lesson. Write your typical external triggers, but this time write a plan of action (in advance) for addressing each of those triggers the next time they occur.

External Triggers

Situation	External trigger	Associated emotion	Behavioral reaction

Plans for Dealing with External Triggers

External trigger	Advance plan of action for addressing trigger

Pitfalls and Planks

DON'T PANIC. PROBLEM SOLVE!
STOP
THINK
GO

The importance of being calm: Understanding the consequences for your thinking

Materials

Handout A: Schematic of Short-term Memory

Thermometer

Picture of the wave

Goals

To learn about the concept of short-term memory and its limited capacity.

To understand that emotions take up space in short-term memory, and as a consequence you have less processing space.

Procedures

1. **Discuss the purpose of the lesson.** Talk about the necessity of being calm. Maintaining calm, or having the ability to regain calm after being upset, are very important abilities.

2. **Explain that being calm makes it easier to get along with others.** It also allows clear thinking and communication. Self-calming is essential so that one can: (1) express one's thoughts effectively (fluently); (2) express strong emotions/needs in an effective way; (3) think clearly to control behavioral choices; (4) stop an ineffective behavior. The purpose of this lesson is to explain why being calm allows a person to do all of these things and why it is impossible to do these things when one is not calm.

3. **Review the two main methods for self-calming from Lesson 1:**

   a. One method is to view a strong emotion as a "wave" that will come, crest, and then subside. Sometimes it is possible (even preferable) to just watch the "wave" come and go until calm returns. Do *nothing*. Leave the upsetting situation and ride the wave until it subsides (it comes and it goes).

   b. Sometimes a person does not have the time to simply watch the upset come and go, but, rather, must actively calm himself. This is necessary when the situation is dangerous or when it is not possible to leave an upsetting situation. In this case, he can use the image of bringing down the mercury in a thermometer. Using the thermometer from Lesson 1, have the student pretend to go out of control, and then self-calm. He should self-calm by taking deep breaths, being mindful of slowing his breathing and relaxing his jaw, counting to ten in his head, and telling himself he can stop and what he can do instead. Tell him to think of the mercury in his thermometer coming down, as he calms down.

4. **Remind the student that calming does not mean he needs to just keep his feelings inside.** In fact, communicating his feelings assertively (as in Lesson 5) may allow him to calm down more effectively (he can even ask for help), and will allow him to remain calm, because he is understood by others.

5. **Practice mindfulness for gaining a relaxed state.** Have the student sit quietly for three minutes, breathing slower and deeper. Have him relax his face muscles. Tell him to drop his jaw, keeping his lips lightly touching. Tell him to be mindful of how his body is feeling as he breathes slowly and deeply and maintains a relaxed jaw, all the while telling himself, "I can stop and be calm."

6. **Now tell your student that you are going to explain why it is impossible to express himself or to behave effectively when he is not calm.** Discuss the concept of short-term memory with your student. (If it is helpful, equate short-term memory to RAM in a computer.) Explain that processing space in short-term memory is limited (holding 7 ± 2 pieces of information).

   Short-term memory is used to formulate and understand language, problem solve, and so on. If the processing space gets filled up with emotions or ineffective thoughts, like preoccupations, there is no room for other, more productive thoughts. When a person is very upset, short-term memory becomes filled with emotions. They take up most of the limited processing space and can stop a person from thinking clearly. It is essential that the student is calm before he speaks. This is because emotions can fill the processing space in short-term memory, stopping a person from problem solving or communicating effectively, because there is not enough processing space left to think. To free processing space, a person must calm down.

   Discuss the idea that processing space in short-term memory can also get filled up with a preoccupation (e.g., civil war, musical theatre, video games), or the need to engage in a repetitive behavior. It is important to help the student understand that he must be mindful of the present context (e.g., ongoing conversation) and push the preoccupation out of the spotlight of attention. He must set the preoccupation aside (knowing that he can "park" it and come back to it at an appropriate time). He must be aware of the preoccupation that is trying to intrude and fill the space in his short-term memory and at the same time work to be completely mindful of the current situation.

7. **Homework: Explain to the student that this week every time before he speaks, he must try to use his calming strategies to settle himself.** This is especially important before he enters a conversation or initiates a topic with others. Some conversation topics bring on a "wave" of anxiety, some bring on anger, and some he cannot attend to because there is already a "wave" of excitement present. Discuss how the student will deal with each of these types of "waves."

Schematic of Short-term Memory

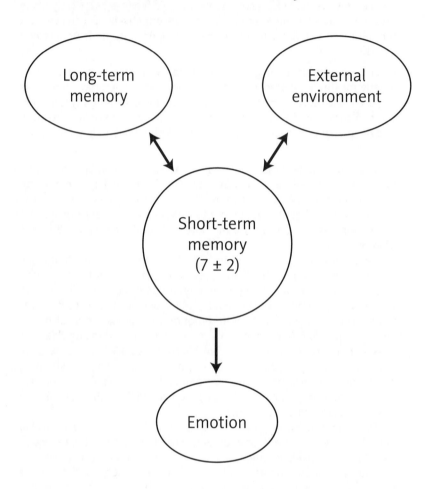

Communicating emotions and the need for help

Materials

Handout A: Strong Feelings People Have

Handout B: Verbal Expression of Emotions

Goal

To learn to communicate thoughts and feelings to others in order to: (a) help oneself remain or regain calm; and (b) problem solve with a trusted friend or adult.

Procedures

1. **Explain the purpose of the lesson:** To learn to communicate thoughts and feelings to others in order to help oneself remain or regain calm and problem solve with a trusted friend or adult:

   a. Why communicate emotions verbally rather than by "acting out" or just hold them inside?

   b. Knowing when and how to express emotions verbally.

2. **Discuss strong feelings people have.** Have the student list strong feelings he and others have on Handout A.

3. **Explain why it is important to express one's thoughts and feelings verbally.** If a person fails to express feelings verbally or expresses their feelings by acting out (e.g., aggressively, with anxiety), it is extremely difficult to understand him or to help solve the problem that is causing the upset. Sometimes people can get their feelings under control and sometimes they have trouble doing this. In either situation it is important and helpful to express one's feelings verbally, as calmly as possible, because:

   a. Verbalizing a feeling defines it and contains it so it is not overwhelming.

   b. Talking about feelings rather than acting out or failing to express feelings builds better relationships with other people. People are more likely to feel empathetic rather than confused and upset if you tell them what is going on.

c. Talking about feelings helps a person to be better understood and validated. Validation can only occur if a person expresses something to others in a way that is understandable. Being understood and validated makes a person feel more connected to others, and as a consequence people feel calmer and are more likely to remain calm.

d. Discussing feelings and why they occurred allows problem solving in the moment and for the future. It is important to learn to anticipate and plan how to deal with emotions in the future.

4. **Discuss when and how to express feelings verbally.** There are three situations in which one should communicate his emotions to another person: (1) if he is upset and having trouble calming down; (2) if he needs to advocate for himself when his rights have been violated; and (3) after he has calmed down and needs help with problem solving.

a. *If you are upset and having trouble calming down.* Sometimes it is necessary to verbalize feelings in order to get help when one is having trouble calming down. If you are having trouble calming down or focusing your attention where it needs to be rather than on your preoccupation, ask a trusted adult or peer for help to get yourself back on track. If you talk to someone about how you are feeling, that person could help you calm down or to come up with a solution (a "plank for your pitfall").

Rules for asking for help with modulating emotions/behavior:

*   STOP

*   THINK: I am out of control. I need help.

*   GO: Tell an adult, "I am feeling too (emotion), please help me calm down" *or* "I am stuck. I can't stop thinking about _____. Can you help me get on track?"

b. *To advocate for yourself when your rights have been violated.* Tell the student that sometimes it is necessary to assertively express feelings and needs when he is upset because his rights have been violated or he is confused. Tell the following stories to illustrate this point.

Story 1

Julia is a high school student who does yard work for her neighbors to earn money to pay for her art lessons. One of her neighbors owes her $100 for the work she has done. Each time she asks to be paid, that neighbor says that he needs to go to his bank to get some cash, and he will pay Julia the next week. Julia is starting to feel upset and angry with her neighbor. What should she do?

Story 2

Jack was at his new job at the supermarket. His boss was in a rush as he asked Jack to set up a new display of cereal in the front of the store. Jack was not sure which kind of cereal should be in the display, and he had never set up a display before. First he asked a co-worker, who had worked in the store for five years, how the display should be arranged. The co-worker explained to Jack that he didn't know which cereal should be put in the display. Jack felt himself starting to panic. He took a few deep breaths to calm down, found his boss, and interrupted him appropriately to ask his question. Should he have done anything differently?

   c. *After you have been upset and you have calmed yourself down.* Discuss how you were feeling with a trusted friend or adult, why you felt that way, the consequences of your behaviors during the time you were upset, and what to do about it next time (figure out the rules).

5. **When there is no one around to talk to about your feelings.** Write down your feelings and what happened in a journal. Write down any solutions to these situations you have used successfully in the past. As soon as you can, talk to a trusted adult or friend about your feelings and the possible solutions for the present and to use in the future.

6. **Homework:** On Handout B, write ten emotions that you experience over the next week. Include the situation where you felt the emotions and how and to whom you verbally expressed them.

Strong Feelings People Have

Feelings

Verbal Expression of Emotions

Emotions	Situation	Who you told	What you said

Emotions	Situation	Who you told	What you said

CHAPTER 3

Voice: Creating a More Oral Timbre

Introduction: The concept of the balanced mix

There are two extreme vocal-timbre conditions which may be present in individuals with ASD. Vocal production may have either a hyper-nasal timbre, which is the more common issue, or a hyper-oral timbre. Either extreme presents a voice that sounds unusual, which can have significant consequences for the individual. Odd vocal timbre can negatively impact the development of relationships and the ability to obtain employment, since one's voice is involved in the first and ongoing social impression one makes. These extreme conditions, if not addressed, can result in further social isolation for the individual with ASD.

If the student naturally produces a hyper-nasal vocal quality when speaking, we teach him to produce a sound which is more oral, giving him a more balanced timbre. This makes his voice not only less odd, but also less abrasive and less intrusive. A hyper-nasal quality can sound annoying, inappropriately loud, or even aggressive to the listener.

On the other hand, if a student does not produce an adequate volume, one possibility is that his timbre is not nasal enough, but rather hyper-oral. A hyper-oral timbre will make the speaker sound less assertive. This quality prohibits one from being heard and understood or even attended to under many circumstances. (Issues with volume are addressed in Chapter 4.)

Timbre, at either extreme, negatively impacts the speaker's ability to effectively communicate. One must understand that an individual's voice is his primary tool for social communication. A balanced timbre offers the speaker a wider variety of expressive colors. It offers the listener(s) a greater opportunity for a more complete understanding of the speaker's ideas and feelings.

What is a balanced-mix timbre? An effective speaking voice is neither too nasal nor too oral in its quality. This chapter contains exercises designed for the manipulation of the velum, tongue, and fleshy tissue which encase the entire acoustic system (filter), all of which are key in directing the flow of air and sound and in producing resonance. The lessons are instrumental in helping the student form acoustic surfaces in the vocal tract, to assist with developing a projected sound which is also less nasal. An individual who has too nasal a timbre is taught to relax the tongue and rest its tip (in neutral position) behind the lower row of front teeth. He is taught to relax his lips and jaw and maintain a vertical position of his mouth as he speaks. The person is also taught to raise the velum by forming his natural position for a yawn, which, in turn, produces an acoustically useful tighter/smoother tissue in the back of the mouth. During the execution of the yawn position, the epiglottis naturally extends to a position out and over the windpipe, partially covering it, thereby directing the flow of air for resonance. The aim in focusing on developing a more oral sound in a student with a hyper-nasal voice is to help the student move towards a more balanced mix between oral and nasal resonance.

Efficient vocal communication is greatly dependent upon the flexibility of the musculature in and around the entire vocal mechanism. Muscular flexibility produces a more agile and adaptable apparatus. It also produces greater richness and range in the acoustic properties of the produced tone. In this chapter and in Chapter 4 the student is taught the physical sensations associated with taking a balanced approach to vocal production. This will help him to produce a greater dynamic vocal range, and will modify resonating overtones, resulting in a more typical and effective timbre.

Our approach to balancing timbre involves multiple modalities. We teach the student the physical sensations associated with the correct anatomical set-up, so that he may gain a more balanced-mix timbre. We also teach the student what that set-up looks like. We show this in pictures, anatomical models, and in our own mouths. We then instruct them in how to produce the desired position with their own mouths. They learn first what it feels and looks like, and then later what it sounds like.

This chapter addresses how to obtain a balanced-mix timbre when the student starts out with a hyper-nasal voice. A hyper-nasal quality in speech occurs when an abnormal nasal resonance dominates the student's vocal tone. This is caused by an unbalanced flow of breath and sound, which travels mostly through the nasal pharynx and then into the nasal resonating chambers located behind the eyes and nose.

According to the source–filter model (Diehl 2008) of vocal production (Figure 3.1), vocal tone (including pitch) is produced at the vocal cords, while the vocal tract acts as a resonator tube which modifies the sound according to how the tube is shaped. Changes in the shape and size of the tube produce the different resonances or timbres we hear. The resonator tube (filter) is comprised of the laryngeal pharynx, the mouth (oral pharynx) (including the tongue), and sometimes through the nose (nasal pharynx). Within the oral pharynx, the palate is comprised of two parts: the hard palate, located just behind the top front teeth; and the soft palate (also known as the velum), which lies adjacent, just behind the hard palate. The anterior region of the soft palate is connected to the posterior region of the hard palate. The uvula is centered at the posterior region of the soft palate. The adjustment of the soft palate is primarily made possible by the musculature surrounding the velopharyngeal opening (which is behind the soft palate/velum at the opening to the nasal pharynx). When the velum lifts, this produces a partial closure of the nasal chamber and an oral vocal timbre is produced. When the velum is relaxed and dropped (and particularly when the back of the tongue is raised), more air and tone advance through the velopharyngeal opening and into nasal resonators and out through the nose. A hyper-nasal timbre is caused by an atypical opening at the nasal pharynx with some degree of occlusion at the oral pharynx.

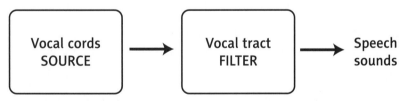

Figure 3.1 Source–filter theory

Muscle tension plays a major role in the production of hyper-nasality. As discussed earlier in Chapter 2, individuals with ASD often have difficulty modulating their emotions and behavior. Strong emotions can create excessive muscle tension in the tongue and the jaw. This muscle tension closes off the vocal passage and constricts the flow of air and sound. We must teach individuals with ASD the emotional modulation rules, so that they can calm and relax their muscles. The ability to calm is required as a first step in improving timbre. The next step is to learn the rules for the optimal positioning of the vocal anatomy to produce a less nasal timbre.

These are:

1. Relax the tongue into a low position and keep its tip behind the lower front teeth. This is associated with a relaxed jaw. The two work together to help maintain an open passage for a more balanced timbre.

2. Breathing in, like a yawn, sets up the vocal anatomy in precisely the correct position to produce a more oral timbre. This is termed the "acoustic yawn." In this position, more sound and air are sent predominantly through the oral pharynx rather than the nasal pharynx. By nature, a yawn is a relaxed and open position. The jaw is dropped vertically (the chin is lowered in a direction straight down – not pointed out or forward – towards the clavicle and sternum). The velum is in its highest position. With the velum and the tongue positioned in opposition at the top and bottom perimeters of the oral acoustic chamber, there is less flesh to obstruct the passageway for air and sound. This open position sets up a smoother, more taut, surface on the inner walls of the mouth to reflect sound as well. A projected tone is produced, with more dynamic presence.

3. Think "tired lion." The student should strive to maintain a relaxed, open, and vertical oral position (of the tired lion, yawning).

4. The student speaks while maintaining the position he has established in the three steps above (like a tired lion yawning).

The goals are: to speak with a more vertically opened mouth, keeping the tongue and the jaw relaxed; and to position the pharyngeal tissue up and out of the way (as in a yawn) by lifting the velum. This positioning creates an ensemble of articulators, which are positioned to give more space.

To firmly establish the motor patterns associated with this new, more oral timbre requires a significant amount of practice. This practice is accomplished during the lessons themselves with direction and feedback from the therapist, and through homework assignments (which generalize the skills to the rest of life). Practice serves to automate the new skills, which allow the student to allocate more of his attentional resources to what he wants to say rather than to how he will produce the sound. The student will keep copies of all handouts, homework, and notes in a three-ring binder, which he can refer to at home in order to practice and must bring to all lessons. The lessons are developmentally ordered. Later lessons refer back to concepts in earlier ones and make repeated use of materials from earlier lessons to solidify the concepts as the student develops the skills.

Learning about timbre

Materials

Handout A: Oral and Nasal Sound Chart

Handout B: Anatomy of the Voice

Handout C: Positioning of Anatomy for Nasal Timbre

Handout D: Positioning of Anatomy for Oral Timbre

Appendix A: Sample of Handout A

Appendix B: Example for How to Color Oral and Nasal Timbre Anatomy Diagrams

Mirror

Recording device

Reading passage

Goals

To practice auditory discrimination of oral versus nasal timbre.

To learn to produce and practice producing vowels and words which have nasal and oral timbres.

To learn about the anatomical structures in the mouth and nasal chamber that are involved in producing oral timbre and to gain a preliminary understanding of how the structures in the mouth are manipulated to produce a more nasal or a more oral sound.

Procedures

1. **Make baseline recordings:**
   a. Have the student read a passage which is at least two paragraphs long. Record this as a baseline for comparison in later lessons.
   b. Have the student talk about a recent vacation or event in school. Record this as a baseline for comparison in later lessons.

2. **Assess the student's ability to discriminate nasal from oral vocal sounds and teach the terminology "nasal" and "oral."** Choose one sentence from the reading passage you just used. You will read that sentence twice, once with a pronounced hyper-nasal timbre and then again with a pronounced hyper-oral timbre.

3. **Ask the student if the sentences are different and what he hears as different:**

   a. Then, **teach him the terminology**, identifying one as "nasal" and the other as "oral."

   b. **Practice discrimination.** Now read another sentence from the passage twice, once with a nasal timbre and once with an oral timbre, but this time make the contrast between the two smaller. After each sentence is read, ask the student to identify which sentence sounds "nasal" and which sounds "oral." Repeat this procedure a few times to make certain he can correctly use the labels associated with each timbre, each time.

   c. **Understanding oral and nasal vowels.** Have the student write all of the vowels in the alphabet on a piece of paper. Read out loud each of the vowels the student wrote, and have the student imitate each. Help him understand that some vowel sounds are naturally more nasal and some are more oral. Now help him enter the vowels into the chart in Handout A, writing each under the appropriate column indicating which are nasal and which are oral. (Use Appendix A as an example.)

4. **Discovering words that are nasal and oral.** Have the student come up with at least five words for each vowel sound and write them into the chart in the appropriate places. Have him read the words containing those vowels out loud. Record him as he does this.

5. **Teach the student about the form and function of the "vocal" anatomy:**

   a. Give your student Handout B. Explain the anatomy depicted in the side, cutout, view of the head and neck in the diagram: point out the lungs, trachea (windpipe), tongue, lips, and vocal cords. Label the nasal pharynx and the oral pharynx. Now explain the inserts, which show the trachea and vocal cords from the top. Explain how the cords open to breathe, close before the onset of a vocalization, and vibrate rapidly, very close to each other, during vocalization. Explain that the vocal cords are the source of the sound. The throat, the oral pharynx, the nasal pharynx, the velum (soft palate), the tongue, and lips form the filter. By changing the shape of the filter, the sound generated at the source (cords) is modified. (To help with clarity, have the student color specific parts of the anatomy diagram: lungs, trachea, diaphragm, vocal cords, soft palate, hard palate, lips, tongue, oral resonators, and nasal resonators.)

   b. Give the student Handouts C and D, which show the mouth, tongue, and throat; then explain and label the parts on each diagram. Color the velum and tongue pink. Make blue dots indicating the flow of air and sound. Label diagrams according to whether the positioning of the anatomy produces a more oral or a more nasal sound (Handout C – nasal; Handout D – oral). Use Appendix B for this lesson as a guide for coloring.

6. **Model for the student with your own mouth how to produce oral and nasal sounds.** As you both look at the corresponding diagram for producing a nasal sound, show him how the back of your tongue is up and the soft palate is lowered when you produce a more nasal sound. Then show him how your entire tongue is relaxed down with the tip of the tongue behind the lower teeth and the soft palate is up (yawn position) when you produce a more oral sound.

7. **Now have the student imitate the positions for the production of more oral sounds (vertical, oval) and the production of more nasal sounds (horizontal, smile, upper lip).** In helping him to produce more oral sounds, the use of the index finger held vertically, with the tip of the finger pressing lightly on the upper lip, may be a helpful reminder of the correct oral mouth.

8. **Homework:** Practice the oral vowel sounds, and the words containing them (on Handout A), in front of a mirror. The list of words on this chart should be repeated ten times this week (approx. two times a day).

Oral and Nasal Sound Chart

	Nasal	Oral
Vowels		
Consonants		
Anatomic gate		

Anatomy of the Voice

Positioning of Anatomy for Nasal Timbre

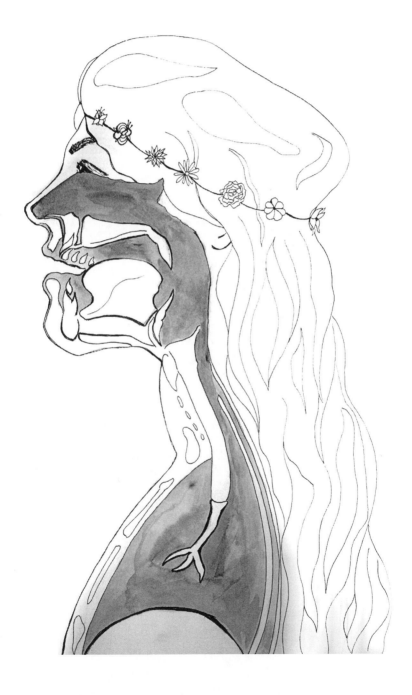

Positioning of Anatomy for Oral Timbre

Sample of Handout A

	Nasal	Oral
Vowels	ee – bee, tree ih – it, sit ay – say, may eh – egg, sled æ – cat, hat	ah – spot, drop uh – cup, mud awh – sought, caught oh – bone, phone ow – cow, now ooh – shoe, moose
Consonants	M, N	P, T, K B, D, G F, S, H V, Z J, ch, sh W, L, R
Anatomic gate	Back of tongue up and soft palate down	Entire tongue relaxed down and soft palate up (yawn position)

Example for How to Color Oral and Nasal Timbre Anatomy Diagrams

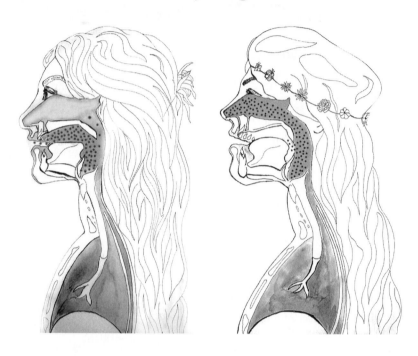

Oral timbre: Tongue position – vowels 1

Materials

Handouts A, C, and D from Lesson 1

Handout A: The Anatomic Gate: Tongue Position for Oral Versus Nasal Sounds

Handout B: Tired Lion

Mirror

Recording device

Flashlight

Goals

To practice the production of nasal and oral vowels and words.

To increase understanding of the form and function of the anatomical structures in the throat, mouth, and nasal chamber involved in producing timbre.

To practice using tongue position to produce a more nasal or oral sounding timbre.

Procedures

1. **Review the chart of oral and nasal vowel sounds, then have the student produce all of the oral vowel sounds.** First let him produce the sounds, naturally, in his own way. Record this.

2. **Then work on making his production of those oral vowel sounds more oral by having him put his fingers on the sides of his mouth, lightly pushing in, with the inside of his cheeks just touching the outer surface of his molars.** This serves to keep his mouth open in a vertical position with his jaw dropped. Record this. Listen to the initial recording from step 1 and the recording from this step with the student and give feedback on the quality of his sound in each.

3. **Develop the contrasting sensations involved in the production of nasal quality versus the production of oral quality.** Show the diagram in Handout A for this lesson, as you have the student produce the following sequences of sounds:

   a. First have the student produce a nasal "ng" sound, sustained for two seconds, to an "a" (as in cat) sound, sustained for two seconds; then an oral "ah" or "oh" sound, sustained for three seconds.

   b. Now use a "breathy" "h" sound to initiate the production of the sequence: "Hung......æ......ah......" First demonstrate and then have him imitate you as you repeat the sequence.

   c. Discuss what he feels in his mouth and hears. As he begins he should feel the back of his tongue in a high position and his velum in a dropped position. This position makes a nasal sound. As he produces the entire sequence, his tongue should drop in the back, and his velum should rise. Use the diagram and explain the change in the position of the back of the tongue as the student produces each sound.

   d. Then have him continue to practice the movement from a nasal position to an oral position, using the following sequence: a nasal "ng" sound, sustained for two seconds, to an oral "ah" or "oh" sound, sustained for three seconds. "Hung......ah......

   e. Hung......oh......"

   f. Now reverse the sequence in this exercise. Have the student produce those sustained sounds, but this time, in order, from an "oral" quality to a "nasal" quality.

4. **Review the anatomic diagrams (Handouts C and D from Lesson 1).** Discuss the "anatomic gate." The anatomic gate, which produces vocal timbre, is comprised of the velum (soft palate) and the tongue. When the velum is raised and the tongue is down, the gate is open, and an oral timbre will be produced. When the tongue is raised in the back and the velum is dropped, the gate to the oral pharynx is closed. Therefore, air and sound will predominantly flow through the nasal pharynx and a nasal timbre is produced:

   a. Fill in information on the chart describing the anatomic gate. (Use Appendix A from Lesson 1 as a guide.)

   b. Help your student to recognize the sensation of the position of the "anatomic gate." As you show him the diagram of the position of the anatomy for producing a nasal sound, again help him to notice that when the back of the tongue is up and the soft palate is lower, a more nasal sound is produced. Reinforce the sensation of the closed "anatomic gate" by having him produce "ng," "k," and a snoring sound. These sounds will help him understand and feel the sensation. When the back of the tongue is up and the soft palate is in a low position, air and sound travel more through the nasal pharynx (thus the more nasal sound).

   c. While looking at the diagram, which shows the vocal anatomy in a position that will produce an oral sound, help him notice that when the entire tongue is relaxed, in the bottom of the mouth, with the tip of the tongue just behind the lower front teeth and the soft palate up (in a yawn position), a more oral sound is produced. Reinforce the sensation by having him produce "ah" and "oh." When the tongue is down and relaxed and the soft palate is in a high position, air and sound travel through the oral pharynx, the mouth, creating a more oral sound.

d. To demonstrate, shine a flashlight into your own mouth and have the student look in, and observe what you do in order to produce a nasal sound or an oral sound.

5. **Tell the student that he will now practice making an oral sound, when speaking the *oral* vowels on his chart.** His tongue will need to be relaxed, in the bottom of the mouth, with the tip of his tongue behind the lower front teeth. Have the student breathe in slowly and calmly as if yawning. Tell him to yawn, with an open mouth, like our picture of a "tired lion" (Handout B for this lesson). This will produce a more vertical position for the mouth. Work with him to maintain that same "tired lion" position when producing sounds. Demonstrate all five "oral" vowels with your mouth in this "tired lion" position and have him imitate. Shine the flashlight into your mouth as you demonstrate, so that he can clearly see what you are doing. Have him use his fingers on his cheeks, as in step 2 above. Ask him if he understands that when his fingers are lightly pushing against his cheeks, it helps him produce a more oral sound.

6. **Tell the student that he will now learn to produce and practice making an oral sound when speaking the *nasal* vowels on his chart.** Again his tongue will need to be relaxed, in the bottom of the mouth, with the tip of the tongue behind the lower front teeth. Tell him to breathe in as he yawns like a "tired lion." This will produce a more vertical mouth position. Work with him and help him to maintain that same position when producing the oral quality with these vowels. Demonstrate all five nasal vowels with your mouth in this "tired lion" position; and then have him imitate you.

Note: Because the dominant character of these vowels is nasal, the back of the tongue will lift. However, the important concept here is that the tongue stays relaxed. Remind the student that if he maintains a relaxed tongue, the sound quality of the vowel will become more oral and will eventually become a more balanced and, thus, effective sound. You should shine the flashlight into your mouth as you demonstrate, so that he can clearly see what you are doing in the process. Have him use his fingers on his cheeks, as in step 2 above.

7. **Have the student write and practice speaking phrases comprised of words containing oral and nasal vowels.** Divide a sheet of loose-leaf paper in half, vertically. Write the word "oral" at the top of one column and "nasal" at the top of the other. Have the student say the phrases,

indicated below, and have him determine which are more oral and which are more nasal in quality. Now have him write the two-to-three-word phrases that emphasize the oral or nasal vowels, under the appropriate columns on the sheet. Have the student produce the phrases out loud. Next you will demonstrate and have him imitate you:

a. **Oral phrases:** box of socks, blue moon, blow snow, cup of mud

b. **Nasal phrases:** red/bed, snack/pack, bees/trees, sit/knit

c. Have the student come up with some more word pairs or phrases, as he tells you whether they are oral or nasal. Have him write them in the appropriate columns on the chart.

8. **Homework:** Continue to practice oral versus nasal sounds on the supplied chart (includes syllables and words).

The Anatomic Gate: Tongue Position for Oral Versus Nasal Sounds

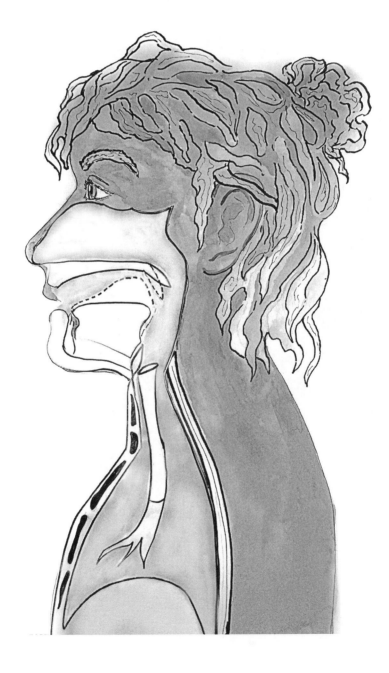

Tired Lion

LESSON 3

Oral timbre: Tongue position – vowels 2

Materials

Handouts C and D from Lesson 1: Anatomy Diagrams

Handout A: Rules for Producing an Oral Timbre

Handout B: Pictures of Tongue Position for Vowels

Handout C: Homework

Mirror

Audio recorder

Flashlight

Selected written passage

Goals

To practice production of nasal and oral vowels with a more oral timbre, using the Rules for Producing an Oral Timbre.

To practice tongue position in order to produce a more nasal or oral sounding timbre.

Procedures

1. **Review the homework from the last lesson.** Have the student produce and practice all "oral" versus "nasal" vowel sounds. Give feedback. Ask the student to tell you where he thinks his tongue should be for the different sounds. Shine a flashlight into your mouth and demonstrate the shape of the vowel sounds. Have him look in and observe what the back of your tongue is doing for each sound. Produce random vowel sounds and have the student tell you which sounds are nasal or oral, while identifying and describing your tongue position to you.

2. **Introduce the Rules for Producing an Oral Timbre.** Give the student the "Rules for Producing an Oral Timbre" chart, Handout A, for this lesson, which lists and visually demonstrates cues for these rules. Explain the rules:

   ✓ Position your *tongue* in a relaxed concave position, in the bottom of your mouth, with the tip of your tongue lightly touching the back of your lower front teeth (maintain this tongue position).

✓ Breathe in through your mouth, in a *yawn* position, like a "tired lion." This will produce a more vertical mouth position.

✓ While still maintaining the same "tired lion" *think* "ah," lowering the jaw.

✓ *Speak* (as if yawning out the sounds/words).

3. **Apply the Rules for Producing an Oral Timbre to connected speech.** First you produce the following sentences with a "nasal" timbre and then again with an "oral" timbre (using the rules in step 2): "Who can say, if I've been changed for the better. Because I knew you, I have been changed, for good" (from the musical *Wicked*, by Stephen Schwartz). Ask the student which sounded more "nasal." Now have your student say the sentences, first with a nasal sound and then with an oral sound. Discuss how each rendition felt to him, physically and emotionally.

4. **Review the two pictures of "vocal" anatomy associated with the production of oral and nasal timbres that he colored in Lesson 1.** Again talk about the anatomic gate and the idea that oral sounds are produced with the tongue down and the soft palate up. For naturally occurring nasal sounds, the back of the tongue is higher and the soft palate is lower. However, to make his overall sound more oral, the student must use the Rules for an Oral Timbre to gain a relaxed tongue, jaw, and lips and a more rounded, vertical shape to the mouth, Handout B.

5. **Visual identification of timbre.** Show the student the vowels and each associated picture of the mouth in Handout B for this lesson. Have him look at each of the pictures. Point out the dotted lines on some of the tongues. Explain that the dotted lines show the level of the middle of the tongue. The solid lines show the level of the sides of the tongue. Discuss the shape of the tongue and the position of the velum in each picture. Just by looking at the pictures, have your student tell you which mouths depict vowels that are naturally nasal and which are naturally oral, based on the position of the tongue and the velum in each of the pictures. Have him fill in the column where he is asked to write "nasal" or "oral."

6. **Teach your student to quickly shift between oral and nasal sounds, recognizing the associated sensations as he speaks the words below:**

   a. You will help the student produce the following sound sequence. Begin with words such as lung, hung, sung, tongue, sing, king, and ring. Have the student sustain the vowel in the word for two seconds, followed by sustaining the nasal "ng" consonant combination for two seconds, and then have him transition into a sustained "oral" "ah" or "oh" for another two seconds, followed, again, by the "nasal" "ng." You should demonstrate the sound sequence for each word and then have your student repeat.

    b. Shine a flashlight into your mouth so the student can see your tongue. Demonstrate the correct positions for the tongue when producing these sound sequences. Discuss what he sees and hears. Review how the tongue position changes, specifically while producing "ng," when the back of the tongue goes up to meet the soft palate and then drops back down for vowels "ah" or "oh."

    c. Have the student repeat the same sound sequences after you, beginning with the same words, first sustaining the vowel for one second, followed by sustaining the nasal "ng" for one second, followed by sustaining the "ah" for one second, and then by a sustained nasal "ng" for one second.

    d. Now have him produce the sound sequences in the reverse order, going from "oh" or "ah" to "ng."

    e. Next, use a small mirror and have the student look into his mouth as he produces the sequence of sounds "ng" followed by "ah."

7. **Have your student read a printed passage out loud to assess how he is applying his rules for producing a more oral sound.**

8. **Homework (Handout C):** (1) Practice producing the sound sequences in your homework chart (using the lion position), once each day. (2) Practice all vowel sounds in your homework chart, using the "tired lion" position, once each day. (3) Record at least one practice session and bring the recording to your next lesson. (*Note:* This week, ignore the word columns in the second chart. You will fill them in at your next lesson.)

Rules for Producing an Oral Timbre

TONGUE	
YAWN	
THINK (of what you will say)	
SPEAK	

Pictures of Tongue Position for Vowels

Vowels	Tongue position	Is the vowel naturally "nasal" or "oral"? (fill in below)
ee (as in bee)		
ih (as in sit)		
ay (as in say) eh (as in egg)		
a (as in cat)		
ah (as in mom) uh (as in cup)		
awh (as in saw)		
oh (as in low) ooh (as in shoe)		

✓

Homework

Remember the Rules for Producing an Oral Timbre:

✓ Position your *tongue* in a relaxed concave position, in the bottom of your mouth, with the tip of your tongue lightly touching the back of your lower front teeth.

✓ Breathe in through your mouth, in a *yawn* position, like a "tired lion." This will produce a more vertical mouth position.

✓ While still maintaining the same "tired lion" *think* "ah," lowering the jaw.

✓ *Speak* (as if yawning out the sounds/words).

Practice the following sounds in front of a mirror.

Try to keep the muscles in your tongue, jaw, or lips relaxed.

Consonants	
ng to ah ng to oh	ng to ah to ng ng to oh to ng

Remember: Use the Rules for Producing an Oral Timbre even for vowel sounds that are naturally nasal. A relaxed tongue, jaw, and lips will give naturally nasal vowels a less nasal/more balanced sound.

Vowels	Word 1	Word 2	Word 3
ee (as in bee)			
ih (as in sit)			
ay (as in say)			
eh (as in egg)			
æ (as in cat)			
ah (as in mom)			
uh (as in cup)			
awh (as in saw)			
oh (as in low)			
ooh (as in shoe)			

LESSON 4

Oral timbre: Tongue position, vowels, consonants, and words

Materials

Handouts A, C, and D from Lesson 1

Handout A from Lesson 3

Handout B from Lesson 3

Mirror

Goals

To practice production of nasal and oral vowels, consonants, and words with a more oral timbre.

To practice effective tongue position to produce a more oral sound.

Procedures

1. **Review the homework from the last lesson.** Listen to your student pronounce all vowel sounds and the sound sequences in his homework chart (Handout C from Lesson 3). Give feedback and correction as needed.

2. **Explain the purpose of the lesson:** To practice production of nasal and oral vowels, consonants, and words with a more oral timbre and to practice tongue position to produce a more oral sound.

3. **Review the Rules for Producing an Oral Timbre while looking at Handout A from Lesson 3:**

   ✓ Position your *tongue* in a relaxed concave position, in the bottom of your mouth, with the tip of your tongue lightly touching the back of your lower front teeth.

   ✓ Breathe in through your mouth, in a *yawn* position, like a "tired lion." This will produce a more vertical mouth position.

   ✓ While still maintaining the same "tired lion" *think* "ah," lowering the jaw.

   ✓ *Speak* (as if yawning out the sounds/words).

4. **Go over the chart of tongue positions for each vowel (Handout B from Lesson 3) and discuss which positions make a "nasal" and which make an "oral" timbre.** Then have your student repeat the vowel sounds,

after you, while at the same time looking in his mouth, using a mirror. Have him label which vowel sounds are more "nasal" and which are more "oral." Discuss how his lips change shape for each vowel.

5. **Practice transitioning between naturally occurring nasal and oral vowels.** Have your student repeat and practice shaping his mouth, while transitioning back and forth from "ee" to "ooh," while looking in a mirror to check tongue positions. He should notice when he begins that, with the vowel "ee," the tongue position is high in the back, and that the sound and anatomic position is closer to a "nasal" one. With the second vowel, "ooh," he should notice that the back of the tongue is in a high position on the sides, and that the back center portion of the tongue drops to form a concave shape. This second sound and anatomic position is closer to an "oral" one.

6. **Practice transitioning between naturally oral vowels and the nasal "ng."** Now have him repeat and practice transitioning back and forth from "uh-ng" to "ah" and then back to "ng"; then repeat, in sequence, for a total of five times, while looking in a mirror to check tongue positions. This time, as we are transitioning back and forth from a vowel to consonant cluster sequence, he should initially notice that, at the beginning of each sequence, the tongue starts in a low and relaxed position, producing a sound "uh" which is "oral," while in the second position he produces the sound "ng," where the back of the tongue is in a high position, just touching the velum (soft palate). This second sound and anatomic position is most certainly a "nasal" one. As the student transitions to the "ah" vowel, he will feel the back of his tongue and the velum separate and produce a more oral sound posture.

7. **Making naturally occurring nasal vowels more oral.** Remind the student that his goal is to form a less nasal and more oral sound, even when he is producing sounds that are naturally more "nasal." He will obtain this by starting in the yawn, "tired lion," position, keeping the tongue relaxed, and then produce the sequence uh-ng-ah. The back of his tongue will rise for the nasal "ng," but he must understand that he is to return to and maintain a vertical "tired lion" position throughout this process. Have him repeat this exercise three times.

8. **Work on the relaxed lip position.** The lip position changes for different vowels. The lips and the musculature surrounding the lips must remain flexible, pliable, and independent of the teeth during these exercises, at all times. Help your student form and maintain a relaxed lip position by having him place his index and middle fingers between his lips (not teeth), with the index finger touching his lower lip and middle finger touching his upper lip. It is very important for the lips to remain *flexible*. They must not tighten or curl in. Have him maintain this position, with his fingers between his lips, as he repeats the following vowels: ah, awh, oh, and ooh. The shape of the lips will change slightly, but finger placement will stop the lips from becoming too tight and curling in,

leaving them flexible. Have the student now say the vowel sounds without his fingers between his lips, still maintaining relaxed lips.

9. **Introduce the way consonants are produced and how they play a role in timbre production.** Discuss the two ways in which consonants can negatively impact the production of a more oral/balanced timbre:

   a. **Some consonants, like some vowels, naturally occur with a nasal quality.** Explain to your student that the consonants M and N, like ng, are naturally nasal in the way they feel. During pronunciation of these consonants the velum is down, sending air and sound through the nasal pharynx. Have your student say each of these consonants while intermittently pinching his nose. The fact that the sound stops whenever he closes his nostrils will indicate to him that the air and sound are moving mostly through his nose.

   To promote a more oral sound, the student will need to learn how to produce the nasal consonants quickly and then quickly return to an oral position where he raises the velum from the position, during pronunciation of M and N. Have your student begin by lightly putting his lips together and then saying mah, mah, mah. Then have him lightly touch the tip of his tongue behind his top front teeth and say nah, nah, nah. This will help him recognize the feeling of going from the nasal consonant to an oral position.

   Write the nasal consonants M and N into the chart you began in Lesson 1 (Handout A in Lesson 1 according to Appendix A in Lesson 1). Write the remaining consonants into the oral column.

   b. **Some consonants can produce muscle tightness in the lips, tongue, and jaw; and tightness is the enemy of an oral timbre.** Explain to the student that if the lips, tongue, and jaw are tight, the tightness will persist and affect/distort the sound of the vowels that are attached to them in words. As an example, have the student say the word "run." First he should pronounce the "r" in "run" in a relaxed way, without bringing his molars together. Then he should pronounce the "r" in "run" by biting down. You should demonstrate pronouncing the word "run" in both ways. Ask for your student's observations. Be clear that the relaxed pronunciation is preferable and that it will promote an oral timbre overall. Discuss again that breath and sound are coming mostly through his nose. Consonants that very often produce tightness are: j, ch, sh, w, l, r.

10. Since the student will now concentrate on maintaining an oral sound while adding in consonants, **write three words containing each of the vowels into the homework chart** (Handout C from Lesson 3). He will be practicing these for homework.

11. **Homework:** (1) Practice producing the sound "ng" to "ah" ("tired lion" position), in front of a mirror. (2) Practice all vowel sounds, and words containing them, in your homework chart, using the "tired lion" position. (3) Record at least one practice session and bring the recording to your next lesson.

Oral timbre: Words and pre-formulated sentences

Materials

Handouts A and B from Lesson 3

Handout A: Homework

Fox in Socks by Dr. Seuss (1965)

Mr. Brown can Moo! Can You? by Dr. Seuss (1970)

Mirror

Flashlight

Goal

To produce nasal and oral vowels, words, and sentences with a more oral timbre.

Procedures

1. **Review the homework from the last lesson.** Have the student read all the words he wrote into his homework chart (Handout C from Lesson 3). Listen carefully for distorted vowels. Provide instruction and feedback as needed.

2. **Explain the purpose of the lesson:** To practice saying all vowels, words, and sentences with a balanced/more oral timbre.

3. **Review the Rules for Producing an Oral Timbre while looking at Handout A from Lesson 3:**

   ✓ Position your *tongue* in a relaxed concave position, in the bottom of your mouth, with the tip of your tongue lightly touching the back of your lower front teeth.

   ✓ Breathe in through your mouth, in a *yawn* position, like a "tired lion." This will produce a more vertical mouth position.

   ✓ While still maintaining the same "tired lion" *think* "ah," lowering the jaw, making a vertical oval.

   ✓ *Speak* (as if yawning out the sounds/words).

4. **Review work on relaxed lip position for all vowels.** Help your student to maintain a more relaxed and vertical oval mouth position by having

him place his index and middle fingers between his lips (not teeth) with the index finger on his lower lip and middle finger on his upper lip. Have him repeat and practice the following three vowels: awh, oh, ooh. Have him practice this five times. The finger placement will stop the lips from curling in. The lips must remain touching the fingers throughout the process. Now have him say the vowels five times without his fingers between his lips, maintaining a relaxed lip position.

5. **Gaining control over timbre.** Have the student say all ten vowels using the rules for a more oral sound while looking in the mirror to check his tongue position. Then have him say those vowels that are more naturally nasal in a very nasal way and then in a very oral way. Have him describe the difference. Help him notice that when he tries to produce a hyper-nasal quality his lips become more tense, trying to create a more horizontal position.

6. **Have the student come up with one word for each of the oral vowel sounds and say them in an oral way.**

7. **Present five words for each of the more nasal vowel sounds (ee (bee), ih (sit), ay (say), eh (egg), æ (cat)) and have him produce them with a more oral sound.** Remind the student of tongue and lip position before he speaks (relaxed tongue, and relaxed lips opened more vertically as if fingers were in mouth, as in step 2). Remind him that even the naturally occurring nasal sounds can be said in a more oral way. The key is relaxation.

   a. Bee, knees, cease, dean, mean

   b. Sit, fit, pink, litter, improve

   c. Say, day, erase, aim, plane

   d. Egg, lemon, pen, let, bed

   e. Cat, math, pat, cap, map

8. **Now work on reading sentences with an oral timbre.** For fun you can use Dr. Seuss books such as *Fox in Socks* or *Mr. Brown can Moo! Can You?* Record and play back for him. Critique and discuss his production together.

9. **Homework:** (1) Review the rules for producing a more oral sound. (2) Practice all vowel sounds and words containing them in your homework chart (Handout A), using the "tired lion" position. (3) Using the chart in Handout A, write ten sentences (one for each vowel), including as many of your words for that vowel (from the last lesson's homework) as you can. Practice the sentences. (4) Record at least one practice session and bring the recording to your next lesson.

Homework

Remember the Rules for Producing an Oral Timbre:

- ✓ Position your *tongue* in a relaxed concave position, in the bottom of your mouth, with the tip of your tongue lightly touching the back of your lower front teeth.

- ✓ Breathe in through your mouth, in a *yawn* position, like a "tired lion." This will produce a more vertical mouth position.

- ✓ While still maintaining the same "tired lion" *think* "ah," lowering the jaw.

- ✓ *Speak* (as if yawning out the sounds/words).

Practice the following vowel sounds in the chart below in front of a mirror.

Write ten sentences (one for each vowel), including as many of your words for that vowel, from the last lesson's homework, as you can. Practice the sentences.

Remember: Even for vowel sounds that are more naturally nasal, use the Rules for Producing an Oral Timbre. Making sure that the tongue is relaxed will give nasal vowels a less nasal (more balanced) sound. Try not to tighten on the consonants.

Vowels	Sentence using the words from the last lesson's homework
ee (as in bee)	
ih (as in sit)	
ay (as in say)	
eh (as in egg)	
æ (as in cat)	
ah (as in mom)	
uh (as in cup)	
awh (as in saw)	
oh (as in low)	
ooh (as in shoe)	

Oral timbre: Consonants in spontaneous speech

Materials

Handout A from Lesson 3: Rules for Producing an Oral Timbre

Handout A from Lesson 5: Homework

Audio recording device

Goals

To practice producing words and sentences with a more oral timbre.

To develop awareness that consonants can distort vowels and that there are preferred positions for producing consonants.

Procedures

1. **Explain the purpose of the lesson:** To practice producing words and sentences with a more oral timbre and develop awareness that consonants can distort vowels and that there are preferred positions for producing consonants.

2. **Review the Rules for Producing an Oral Timbre:**

   ✓ Position your *tongue* in a relaxed concave position, in the bottom of your mouth, with the tip of your tongue lightly touching the back of your lower front teeth.

   ✓ Breathe in through your mouth, in a *yawn* position, like a "tired lion." This will produce a more vertical mouth position.

   ✓ While still maintaining the same "tired lion" *think* "ah," lowering the jaw.

   ✓ *Speak* (as if yawning out the sounds/words).

3. **Review the homework from the last lesson.** Have the student read the sentences he generated and practiced for homework (Handout A from Lesson 5). Record him as he does this. Give feedback and correction as needed. Pay close attention to whether he tightens up the muscles in his throat, mouth, and lips. Remind him to relax those muscles to help produce a more oral sound. In his reading of his sentences, insist that he pause and take a deep breath before each and that he use the rules for oral timbre. Review the recording with the student and point out places

where his timbre becomes too nasal. Explain that it is important for him to be calm, mindful, and focused in order to produce an oral timbre.

4. **Collect a spontaneous language sample.** Ask the student to tell you something about what he did since the last lesson. Record this spontaneously generated speech sample (it should be about two minutes long). Listen back to this speech sample with the student. Comment on and make a list of the sounds the student needs to work on. Put this in his notebook. Give individualized homework based on the list of sounds that need work. For example, if your student were to pronounce words such as dog and coffee as dawg and cawfee, instead of in a more oral way (i.e., dahg, cahfee), give him a homework assignment to practice the following words containing the "awh" vowel sound in isolation, then in words (e.g., bought, sought, coffee, dog, for, talk, walk, caught, fraud, awful), and finally practice those words in sentences that he makes up. He should watch himself in a mirror as he does this, to be certain he is applying the Rules for Producing an Oral Timbre.

5. **Begin work on producing specific consonants in a way that will promote a more oral sound.** Remind the student that there are two reasons that consonants can interfere with producing an oral timbre: (1) when the velum drops and closes the anatomic gate to the oral pharynx, as in the consonants M and N; and (2) when the consonants produce muscle tension, which can distort the vowels to which those consonants are attached.

6. **Explain to your student that in the next set of lessons, beginning at the next lesson, he will learn the most effective way to pronounce consonants in the context of words and sentences, to promote a balanced/more oral timbre.** He will work on specific subsets of consonants. He will begin with the consonants that interfere least with a balanced/more oral timbre (e.g., P, T, K, B, D, G) and work his way up to the most difficult (e.g., M and N, which promote a nasal sound; R, L, and W, which produce muscle tension).

7. **Homework:** Practice the sentences you wrote for the last lesson's homework. PLUS complete individualized homework, developed in step 4.

Oral timbre: Consonants P, T, and K in consonant–vowel syllables and words

Materials

Handout A: Words with P, T, K

Goal

To maintain an oral timbre when the consonants P, T, and K, in both initial and final positions, are combined with all vowel sounds.

Procedures

1. **Explain the purpose of the lesson:** Tell the student that he will be practicing maintaining an oral timbre while he says words that combine the consonants P, T, and K with all vowels.

2. **Explain to the student that P, T, and K are considered oral consonants, since they do not promote a nasal quality.** Therefore, they provide a good starting point for combining consonants with vowels while using a balanced/more oral timbre.

3. **Briefly instruct the student to keep his lip and tongue muscles relaxed as he pronounces consonant–vowel combinations involving these consonants.** He should not press his lips together or push his tongue into his teeth or the roof of his mouth. Rather, the movements he uses to produce these consonants should be gentle, small, and isolated. P begins with the lips lightly touching. T begins with the tip of the tongue lightly touching behind the upper front teeth. For K, the middle of the tongue, in isolation, begins by touching the hard palate.

4. **Review the Rules for Producing an Oral Timbre:**

   ✓ Position your *tongue* in a relaxed concave position, in the bottom of your mouth, with the tip of your tongue lightly touching the back of your lower front teeth.

   ✓ Breathe in through your mouth, in a *yawn* position, like a "tired lion." This will produce a more vertical mouth position.

   ✓ While still maintaining the same "tired lion" *think* "ah," lowering the jaw.

   ✓ *Speak* (as if yawning out the sounds/words).

5. **Use Handout A:** You speak the words of each column and have the student listen and repeat words with P, T, and K in initial position followed by all vowel sounds; and then have him listen and repeat words with P, T, and K in final position preceded by all vowel sounds (three times each). Make sure the student is applying the rules for a more oral timbre as he repeats.

6. **Homework:** Practice the words on Handout A.

Words with P, T, K

	Initial			Final		
	P	**T**	**K**	**P**	**T**	**K**
ee – bee, tree	peas peek piece	teen teal tear	keep keel keen	steep cheap leap	peat seat delete	teak leak sneak
ih – it, sit	pit picture pig	tin till tier	kin kitty kiss	tip chip trip	sit pit mitt	nick chick stick
ay – say, may	pay pain paste	tape taste tailor	care cane kale	ape cape drape	late rate gate	lake take rake
eh – egg, sled	peg pest pet	test tell ten	Celtic kettle keg	step pep schlep	let debt set	wreck neck check
æ – cat, hat	pan past pat	tap tag tan	camel candy cast	tap nap trap	pat sat cat	sack lack crack
ah – spot, drop	pot pop pocket	tot top toxic	cottage conquer cobble	top cop lop	tot cot lot	lock sock mock
uh – cup, mud	pup pun putty	ton touch tub	cup come custard	up cup syrup	shut cut gut	muck truck luck
awh – sought, caught	pawn paw palm	toss taught talk	cost caulk call	—	caught naught onslaught	talk caulk chalk
oh – bone, phone	post poll pony	toast tone toll	cope cone coal	soap pope nope	mote tote goat	soak joke broke
ooh – shoe, moose	poor pool	tube tool tooth	coo cool cougar	troop loop snoop	boot chute loot	fluke rebuke juke

Oral timbre: Consonants P, T, and K in pre-formulated sentences

Materials

Handout A from Lesson 7: Words with P, T, K

Handout A: Sentences Containing Words with Consonants P, T, K

Goal

To maintain an oral timbre when the consonants P, T, and K, in both initial and final positions, are combined with all vowel sounds and said in the context of pre-formulated sentences.

Procedures

1. **Review the homework from the last lesson.** Listen to the student read words on Handout A from Lesson 7. Give feedback and correction as needed.

2. **Explain the purpose of the lesson:** To continue to practice the consonants P, T, and K in words but now in the context of pre-formulated sentences.

3. **Review the Rules for Producing an Oral Timbre:**

   ✓ Position your *tongue* in a relaxed concave position, in the bottom of your mouth, with the tip of your tongue lightly touching the back of your lower front teeth.

   ✓ Breathe in through your mouth, in a *yawn* position, like a "tired lion." This will produce a more vertical mouth position.

   ✓ While still maintaining the same "tired lion" *think* "ah," lowering the jaw.

   ✓ *Speak* (as if yawning out the sounds/words).

4. **Remind the student that he should not press his lips together or push his tongue into his teeth or the roof of his mouth, but rather keep his tongue and lips relaxed.** He should use movements that are gentle, small, and isolated to say these consonants. P begins with the lips lightly touching. T begins with the tip of the tongue lightly touching behind the upper front teeth. For K, the middle of the tongue only begins by touching the hard palate.

5. **Now have the student read the accompanying sentences (two times each).** Make sure the student is applying the Rules for Producing an Oral Timbre as he reads. Make corrections as needed.

6. **Homework:** Practice saying the sentences in Handout A, employing an oral timbre.

Sentences Containing Words with Consonants P, T, K

P–T–K SENTENCES: (ee) tree

Our dinner includes corn, mashed potatoes, and peas.

We carefully drove over the mountain peak.

You can trust that the teen will do a good job.

My wedding colors will be teal and orange.

Our sailboat's keel is nine feet long.

The eagle has a very keen vision.

The mountain trail is very steep.

Our school's bake sale sold everything at cheap prices.

The neighbor's yard was fertilized with peat.

Be very careful not to delete your homework.

My mother's salad bowl is made of teak wood.

The ship had a massive leak after the crash.

P–T–K SENTENCES: (ih) sit

The huge pit contained a pond.

We had a very funny picture of a pig.

Don't come out till you hear my whistle.

My seat is way up on the third tier.

There are eight kitties in the box.

My sister gave a kiss to the little baby.

The tip of the iceberg rose one hundred feet out of the water.

Our trip to California seemed very long.

Try to sit on the tree log.

We visited the tar pit for three hours.

Our hen had lost her chick for fifteen minutes.

Rover, our poodle, loved to chew her stick.

P–T–K SENTENCES: (ay) say

Please pay the store clerk for the book.

This paste will glue all the parts.

We will tape the torn magazine.

Tomorrow I will pick up my suit from the tailor.

My parents would take care of me and my brother, no matter what.

We prefer to use pure cane sugar.

I saw an ape at the zoo.

Our grandfather wears a cape when he dresses up.

We cannot stay up too late tonight.

Our dog won't be able to jump over the gate.

This weekend we will go to the lake.

Please rake the leaves today.

P–T–K SENTENCES: (eh) egg

In this game you will put the peg in the hole.

May I borrow your pen?

Tomorrow we will have a test.

My grandmother will tell us a nice story.

We love to listen to Celtic music.

We will cook the chicken in the old black kettle.

Our choir learns songs step by step.

Coffee gives me a real pep in the morning.

Please let me fly your kite.

I would like to have the table set for dinner.

The bus was involved in a minor wreck.

I will pick up my check on Thursday.

P–T–K SENTENCES: (æ) cat

The cast iron pan was very heavy.

In the past we have always planted tomatoes.

We heard a tap on the window.

After three hours I was very tan.

The camel made a strange sound.

We love to get candy on Halloween.

We took a long nap yesterday.

The squirrel was very excited inside the trap.

My family cat was a mother this year.

We sat in the theatre for the entire show.

We brought a big sack of oranges.

We found a crack in the foundation.

P–T–K SENTENCES: (ah) spot

The small pot will not hold the soup.

I found a hole in my pocket.

The tot crawled into the next room.

Toxic chemicals were cleaned out of the Hudson River.

The tired uncle slept on the cot.

Cobblestones cover most of the streets in Europe.

We must stop wasting our natural resources.

My bumper crop will be wheat this year.

The car lot would be full of customers.

The tot ate pancakes for breakfast.

My sock appears to be lost again.

I have not seen a lock on the patio gate.

P–T–K SENTENCES: (uh) cup

My aunt gave us a very cute puppy.

Dad used putty to repair the hole in the wall.

My mom didn't want to touch the broken glass.

We washed our puppy in the tub.

Please give me a cup of coffee.

I will try the custard after my dinner.

Combine one cup of flour with the other ingredients.

Please put maple syrup on my pancakes.

Please don't shut the door if your hands are in the doorway.

We could not cut the frozen cake.

Our family drives a truck to our mountain home.

My dad went fishing and had very good luck.

P–T–K SENTENCES: (awh) caught

We found a splinter in our cat's paw.

I ate some very good tropical food on palm leaves.

Please toss the car keys to me.

The teacher taught us how to manage our time.

Talk slowly for your friends.

Why does the book cost so much?

Please call the doctor.

My shower needed new caulking.

My brother caught a twelve-pound catfish.

Our entire winter was an onslaught of snowstorms.

When you talk please let me see your eyes.

When my teacher writes on the board he uses orange chalk.

P–T–K SENTENCES: (oh) bone

We will post our invitation on the web site.

The little pony trotted alongside.

Please bring me whole-wheat toast.

The tone of your voice was well projected today.

I ate ice cream on a cone every day this summer.

Eastern Europe uses a lot of coal.

The soap that I used this morning smells like lavender.

The new rope needs to be loosened up.

The tote bag will easily carry my muddy boots.

I made my voice carry past the goat on the other mountain.

We will soak the dishes in the sink.

When I made a joke my brother wouldn't stop laughing.

P–T–K SENTENCES: (ooh) shoe

My family helps the poor as much as they can.

Our pool stays warm in the winter.

Please replace my old tube of toothpaste.

When I was young one tooth came out all by itself.

My baby sister is so cute.

Perhaps you should bring a sweater for the cool weather.

We saw a troop of soldiers in the airport.

The mountain climber secured my rope with a strong loop.

My dad's boot needs to be repaired.

The skydiver's chute opened in time.

Mom caught a fluke when she went fishing.

We will not rebuke the concept of evolution.

LESSON 9

Oral timbre: Consonants P, T, and K in spontaneously formulated sentences

Materials

Handout A from Lesson 7: Words with P, T, K

Goal

To maintain an oral timbre when the consonants P, T, and K, in both initial and final positions, are combined with all vowel sounds and said in the context of spontaneously formulated sentences.

Procedures

1. **Explain the purpose of the lesson:** To apply what the student has learned about saying the consonants P, T, and K in words and connected speech to his spontaneous speech.

2. **Review the Rules for Producing an Oral Timbre:**

   ✓ Position your *tongue* in a relaxed concave position, in the bottom of your mouth, with the tip of your tongue lightly touching the back of your lower front teeth.

   ✓ Breathe in through your mouth, in a *yawn* position, like a "tired lion." This will produce a more vertical mouth position.

   ✓ While still maintaining the same "tired lion" *think* "ah," lowering the jaw.

   ✓ *Speak* (as if yawning out the sounds/words).

3. **Review all words in Handout A from Lesson 7.** Have the student read the words out loud. Listen to his pronunciation. Provide feedback and correction to help him produce a more oral timbre.

4. **Have the student make up sentences (at least 20) containing at least two of the words listed in Handout A from Lesson 7 in each.** Have the student recite his sentences. Make sure the student is applying the Rules for Producing an Oral Timbre as he recites. Make corrections as needed.

5. **Homework:** Practice saying the sentences in Handout A, employing an oral timbre.

LESSON 10

Oral timbre: Consonants B, D, and G in consonant–vowel syllables and words

Materials

Handout A: Words with B, D, G

Goal

To maintain an oral timbre when the voiced stop consonants B, D, and G, in both initial and final positions, are combined with all vowel sounds.

Procedures

1. **Explain the purpose of the lesson:** Tell the student that he will be practicing maintaining an oral timbre while he says words that combine the consonants B, D, and G with all vowels.

2. **Explain to the student that B, D, and G are considered oral consonants.** The only difference from P, T, K is that B, D, G are voiced consonants. This means that a sound is produced by the vocal cords as these consonants are said. P, T, K are unvoiced.

3. **Briefly instruct the student to keep his lip and tongue muscles relaxed as he pronounces consonant–vowel combinations involving these consonants.** He should not press his lips together or push his tongue into his teeth or the roof of his mouth. Rather, the movements he uses to produce these consonants should be gentle, small, and isolated. B begins with the lips lightly touching. D begins with the tip of the tongue lightly touching behind the upper front teeth. For G, the middle of the tongue only begins by touching the hard palate.

4. **Review the Rules for Producing an Oral Timbre:**

    ✓ Position your *tongue* in a relaxed concave position, in the bottom of your mouth, with the tip of your tongue lightly touching the back of your lower front teeth.

    ✓ Breathe in through your mouth, in a *yawn* position, like a "tired lion." This will produce a more vertical mouth position.

    ✓ While still maintaining the same "tired lion" *think* "ah," lowering the jaw.

    ✓ *Speak* (as if yawning out the sounds/words).

5. **Now use the accompanying chart:** Have the student listen and repeat words with B, D, and G in initial position followed by all vowel sounds; and then have him listen and repeat words with B, D, and G in final position preceded by all vowel sounds (three times each). Make sure the student is applying the Rules Producing an Oral Timbre as he repeats.

6. **Homework:** Practice the words in Handout A, employing a balanced/ more oral timbre.

Words with B, D, G

	Initial			Final		
	B	**D**	**G**	**B**	**D**	**G**
ee – bee, tree	beat bean beam	deep dean deal	geek geezer gear	dweeb	read mead lead	league Grieg colleague
ih – it, sit	bit built big	dip dish did	gill give giddy	bib crib glib	rid slid lid	big pig rig
ay – say, may	bay brain bait	day date daily	gain gable gate	babe	paid trade stayed	plague Hague vague
eh – egg, sled	beg bed bet	dead dell	get gecko gelding	web Debb	dead sled bled	keg leg beg
æ – cat, hat	bat banned battle	dab dash dam	gather gas gander	slab nab gab	lad dad mad	rag stag hag
ah – spot, drop	bottle Bonnie bother	dot doctor D.O.S.	god gobble got	slob job snob	odd sod nod	dog hog log
uh – cup, mud	butter buzz bun	done dull dusk	gust gull guts	tub rub stub	thud crud dud	jug lug mug
awh – sought, caught	ball boss bark	dawn daughter dabber	gone gall gawk	daub	clawed flawed Maude	dialogue epilogue prologue
oh – bone, phone	bone boast boil	donut don't doze	go goal ghost	probe lobe robe	ode slowed crowed	vogue rogue
ooh – shoe, moose	boost boom boots	doom dude duel	goon goo Google	tube lube	food dude crude	Moog fugue

Oral timbre: Consonants B, D, and G in pre-formulated sentences

Materials

Handout A from Lesson 10: Words with B, D, G (nasal consonants)

Handout A: Sentences Containing Words with Consonants B, D, G

Goal

To maintain an oral timbre when the consonants B, D, and G, in both initial and final positions, are combined with all vowel sounds and said in the context of pre-formulated sentences.

Procedures

1. **Review the homework from the last lesson.** Listen to the student read the words on Handout A from Lesson 10. Give feedback and correction as needed.

2. **Explain the purpose of the lesson:** To continue to practice the consonants B, D, and G in words but now in the context of pre-formulated sentences.

3. **Review the Rules for Producing an Oral Timbre:**

    ✓ Position your *tongue* in a relaxed concave position, in the bottom of your mouth, with the tip of your tongue lightly touching the back of your lower front teeth.

    ✓ Breathe in through your mouth, in a *yawn* position, like a "tired lion." This will produce a more vertical mouth position.

    ✓ While still maintaining the same "tired lion" *think* "ah," lowering the jaw.

    ✓ *Speak* (as if yawning out the sounds/words).

4. **Remind the student that he should not press his lips together or push his tongue into his teeth or the roof of his mouth, but rather keep his tongue and lips relaxed.** He should use movements that are gentle, small, and isolated to say these consonants. B begins with the lips lightly touching. D begins with the tip of the tongue lightly touching behind the upper front teeth. For G, the middle of the tongue only begins by touching the hard palate.

5. **Now have the student read the accompanying sentences (two times each).** Make sure the student is applying the Rules for Producing an Oral Timbre as he repeats. Make corrections as needed.

6. **Homework:** Practice saying the sentences in Handout A, employing an oral timbre.

Sentences Containing Words with Consonants B, D, G

B–D–G SENTENCES: (ee) tree
> Beat the drum loudly.
> We saw the yellow beam of light.
> The starfish was found deep in the red sea.
> The dean of the school awarded the student.
> The old geezer drove his car too slow.
> You'll need camping gear for your trip.
> We honored the dweeb for saving our city.
> Please read the instructions carefully.
> I will lead the troops into battle.
> The soccer league included fifty teams.
> My colleague played the Beethoven piano sonata.

B–D–G SENTENCES: (ih) sit
> My dog bit his own tail.
> There is a big valley near my cabin.
> You may dip your paintbrush briefly.
> My Italian dish was delicious.
> The fish has a huge gill on either side.
> Give my shovel to the teenager.
> There was food on the baby's bib.
> The newborn slept in his crib.
> We will get rid of the old sink.
> The boy's bicycle slid into the fence.
> The pig was full of corn.
> The lady drove the big rig across the country

B–D–G SENTENCES: (ay) say
> We were sailing in the bay.
> He put the live bait on the fishing hook.
> He asked the girl on a date to the movies.
> I consult my planner daily.
> Our team will gain six points in this game.
> The gate was locked with four padlocks.

The ox named "Babe" was blue and huge.

We paid for all of our tickets.

Our tent stayed secure all night.

The "black plague" was devastating for Europe.

The vague movements of the dancer confused me.

B–D–G SENTENCES: (eh) egg

My dog begs for his dinner.

When you finish your homework, go to bed.

Debbie will run the hundred-yard dash.

Our car sputtered and then was dead.

It's time to get our work done.

My sister has a very colorful gecko.

I get all my information from the web.

We will visit the Dead Sea while on our vacation.

The boy's nose bled all over his clothes.

The old wooden keg was full of wine.

My leg was injured in the soccer game.

B–D–G SENTENCES: (æ) cat

We were watching the bat very closely.

The old sailor was banned from the treasure hunt.

The hundred-yard dash was his best event.

The Hoover Dam protected our valley.

We will gather under the old pecan tree.

The gas from the coal mine was toxic.

There was a cracked slab of concrete.

Our boys had the gift of the gab.

The lad was a great dancer.

Our dad wanted to watch the game.

We were photographing the stag.

Our mother used a special rag for her cleaning.

B–D–G SENTENCES: (ah) spot

My brother drinks milk from a bottle.

Please don't bother her mother tonight.

Our doctor lives in Manhattan.

A dot marks the end of a sentence.

How do you gobble down a hotdog so fast?

What have you got in your hand?

My job was to serve the public.
The girl should lob the ball back across the net.
We planted the yard completely with sod.
The pilot gave us a reassuring nod.
Our best pet was a tiny little hog.
The brave dog jumped up on the log.

B–D–G SENTENCES: (uh) cup

Please put butter on my toast.
The small plane would buzz our position nightly.
The turkey was done after four hours.
The paint coating seemed dull to me.
Our house shook from the massive gust of wind.
When we visit the beach we watch the sea gulls.
We will bathe our dog in the metal tub.
You must rub the sticks together to make a fire.
When the piano fell it made a huge thud.
When mom cleaned out the filter she found lots of crud.
We brought a jug of water on our camping trip.
My grandfather always drinks from a steel mug.

B–D–G SENTENCES: (awh) caught

Let's go and play catch with the ball.
Our dog barks all night long.
My daughter plays the piano.
At dawn we will sail across the lake.
Our uncle's family stays gone for the winter.
My dad went to the hospital to have his gall stone removed.
Use your marker to daub the correct numbers on the paper.
The tiger clawed the antelope with his claws.
The lab results were flawed because of the data.
Her dialogue seemed clear and smooth.
The prologue to the performance was very exciting.

B-D-G SENTENCES (oh) bone

We painted the blue boat.
I couldn't take the dog's bone.
Our new lunchroom is a real bonus.
A bolt of lightning struck the banana tree.
The apple spice donut is my favourite one.

I told my sister that I saw a picture of the extinct Dodo bird.

Don't feed table scraps to our dog.

My brother dove into the deep water.

Go pick up your clothes and put them in the laundry.

Our pet goat eats everything you give him.

At the beginning of the school year I set a difficult goal for myself.

Some people say a ghost lives in the old lighthouse.

B-D-G SENTENCES (Ooh) shoe

My little brother cried when I said, "Boo!"

I like to wear cowboy boots.

My dad got a real boost when his boss gave him the award.

When the train crashed into the platform, I heard a loud boom!

The four super heroes felt they were doomed.

Do you like puppies or kittens?

Staying at the dude ranch gave me some really great memories.

The Duke had a bad reputation.

My father used goo to hold the model airplane together.

My mother saw dark green goop coming from underneath the garbage pail.

I sleep with my head on a goose down pillow.

Google helped me get through my assignments all year.

Oral timbre: Consonants B, D, and G in spontaneously formulated sentences

Materials

Handout A from Lesson 10: Words with B, D, G

Goal

To maintain an oral timbre when the consonants B, D, and G, in both initial and final positions, are combined with all vowel sounds and said in the context of spontaneously formulated sentences.

Procedures

1. **Explain the purpose of the lesson:** To apply what the student has learned about saying the consonants B, D, and G in words and connected speech to his spontaneous speech.

2. **Review the Rules for Producing an Oral Timbre:**

   ✓ Position your *tongue* in a relaxed concave position, in the bottom of your mouth, with the tip of your tongue lightly touching the back of your lower front teeth.

   ✓ Breathe in through your mouth, in a *yawn* position, like a "tired lion." This will produce a more vertical mouth position.

   ✓ While still maintaining the same "tired lion" *think* "ah," lowering the jaw.

   ✓ *Speak* (as if yawning out the sounds/words).

3. **Using an oral timbre, have the student read the words in Handout A from Lesson 10 out loud.** Listen to his pronunciation. Provide feedback and correction to help him produce a more oral timbre.

4. **Have the student make up sentences (at least 20) containing at least two of the words listed in Handout A from Lesson 10 in each.** Have the student recite his sentences. Make sure the student is applying the Rules for Producing an Oral Timbre as he recites. Make corrections as needed.

5. **Homework:** Practice saying the sentences in Handout A, employing an oral timbre.

Oral timbre: Consonants M and N in consonant–vowel syllables and words

Materials

Handout A: Words with M and N (nasal consonants)

Goal

To maintain an oral timbre when the nasal consonants M and N, in both initial and final positions, are combined with all vowel sounds.

Procedures

1. **Explain the purpose of the lesson:** Tell the student that he will be practicing maintaining an oral timbre while he says words that combine the consonants M and N with all vowels.

2. **Explain to the student that M and N are considered nasal consonants.** This means that when they are pronounced, the velum drops, closing the gate to the oral pharynx. When M and N are said, all of the air and sound comes through the nasal pharynx. Remind the student that he knows this, because if he pinches his nose as he is saying these sounds, all sound will stop.

3. **Explain that since M and N are nasal consonants, they will promote a nasal timbre.** Tell your student he must try to get back to an oral position with his tongue relaxed and down and his velum lifted after he briefly pronounces these consonants.

4. **Instruct the student to keep his lip and tongue muscles relaxed as he pronounces consonant–vowel combinations involving these consonants.** He should not press his lips together or push his tongue into his teeth. Rather, the movements he uses to produce these consonants should be gentle, small, and isolated. M begins with the lips lightly touching. N begins with the tip of the tongue lightly touching behind the upper front teeth. (These consonants are similar in character to "ng" where the middle of the tongue begins by touching the hard palate.)

5. **Review the Rules for Producing an Oral Timbre:**

   ✓ Position your *tongue* in a relaxed concave position, in the bottom of your mouth, with the tip of your tongue lightly touching the back of your lower front teeth.

✓ Breathe in through your mouth, in a *yawn* position, like a "tired lion." This will produce a more vertical mouth position.

✓ While still maintaining the same "tired lion" *think* "ah," lowering the jaw.

✓ *Speak* (as if yawning out the sounds/words).

6. **Now use the accompanying chart:** Have the student listen and repeat words with M and N in initial position followed by all vowel sounds; and then have him listen and repeat words with M and N in final position preceded by all vowel sounds (three times each). Make sure the student is applying the Rules for Producing an Oral Timbre as he repeats.

7. **Homework:** Practice the words in Handout A, employing a balanced/ more oral timbre.

Words with M and N (nasal consonants)

	Initial		Final	
	M	**N**	**M**	**N**
ee – bee, tree	meet meal meek	need near knee	steam beam dream	lean teen screen
ih – it, sit	Mitt mist miss	nick nib nip	skim trim slim	thin gin tin
ay – say, may	make may made	nail neigh name	same came fame	rain gain plane
eh – egg, sled	met mess men	nest neck net	hem gem stem	again glen ten
æ – cat, hat	map mask man	nap nab nag	gram jam slam	than clan plan
ah – spot, drop	mop masque mom	knot knock nod	.com tom-tom bomb	bon-bon on Tron
uh – cup, mud	mud mutt mug	nut nub null	drum from slum	sun run ton
awh – sought, caught	morn moss mall	naught gnaw notch	norm storm form	lawn drawn yawn
oh – bone, phone	moan moat mode	note nose gnome	roam foam chrome	bone clone drone
ooh – shoe, moose	mood moon mooch	new noon nuke	tomb groom broom	tune loon soon

LESSON 14

Oral timbre: Consonants M and N in pre-formulated sentences

Materials

Handout A from Lesson 13: Words with M and N (nasal consonants)

Handout A: Sentences Containing Words with Consonants M and N

Goal

To maintain an oral timbre when the consonants M and N, in both initial and final positions, are combined with all vowel sounds and said in the context of pre-formulated sentences.

Procedures

1. **Review the homework from the last lesson.** Listen to the student read words on Handout A from Lesson 13. Give feedback and correction as needed.

2. **Explain the purpose of the lesson:** To continue to practice the consonants M and N in words but now in the context of pre-formulated sentences.

3. **Review the Rules for Producing an Oral Timbre:**

   ✓ Position your *tongue* in a relaxed concave position, in the bottom of your mouth, with the tip of your tongue lightly touching the back of your lower front teeth.

   ✓ Breathe in through your mouth, in a *yawn* position, like a "tired lion." This will produce a more vertical mouth position.

   ✓ While still maintaining the same "tired lion" *think* "ah," lowering the jaw.

   ✓ *Speak* (as if yawning out the sounds/words).

4. **Remind the student that he should not press his lips together or push his tongue into his teeth, but rather keep his tongue and lips relaxed.** He should use movements that are gentle, small, and isolated to say these consonants. M begins with the lips lightly touching. N begins with the tip of the tongue lightly touching behind the upper front teeth.

5. **Now have the student read the accompanying sentences (two times each).** Make sure the student is applying the Rules for Producing an Oral Timbre as he repeats. Make corrections as needed.

6. **Homework:** Practice saying the sentences in Handout A, employing an oral timbre.

Sentences Containing Words with Consonants M and N

M–N SENTENCES: (ee) tree

I will meet my family for lunch.

The meek boy roared like a lion.

We need to sing more.

I hurt my knee yesterday.

My dream was a happy one.

Please steam my vegetables.

Don't sit too close to the screen.

My friend is also a teen.

M–N SENTENCES: (ih) sit

The mist was very thick.

I will miss you today.

The puppy gave me a nip.

Nick was my best friend.

Trim the shrubs carefully.

My brother is very slim.

The paper is too thin.

My favorite cup is made of tin.

M–N SENTENCES: (ay) say

I will make my bed.

May I eat cherries?

My name is _____.

Pull the nail out carefully.

I came at the same time today.

The horse seems very tame.

This rain is heavy.

The plane is very fast.

M–N SENTENCES: (eh) egg

I met my teacher today.

The men are well dressed.

I found a bird's nest.

My friend has an insect net.

The shiny gem is a diamond.

My mom will hem my trousers.

My brother's name is Glen.

There are ten minutes left.

M–N SENTENCES: (æ) cat

Find the campus map.

The man wore a funny mask.

I took a nap for energy.

The boy's sister will nag him all morning.

The element weighs one gram.

I want to try the grape jam.

The ancient clan worshiped the sun.

My plan is to use my planner every day.

M–N SENTENCES: (ah) spot

The moss is growing near the rocks.

I will mop the kitchen floor for my mom.

He tied the knot too tight.

Please nod yes or no.

My little brother likes to hit the tom-tom.

When I hit my head on the floor, it felt like a bomb!

My aunt wants to eat one bon-bon.

This arcade reminds me of the movie "Tron."

M–N SENTENCES: (uh) cup

I stepped in the mud this morning.

That mutt is the cutest puppy ever.

My bike has a loose nut.

The tire nubs give me good traction.

Play the drum loudly.

She comes from a tropical island.

I love to run out in the sun.

The tiny little car only weighs a ton.

M–N SENTENCES: (awh) caught

This is a productive morning.

We always shop in the mall.

They traveled one nautical mile.

My dog will gnaw on his bone.

The storm will last all night.

The sand castle began to take form.

The lawn was well manicured.

Let yourself yawn and you will relax your jaw.

M–N SENTENCES: (oh) glow

The moat was filled with water.

The gyroscopic mode gave the vehicle stability.

Send yourself a note for a reminder.

My nose is hyper-sensitive.

Oh give me a home where the buffalo roam.

The coastline was full of foam.

We will clone the primate.

Our military will deploy the drone.

M–N SENTENCES: (ooh) shoe

The moon affected the tide.

She is in a happy mood.

We will meet her at noon today.

My plate of pasta was one long noodle.

We explored the ancient tomb.

I will be happy to groom the horse.

That last tune needed a better melody.

We saw a single loon on the lake.

Oral timbre: Consonants M and N in spontaneously formulated sentences

Materials

Handout A from Lesson 13: Words with M and N (nasal consonants)

Goal

To maintain an oral timbre when the consonants M and N, in both initial and final positions, are combined with all vowel sounds and said in the context of spontaneously formulated sentences.

Procedures

1. **Explain the purpose of the lesson:** To apply what the student has learned about saying the consonants M and N in words and connected speech to his spontaneous speech.

2. **Review the Rules for Producing an Oral Timbre:**

   ✓ Position your *tongue* in a relaxed concave position, in the bottom of your mouth, with the tip of your tongue lightly touching the back of your lower front teeth.

   ✓ Breathe in through your mouth, in a *yawn* position, like a "tired lion." This will produce a more vertical mouth position.

   ✓ While still maintaining the same "tired lion" *think* "ah," lowering the jaw.

   ✓ *Speak* (as if yawning out the sounds/words).

3. **Review all words in Handout A from Lesson 13.** Have the student read the words out loud. Listen to his pronunciation. Provide feedback and correction to help him produce a more oral timbre.

4. **Have the student make up sentences (at least 20) containing at least two of the words listed in Handout A from Lesson 13 in each.** Have the student recite his sentences. Make sure the student is applying the Rules for Producing an Oral Timbre as he recites. Make corrections as needed.

5. **Homework:** Practice the words in Handout A, employing a balanced/ more oral timbre.

Oral timbre: Consonants J and ch in consonant–vowel syllables and words

Materials

Handout A: Words with J and ch

Goal

To maintain an oral timbre when the voiced stop consonants J and ch, in both initial and final positions, are combined with all vowel sounds.

Procedures

1. **Explain the purpose of the lesson:** Tell the student that he will be practicing maintaining an oral timbre while he says words that combine the consonants J and ch with all vowels.

2. **Explain to the student that J and ch are consonants that can greatly increase muscle tension and thereby make it quite difficult to achieve or maintain an open, balanced timbre.** For both of these consonants the molars may come together to produce the sound. It is easy to press the molars together hard and create muscle tension throughout the jaw and tongue.

3. **Instruct the student in how to produce J and ch so that he does not create an abundance of muscle tension as he does.** He should not "chew" these consonants by crunching his teeth together. Rather, the movements he uses to produce these consonants should be gentle, small, and isolated. To pronounce J and ch, he should extend his lips outward in the shape of a vertical "O" (like a fish). Instruct him to begin by touching the front of his tongue to the hard palate right behind his upper front teeth. This will stop him from biting down hard and producing muscle tension.

4. **Review the Rules for Producing an Oral Timbre:**

   ✓ Position your *tongue* in a relaxed concave position, in the bottom of your mouth, with the tip of your tongue lightly touching the back of your lower front teeth.

   ✓ Breathe in through your mouth, in a *yawn* position, like a "tired lion." This will produce a more vertical mouth position.

   ✓ While still maintaining the same "tired lion" *think* "ah," lowering the jaw.

✓ *Speak* (as if yawning out the sounds/words).

5. **Now use the accompanying chart:** Have the student listen and repeat words with J and ch in initial position followed by all vowel sounds; and then have him listen and repeat words with J and ch in final position preceded by all vowel sounds (three times each). Make sure the student is applying the Rules for Producing an Oral Timbre as he repeats.

6. **Homework:** Practice the words in Handout A, employing a balanced/more oral timbre.

Words with J and ch

	Initial		Final	
	J	ch	J	ch
ee – bee, tree	jeer jeep jeans	cheek cheese cheap	siege	screech bleach beach
i – it, sit	jig gym gin	chilly chicken chin	ridge fridge bridge	rich stitch pitch
ay – say, may	jay jail Jane	chain chase change	age page wage	"H"
e – egg, sled	Jello gel Jed	check checkers chess	edge ledge hedge	wretch fetch sketch
æ – cat, hat	January jam Jasper	champion chant charity	badge	catch batch match
ah – spot, drop	jolly job jog	Chinese chop chocolate	Hodge lodge garage	botch scotch watch
uh – cup, mud	justice jug just	chum chug chuck	smudge grudge sludge	much such crutch
awh – sought, caught	jaw jaunt Johnson	chalk Charles chomp		
oh – bone, phone	joke jovial join	choke chose chore		roach coach poach
ooh – shoe, moose	June July juniper	choose chew chewed		hooch pooch smooch

Oral timbre: Consonants J and ch in pre-formulated sentences

Materials

Handout A from Lesson 16: Words with J and ch

Handout A: Sentences Containing Words with Consonants J and ch

Goal

To maintain an oral timbre when the consonants J and ch, in both initial and final positions, are combined with all vowel sounds and said in the context of pre-formulated sentences.

Procedures

1. **Review the homework from the last lesson.** Listen to the student read the words on Handout A from Lesson 16. Give feedback and correction as needed.

2. **Explain the purpose of the lesson:** To continue to practice the consonants J and ch in words but now in the context of pre-formulated sentences.

3. **Review the Rules for Producing an Oral Timbre:**

   ✓ Position your *tongue* in a relaxed concave position, in the bottom of your mouth, with the tip of your tongue lightly touching the back of your lower front teeth.

   ✓ Breathe in through your mouth, in a *yawn* position, like a "tired lion." This will produce a more vertical mouth position.

   ✓ While still maintaining the same "tired lion" *think* "ah," lowering the jaw.

   ✓ *Speak* (as if yawning out the sounds/words).

4. **Remind the student that he should not "chew" these consonants by crunching his teeth together.** This creates a great deal of muscle tension throughout the jaw and tongue, leading to distorted vowels and restricted ability to create a balanced/more oral timbre. Rather, the movements he uses to produce these consonants should be gentle, small, and isolated. To pronounce J and ch, he should extend his lips outward in the shape of a vertical "O" (like a fish). Instruct him to begin by touching the front of his tongue to the hard palate right behind

his upper front teeth. This will stop him from biting down hard and producing muscle tension.

5. **Now have the student read the accompanying sentences (two times each).** Make sure the student is applying the Rules for Producing an Oral Timbre as he repeats. Make corrections as needed.

6. **Homework:** Practice saying the sentences in Handout A, employing an oral timbre.

Sentences Containing Words with Consonants J and ch

J–CH SENTENCES: (ee) tree

My dad has an old army jeep.

May I take my jeans out of the dryer?

My grandmother kissed me on the cheek.

I love Gouda cheese.

The soldiers were defending the fort during the siege.

The hawk made a very loud screech.

My family loves to go to the beach.

J–CH SENTENCES: (ih) sit

We will go to the gym to exercise.

The fish pulled my jig under the water and took off.

The chilly weather is a good time for indoor activities.

My grandmother had a chicken in her yard.

I kept my lunch in the fridge.

Tomorrow we will cross the bridge.

The desert was rich with honey.

Please use a higher pitch when you say those words.

J–CH SENTENCES: (ay) say

The jay hawk landed on our patio.

My aunt's name is Jane.

We were unable to go past the chain.

I love to play chase with my friends.

What is the age of your brother?

Our family picture is on the first page.

My name begins with the letter "H."

J–CH SENTENCES: (eh) egg

"Jello" is fun to eat.

I do not use gel in my hair.

My sister and I play chess after school.

Sometimes we play checkers instead.

The front edge of the storm came across our town.

We never touch the sculptures up on the ledge.

Jumper, my poodle, loves to play fetch.

I will try to sketch a picture of you.

J–CH SENTENCES: (æ) cat

We will have toast and jam.

Jasper is a beautiful mineral.

Our team is the state champion.

The Gregorian chant is very beautiful.

The officer lost his badge.

Let's play catch today.

That match was so exciting.

J–CH SENTENCES: (ah) spot

My dad's job will help our community.

I will jog five miles every day.

Do you sell chocolate bars?

This week we will have to chop ice again.

The old Dodge pick-up was in good shape.

Last summer we stayed at the lodge.

I love to play the game called "hop scotch."

This watch is my most reliable.

J–CH SENTENCES: (uh) cup

Bring the jug of iced tea.

Our community stands for justice.

The tugboat goes "chug-a-chug-a-chug-a."

We poured out chum to attract the large creature.

There is a smudge below your eye.

The ice and snow turned into sludge.

I will not eat too much dessert.

When I broke my ankle, I had to use a crutch to walk.

J–CH SENTENCES: (awh) caught

My jaw is still very sore.

His jaunty attitude proved he was interested.

Red chalk doesn't show on my black board.

We have to finish our chores before we come out.

J–CH SENTENCES: (oh) bone

My dad told another joke.

I would like to join the team.

She choked on a peanut.

I chose her because I love her.

✓

I saw a huge roach in the restaurant.
The tennis coach was a pro.

J–CH SENTENCES: (ooh) shoe

June is a great month to visit Minnesota.
Our yard is full of Juniper bushes.
Please chew your food carefully.
The old Eskimo lady chewed the leather for days.
The hillbilly took his pooch to the river.
This canyon is known as a place to smooch.

Oral timbre: Consonants J and ch in spontaneously formulated sentences

Materials

Handout A from Lesson 16: Words with J and ch

Goal

To maintain an oral timbre when the consonants J and ch, in both initial and final positions, are combined with all vowel sounds and said in the context of spontaneously formulated sentences.

Procedures

1. **Explain the purpose of the lesson:** To apply what the student has learned about saying the consonants J and ch in words and connected speech to his spontaneous speech.

2. **Review the Rules for Producing an Oral Timbre:**

    ✓ Position your *tongue* in a relaxed concave position, in the bottom of your mouth, with the tip of your tongue lightly touching the back of your lower front teeth.

    ✓ Breathe in through your mouth, in a *yawn* position, like a "tired lion." This will produce a more vertical mouth position.

    ✓ While still maintaining the same "tired lion" *think* "ah," lowering the jaw.

    ✓ *Speak* (as if yawning out the sounds/words).

3. **Review all words in Handout A from Lesson 16.** Have the student read the words out loud. Listen to his pronunciation. Provide feedback and correction to help him produce a more oral timbre.

4. **Have the student make up sentences (at least 20) containing at least two of the words listed in Handout A from Lesson 16 in each.** Have the student recite his sentences. Make sure the student is applying the Rules for Producing an Oral Timbre as he recites. Make corrections as needed.

5. **Homework:** Finish step 4. Practice saying the sentences in Handout A, employing an oral timbre.

Oral timbre: Consonants W, L, and R in consonant–vowel syllables and words

Materials

Handout A: Words with W, L, R

Goal

To maintain an oral timbre when the voiced stop consonants W, L, and R, in both initial and final positions, are combined with all vowel sounds.

Procedures

1. **Explain the purpose of the lesson:** Tell the student that he will be practicing maintaining an oral timbre while he says words that combine the consonants W, L, and R with all vowels.

2. **Explain to the student that W, L, and R are likely the most challenging consonants to produce without muscle tension.** Consonants produced in such a way that they create muscle tension distort the sound of the vowels to which they are attached. When the tongue, lips, and jaw muscles are tight, they constrict airflow and sound, making the sound less balanced/less oral.

3. **Instruct the student in how to keep his lips, tongue, and jaw muscles relaxed as he pronounces consonant–vowel combinations involving these consonants.** It is important that your student learns to pronounce these consonants with a relaxed tongue, lips, and jaw, and with a vertical shape to his mouth. In addition, there is a preferred position for producing each of these consonants. It is very important that you instruct your student to take great care as he pronounces the L and the R. They involve a much larger portion of the tongue muscle and require that your student works very hard to control the movement and tension of the tongue. The key for L and R is to not clamp down. Pressure creates tension. There needs to be "openness" within the mouth. Have him start the production of each consonant with a "yawn" (base of tongue down; velum up).

   a. Pronouncing W is relatively straightforward. Your student should be told to extend his lips outward as he produces the sound.

   b. Many people generate the L sound in an ineffective way by sticking the tongue out, between the upper and lower teeth (not preferred). This tightens the jaw and tongue. The preferred method is by starting with the tip of the tongue touching the edge of the upper front teeth or behind the upper front teeth. This maintains the mouth in a more open posture. It promotes a relaxed tongue and jaw and an oral sound.

c. Many people produce the R sound by crunching their molars together, creating great tension throughout the jaw, lips, and tongue (ineffective). The R should be pronounced in a similar way to J and ch. Instruct the student to extend his lips outward in the shape of a vertical "O" (like a fish). His molars should *not* touch each other. The sides of his tongue should come up to meet his upper molars. This will stop him from biting down hard and producing muscle tension. Again, his mouth is maintained in a more open posture.

4. **Review the Rules for Producing an Oral Timbre:**

   ✓ Position your *tongue* in a relaxed concave position, in the bottom of your mouth, with the tip of your tongue lightly touching the back of your lower front teeth.

   ✓ Breathe in through your mouth, in a *yawn* position, like a "tired lion." This will produce a more vertical mouth position.

   ✓ While still maintaining the same "tired lion" *think* "ah," lowering the jaw.

   ✓ *Speak* (as if yawning out the sounds/words).

5. **Now use the accompanying chart:** Have the student listen and repeat words with W, L, and R in initial position followed by all vowel sounds; and then have him listen and repeat words with W, L, and R in final position preceded by all vowel sounds (three times each). Make sure the student is applying the Rules for Producing an Oral Timbre as he repeats.

6. **Homework:** Practice the words in Handout A, employing a balanced/more oral timbre.

Words with W, L, R

	Initial			Final		
	W	**L**	**R**	**W**	**L**	**R**
ee – bee, tree	weed weave weeks	leap leaf leak	read real reef	—	peel wheel squeal	peer sheer deer
ih – it, sit	wit wick width	lip lid lick	rip riff rig	—	pill will sill	—
ay – say, may	way waste wade	lay lace lake	ray rage rail	—	pail whale snail	lair layer mayor
eh – egg, sled	wet web west	led left leg	red ref R.E.M.s	—	fell quell smell	err
æ – cat, hat	whack wares wham	lab lack lads	rat rack raft	—	pal gal	air snare care
ah – spot, drop	what watch watts	lot lava like	rotten rocks rods	—	doll hall mall	are tar star
uh – cup, mud	wonder one	luck love lump	run rub rump	—	gull hull null	fur slur culture
awh – sought, caught	warm warts walls	lawn laws loft	raw wrought wrong	—	all wall call	—
oh – bone, phone	whoa woke woe	loan loaf lobe	wrote road roam	owe glow crow	hole goal mole	floor snore door
ooh – shoe, moose	wound wooed wool	loot loofa loom	root rude rune	chew threw grew	pool drool spool	poor sewer moor

Oral timbre: Consonants W, L, and R in pre-formulated sentences

Materials

Handout A from Lesson 19: Words with W, L, R

Handout A: Sentences Containing Words with Consonants W, L, R

Goal

To maintain an oral timbre when the consonants W, L, and R, in both initial and final positions, are combined with all vowel sounds and said in the context of pre-formulated sentences.

Procedures

1. **Review the homework from the last lesson.** Listen to the student read the words on Handout A from Lesson 19. Give feedback and correction as needed.

2. **Explain the purpose of the lesson:** To continue to practice the consonants W, L, and R in words and now learn to use them in pre-formulated sentences.

3. **Review the Rules for Producing an Oral Timbre:**

   ✓ Position your *tongue* in a relaxed concave position, in the bottom of your mouth, with the tip of your tongue lightly touching the back of your lower front teeth.

   ✓ Breathe in through your mouth, in a *yawn* position, like a "tired lion." This will produce a more vertical mouth position.

   ✓ While still maintaining the same "tired lion" *think* "ah," lowering the jaw.

   ✓ *Speak* (as if yawning out the sounds/words).

4. **Remind your student that once his mouth is in the yawn position he will produce W, L, and R in the following ways.** W is produced by extending his relaxed lips outward as he pronounces the sound. For L, the preferred method is by starting with the tip of the tongue touching the edge of the upper front teeth or behind the upper front teeth. For R, he should extend his lips outward in the shape of a vertical "O" (like a fish). His molars should not touch each other. The sides of his tongue should come up to meet his upper molars. Each of these positions

maintains a shape in the mouth for a more open position, promoting a relaxed tongue and jaw and balanced/more oral sound.

5. **Now have the student read the accompanying sentences (two times each).** Make sure the student is applying the Rules for Producing an Oral Timbre as he repeats. Make corrections as needed.

6. **Homework:** Practice saying the sentences in Handout A, employing an oral timbre.

Sentences Containing Words with Consonants W, L, R

W–L–R SENTENCES: (ee) tree

Remove the weed from the garden.

Three weeks have passed.

Leap over the ditch.

I saw a maple leaf.

Read the page carefully.

The reef was very colorful.

Please peel my orange.

My bicycle wheel is very strong.

I saw a deer in the path.

I will sheer off the twig.

W–L–R SENTENCES: (ih) sit

The wick for the candle is too short.

My wish was for world peace.

His lip was bleeding.

Take the lid off of the jam.

The big rig was out of control.

Rip off the tab so that the cartridge will work.

I will follow the rules.

You will find the key on the window sill.

The steer was big and healthy.

We were standing on the pier.

W–L–R SENTENCES: (ay) say

Which way shall we proceed?

This city will waste too much electricity.

Please lay down your pencils.

The lake is very muddy.

Ask your brother, Ray, to our party.

Many people have too much rage.

I love to see a whale up close.

This train is as slow as a snail.

I will share my paper with you.

The hunter will snare the rabbit.

W–L–R SENTENCES: (eh) egg
> The towel is still wet.
> We might find the game on the web.
> She led her sisters to the museum exhibit.
> My left leg is still in pain.
> You will find the red shirt in your closet.
> You must sleep soundly to accomplish R.E.M.s.
> I fell down on the ice.
> The smell of oranges filled the air.
> To err is human.

W–L–R SENTENCES: (æ) cat
> The shopkeeper's wares were very interesting.
> "Wham" was the sound of the basketball on the wall.
> This week I will be working in the lab.
> This is a happy group of lads.
> My mother saw a rat.
> We had so much fun on the raft.
> Your pal seemed quite nice.
> The gal on the horse rode nicely.
> Breathe the air and smell the roses.
> My friend really does care about me.

W–L–R SENTENCES: (ah) spot
> What will happen after this game?
> The bulb puts out 60 watts of illumination.
> I saw the lava and I was scared.
> I like my brothers and sisters.
> The fruit is rotten.
> We built our house on a hill of solid rocks.
> The girl brought her favorite doll.
> Wait for me in the hall.
> We are all stronger than you are.
> My favorite beach was covered in pieces of tar.

W–L–R SENTENCES: (uh) cup
> Wonder Woman conquered the Amazon people.
> My planner guides me one day at a time.
> My luck has been good on this trip.
> My sadness put a lump in my throat.
> The dog run was very active.
> Aladdin will rub the lamp.

I woke up and heard a sea gull.

I broke the pecan hull to reveal the nut's meat.

The dog's fur was very soft.

Our culture had many shortcomings.

W–L–R SENTENCES: (awh) caught

My blanket is too warm.

Please paint my walls orange.

My lawn is very green.

The new loft is very roomy.

We prefer our diet of raw vegetables.

The teacher proved the student wrong.

My walls are very dirty.

Call the plumber immediately.

All of our family will stay in the hotel.

W–L–R SENTENCES: (oh) phone

When my brother woke he went to have breakfast.

The driver of the wagon said, "Whoa you horses!"

Please loan me your tools.

My sister made a very good loaf of bread.

This week we wrote a new report.

My house is at the end of the road.

My teacher said that I owe her an essay.

The man brought his pet crow.

My dad's car drove over the deep hole.

The soccer team scored a goal.

Please sweep the floor for your mom.

I could hear the music through the door.

W–L–R SENTENCES: (ooh) shoe

My dog's leg wound is going to heal nicely.

My favorite sweater is made of one hundred percent wool.

I always scrub my back with a loofa.

The old woman made the blanket on her loom.

My favorite drink is root beer.

The boy in my class told me I was acting rude.

Please chew your food completely.

This summer I grew two inches taller.

We had so much fun in the pool.

When your dog gets too hot he will always drool.

This summer I will tour Italy.

My friend's lure is attracting all the fish.

Oral timbre: Consonants W, L, and R in spontaneously formulated sentences

Materials

Handout A from Lesson 19: Words with W, L, R

Goal

To maintain an oral timbre when the consonants W, L, and R, in both initial and final positions, are combined with all vowel sounds and said in the context of spontaneously formulated sentences.

Procedures

1. **Explain the purpose of the lesson:** To apply what the student has learned about saying the consonants W, L, and R in words and connected speech to his spontaneous speech.

2. **Review the Rules for Producing an Oral Timbre:**

   ✓ Position your *tongue* in a relaxed concave position, in the bottom of your mouth, with the tip of your tongue lightly touching the back of your lower front teeth.

   ✓ Breathe in through your mouth, in a *yawn* position, like a "tired lion." This will produce a more vertical mouth position.

   ✓ While still maintaining the same "tired lion" *think* "ah," lowering the jaw.

   ✓ *Speak* (as if yawning out the sounds/words).

3. **Review all words in Handout A from Lesson 19.** Have the student read the words out loud. Listen to his pronunciation. Provide feedback and correction to help him produce a more oral timbre.

4. **Have the student make up sentences (at least 20) containing at least two of the words listed in Handout A from Lesson 19 in each.** Have the student recite his sentences. Make sure the student is applying the Rules for Producing an Oral Timbre as he recites. Make corrections as needed.

5. **Homework:** Finish step 4. Practice saying the sentences in Handout A, employing an oral timbre.

LESSON 22

Oral timbre: Persistent problems

Materials

Handout A: Specific Problematic Vowel–Consonant Combinations

Green Eggs and Ham by Dr. Seuss (1960)

Audio recording device

Goals

To practice saying persistently problematic words in isolation and in sentences, with a more oral timbre.

To develop an awareness of what is causing the difficulty with producing specific sounds and words with a balanced/more oral timbre and how to correct it.

Procedures

1. **Explain the purpose of the lesson:** To identify and make the student aware of persistent problems in producing a balanced/more oral timbre and how to overcome them.

2. **Record a language sample from your student.** Ask your student to talk about something that happened in his life between the last lesson and today. Record this. Listen to the language sample together and identify words that are still too nasal. Write a list of those words.

3. **Identify vowels and/or consonant–vowel combinations which continue to be difficult for your student to produce with a balanced/more oral timbre.** Make a chart with the student of vowels or consonant–vowel combinations in words that are persistently difficult for him to produce in a discourse. This includes vowel distortions or a constriction of airflow and sound, which should be coming through the oral pharynx (filter) without constriction. Write them into the chart in Handout A for this lesson. Then write examples of words fitting each category into the chart. Examples can come from the language sample or be new ones that fit the category. See the table for an example.

Problematic consonant–vowel combinations	
Vowels	**Words**
æ (as in cat) before n	can, advanced, mechanic, banana, channel, candle, grandma
æ (as in cat) before m	hammer, famished, ram, clam
æ (as in cat) before l	shall, shallow, foul, growl, howl, malady
æ (as in cat) before r	marry, daring, hairy
eh before r	perish, error, ferry, very, merry, terror, berry
awh	for, dog, coffee, sought, bought, awful, ball, fallen, trough, draw
er	world, turn, blur, slurp, chirp, stir

4. **Review the Rules for Producing an Oral Timbre** (*looking at handout, have the student demonstrate each step after he says it*):

   ✓ Position your *tongue* in a relaxed concave position, in the bottom of your mouth, with the tip of your tongue lightly touching the back of your lower front teeth.

   ✓ Breathe in through your mouth, in a *yawn* position, like a "tired lion." This will produce a more vertical mouth position.

   ✓ While still maintaining the same "tired lion" *think* "ah," lowering the jaw.

   ✓ *Speak* (as if yawning out the sounds/words).

5. **Review the words that contain difficult sounds for the student.** Have him speak them. Help him to correct his production. Make sure he pauses before each word, takes a deep breath, and starts from the "tired lion"/yawn position.

6. **Now have the student spontaneously generate a sentence for each word on the list**. Again, make sure he pauses before each sentence, takes a deep breath, and starts from the "tired lion" position.

7. **Now have the student read the Dr. Seuss book *Green Eggs and Ham* using an oral timbre.**

8. **Homework:** Practice the problematic words on your list, both in isolation and in the context of sentences. Before you begin to speak each word and sentence, pause, take a deep breath, as if yawning, drop your jaw, and relax your tongue ("tired lion" position). While maintaining the position, speak the words and sentences.

Specific Problematic Vowel–Consonant Combinations

Problematic consonant–vowel combinations	Words	Sentences
Problem 1		
Problem 2		
Problem 3		

Oral timbre: Connected speech 1

Materials

Handout A from Lesson 22: Specific Problematic Vowel–Consonant Combinations

Audio recording device

Goals

To produce connected speech with an oral timbre.

To produce persistently problematic words in isolation and in sentences, with a more oral timbre.

To be aware of what is causing the persistent problems with production and how to correct them.

Procedures

1. **Discuss the purpose of this lesson:** To help your student apply a more oral timbre to persistently problematic words and to practice producing a balanced/more oral timbre in connected speech.

2. **Review the homework from the last lesson.** Listen to the student produce his problematic words. Making certain he uses the Rules for Producing an Oral Timbre, have him say them in isolation and in sentences he makes up on the spot. He must take a breath and start from the yawn position each time. Record this and review with the student, correcting and practicing.

3. **Have the student read the following sentences with a balanced/more oral timbre.** (*Note:* You can make new sentences, which contain vowels with oral sounds.) Record him as he does this. Allow him to listen back and make observations about his own production. (*Note:* As you listen to the student's speech, add to the list of problematic words as needed.)

   a. The daring sloth took a drink from the trough.

   b. Harry growled at the owl.

   c. Mary slammed a foul ball into the stands.

   d. The bird gave a very merry chirp because he preferred the berry.

   e. The famished man had bananas and berries by candlelight.

   f. The local animal protection laws prohibit us from hurting this ram.

4. **Apply the Rules for Producing an Oral Timbre to spontaneous speech:**

   - Have the student read a short magazine article out loud with an oral timbre, making sure to breathe and resettle before speaking, with his mouth in the "tired lion"/yawn position before each sentence.

   - When he finishes, make a Web Graphic Organizer to outline the main topic, subtopics, and details from the article.

   - Ask the student to summarize the article using the Graphic Organizer to cue him. Record him as he does this.

   - Listen back with him and review. Discuss timbre issues which occur. Also discuss his breathing and resettling.

   - When he is finished, tell him that this is also a story he can tell his relatives and peers. He should keep his Graphic Organizer in his binder so that he can plan, practice, and use this pre-planned story with others, while in conversation. Discuss how it is important that he uses a balanced/more oral timbre in all situations.

5. **Homework:** Practice the words which continue to be problematic for you in isolation and in sentences that you will make up.

LESSON 24

Oral timbre: Connected speech 2

Materials

Audio recording device

Goal

To assess the student's progress since he began the intervention for his hyper-nasal timbre.

Procedures

1. **Review the homework from the last lesson.** First check his Graphic Organizer for completeness. Then have the student verbally summarize the television show he saw, using his Graphic Organizer to cue him. Record him as he tells you about the show.

2. **Listen to and compare the recordings of your student's summary of the television show and the baseline recording you made of him reading a passage in Lesson 1.** Ask for his observations about his timbre and breathing.

3. **Record a spontaneous language sample to compare with the spontaneous language sample you collected in Lesson 1.** Have your student tell you about a recent vacation, or event in school, or perhaps about a goal he has. If necessary, remind the student that if he is talking about a topic that is emotionally charged for him he will have more trouble modulating his timbre and he should employ the emotional modulation strategies he has been taught in the lessons in Chapter 2.

4. **Play the baseline recording of his spontaneous language that you made at his first lesson.** Compare the recordings. Discuss the student's progress in timbre and how his improvements have made him a more effective communicator. Be specific in your observations. Ask him what he believes the consequences of his improvements to be for his future.

5. **Discuss what your student can do to maintain the gains in timbre he has made and continue to improve.**

6. **Homework:** Practice the words which continue to be problematic for you in isolation and in sentences that you will make up.

CHAPTER 4

Voice: Volume

Introduction: Increasing volume

Some individuals on the autism spectrum may speak at too low a volume. Speaking with a low volume prohibits one from being heard and understood, or even attended to, under many circumstances. Clearly this negatively impacts communication. It can even be dangerous.

The volume of the voice can be compromised at a number of levels. When a person speaks, the vocal cords open to breathe and close just before phonation and the onset of a vocalization (speech, etc.). Then, once enough air pressure builds, it is released and the vocal cords begin to vibrate rapidly. The cords are positioned very close to each other during the vocalization. The air and sound are projected up through the throat, and into the oral pharynx and the nasal pharynx. The velum (soft palate), tongue, and lips direct the flow of air and sound.

Source–filter theory (Diehl 2008; see Figure 3.1) frames vocal production as involving a two-stage process, where, first, a sound (including pitch) is generated at the source, specifically the vocal cords/folds, and is then filtered by the vocal tract through the shape of the resonators involved and the articulators (tongue, soft palate, teeth, and lips). The vocal tract resonators are the throat, mouth, and nasal passages (including the sinuses). These resonators modify timbre and amplify the sound produced at the source, through changes in their positioning which direct the movement of air and sound. By changing the shape of the filter, the sound generated at the source (cords) is modified and regulated. When one has a voice with inadequate volume, the issue can be identified at the level of breath support, sound source, and/or sound filter. For example, the quality can be throaty, which indicates a problem with the shape of the "filter" (shape of the throat and mouth), or creaky, which indicates that the problem is at the source (vocal cords). This quality indicates an issue with the movement of breath through the cords.

Developing the ability to speak with a louder voice must be approached in a combination of ways, including more effective breath support/air release and phonation (at the source/cords), as well as through more effective positioning of the resonators and articulators which filter and amplify the sound. Therefore, this chapter's program is divided into five sections:

- Section 1: Baseline assessment

- Section 2: Developing a more nasal timbre to increase volume

- Section 3: Developing breath support to increase volume (including expansion of the chest cavity to increase air capacity and managing the release of breath)

- Section 4: Developing a more open passage to increase volume

- Section 5: Putting it all together (to coordinate open passage, and nasal timbre, with breath support and to show the student how volume is used to communicate effectively).

Developing a more nasal timbre to increase volume

As discussed in Chapter 3, there are two extreme vocal-timbre conditions which may be present in individuals with ASD. While a hyper-nasal timbre is more often observed in these individuals, some individuals on the spectrum produce a hyper-oral (throaty) timbre with low volume. A hyper-oral timbre makes the speaker sound less assertive. If a student has issues with producing an adequate volume, one aspect of what he must learn is to produce a more nasal timbre to gain a more balanced mix. An effective speaking voice is neither too oral nor too nasal in its quality. If a student's vocal timbre presents at one extreme or the other, his work will be to obtain a balanced timbre by emphasizing the opposite extreme. A hyper-oral quality in speech occurs when a lack of nasal resonance is present during voice production. This is due to unbalanced and ill-positioned articulators in the vocal tract, and failure to move air, resulting from muscular tension. Tension in the vocal tract compromises tone production and reduces volume.

Developing breath support to increase volume

Breath support, first, involves establishing an adequate air supply through chest expansion. Air-filled lungs are the foundation for the production of effective speech. Lessons in this chapter develop an understanding of anatomic sensations associated with adequately filling the lungs, which is associated with chest, back, and abdominal expansion. Breath support also involves management of breath release. Efficient coordination of breath release is a highly skilled activity. The student must develop the ability to stop and start the flow of air and sound as well as regulate the increase or decrease of the velocity of the air being released from the lungs, based on the volume and duration of the sound he wants to make. The student must learn to maintain expansion and not collapse his chest, releasing all of his air too quickly. Maintaining expansion will increase the length of time he is able to sustain any vocalized sound, word, or phrase at an appropriate volume.

We teach the student to manage the flow of air coming from the lungs using the *Breath–Pause technique*, which uses the vocal cords as an air flow valve. When the flow of breath is paused or held, air pressure is built up below the vocal cords. (This is a sensation similar to the sensation experienced when lifting a heavy object.) The release of this back pressure produces more air velocity. This increase in the velocity of air will produce a more assertive and a louder sound.

The Breath–Pause technique will improve vocal issues related to difficulty producing an adequate volume, which are generated at the source (vocal cords), specifically a creaky voice, because the back pressure established with Breath–Pause produces a more exact phonation as the breath is released, producing a purer quality of tone.

At the same time that the student learns to stop and start air flow from the lungs, he must also learn to move his breath and maintain a steady stream of air (whether slow or fast) as he speaks. To coordinate this, your student must understand the structure of speech with regard to sentences and phrases, so that he can plan a smooth release of air over the entire duration of a phrase ("phrase arc"). A halting, interrupted release, or over-conservation of air, results in inadequate vocal volume. In this case, the student ends up speaking with an inadequate amount of air to support the sound.

Developing a more open passage to increase volume

To produce a more projected sound it is important for the throat, jaw, tongue, and lip muscles to be flexible and in a relaxed state. Efficient vocal communication is greatly dependent upon the flexibility of the musculature in and around the entire vocal mechanism. Being calm and relaxed increases muscular flexibility. Tension decreases flexibility and can close the vocal passage, inhibiting its natural function. To produce enough volume, the vocal passage (filter) must be opened to an optimal position.

This may be counter-intuitive for some students, who may feel that they need to try harder to speak louder. These students exert extra muscular effort and produce unnecessary muscular tension in the throat, tongue, jaw, shoulders, and chest. Relaxation allows the student to produce a more projected sound because it removes anatomic obstructions. Muscular flexibility produces a more agile and adaptable apparatus. It produces greater richness and range in the acoustic properties of the produced tone. This will help the student to produce a greater dynamic vocal range, and will modify and increase resonating overtones. Although we teach the student to produce a more nasal timbre to create volume, which requires that the back of the tongue be raised, the student must understand that he can maintain a relaxed tongue and jaw, even when the back of the tongue is raised.

Rules for increasing the volume of the voice

Throughout this chapter we teach the student a set of specific rules, which remind him to use a nasal timbre, use breath support (including expansion and management of breath release), and maintain an open passage (with relaxed jaw, tongue, and lips). Though we have not yet taught all of these skills, they are introduced for the first time in Lesson 3. Then the ability to use the rules more and more effectively is built throughout the remaining lessons in this chapter.

The rules for increasing the volume of the voice (see Handout A from Lesson 3) are:

1. Relaxing the tongue and keeping its tip behind the lower front teeth produces a sensation associated with a relaxed jaw. The two sensations work together to help maintain an *open passage* for the desired sound.

2. The concept of a "Sneeze–Pause" does three things to position the optimal anatomical setup to increase the volume of the voice:

   a. Just before a sneeze, a person fills with air and *expands* the chest cavity.

   b. The mouth and throat position associated with a sneeze is precisely the position which produces a *nasal timbre*. The back of the tongue is lifted, though not tensed, with the back corners of the tongue positioned to touch the upper molars. The soft palate is lowered somewhat, to meet the back corners of the tongue. This merge between the two articulators produces a "joining together" sensation. This, in turn, creates a clear track through the nasal pharynx, directing the breath into the nasal cavity, nasal resonators, and finally through the nose. This position happens naturally, in that instant just before you sneeze. The physical sensations associated with nasal timbre are clearly recognized.

   c. The "pause" part of "Sneeze–Pause" involves *managing the release of air*. The student stops and holds back the release of air at the vocal cords. The momentary pause and hesitation of breath at the cords helps to define the exact, initial phonation of the student's vocalization, as the airflow speed is increased by the momentary burst of air which had been held back by the cords.

3. The third step requires the student to think of the nasal sound a goat makes. This maintains the sneeze position and gets the student ready to produce the desired timbre and speed and duration of airflow (*managing the release of air*), as the student simply tries to emulate the *nasal timbre* of a goat. This, in coordination with the propelled air from the expanded lungs as the breath is released, creates the preferred assertive and appropriate vocal volume.

4. The student then speaks while maintaining the position (established in the first three steps).

To firmly establish the motor patterns associated with this new way of producing vocal sound requires a significant amount of practice. This practice is accomplished during the lessons themselves, enforced with direction and feedback from the therapist and through homework assignments (which generalize the skills to the rest of life). Practice serves to automate the newly acquired motor skills, which then allows the student to allocate more of his attentional resources to what he wants to say rather than to how he will produce the sound. The student will keep copies of all handouts, homework, and notes in a three-ring binder, which he can refer to at home for practice and *must* bring to all lessons. The lessons are developmentally ordered. The later lessons refer back to concepts found in earlier ones, and make repeated use of materials from earlier lessons to solidify the concepts as the student develops the skills.

Section 1: Baseline assessment

Materials

Handout A: Reading Passage 1

Handout B: Reading Passage 2

Appendix A: Assessment Forms

Audio and video recording devices

Pre-recorded restaurant noise (*this may be found online*)

Goals

To qualitatively assess perception and production of volume.

To assess modulation of volume for the purpose of effective communication in response to different situations:

a. *To be heard when the ambient sound is loud.*

b. *To be heard at a distance.*

c. *To adjust to a given social context.*

d. *To convey emotion (e.g., anger, fear) and to be socially assertive.*

Procedures

1. **Explain the purpose of the lesson:** To assess perception and production of volume and the student's modulation of volume in different situations. Discuss that it is necessary to have an appropriate and adequate volume in order to communicate effectively and be understood.

2. **Baseline assessment of volume in connected speech.** Have the student read a passage (Handout A). (This is the best way to assess the student's voice because it removes the confound of other linguistic issues that affect prosody, such as expressive formulation issues.) Audio record this as a baseline for comparison in later lessons. Write your observations in Appendix A.

3. **Assess volume discrimination.** Record your observations in Appendix A:

   a. Speak the word pairs found in Assessment Form A. The words in each pair will be produced at either the same or at different volumes, per the instructions. Ask the student to identify whether you got louder or softer or remained at the same volume. While it is understood that this is not a standardized test, it will provide the clinician with information about the student's perception of volume of voice. You may want to begin by making the distinction in volume between the two words as small as possible in order to understand the student's sensitivity to differences in volume. Record your observations on the form.

b. Say the sentences in Assessment Form B, beginning at one volume and ending at another, and ask the student to identify whether you got louder or softer, according to the instructions in the table. Record your observations.

4. **Assess production of volume:**

a. Now have the student produce the word pairs in Assessment Form C at the same volume or different volumes, per instructions in the chart. Audio record as a baseline. Write your observations in the form.

b. Now, give the student a sentence from Assessment Form D and ask him to say it in what he considers a normal volume. Then he should say it in a whisper voice, a loud outdoor voice, and then in his yelling (emergency) voice. Audio record this as a baseline. Write your observations.

5. **Make a baseline video to anecdotally assess the student's breath support, posture, inhalation, chest and abdominal expansion, and regulation of exhalation:**

a. Videotape the student's breathing while he is standing. Observe and take notes (using the chart in Assessment Form E) on the steadiness of the student's posture throughout the expansion of his chest, back, and lower abdominal area. These are all directly associated with the student's existing level of strength of these muscles. (*Note:* The beginning student may lack the muscular strength to maintain an extended posture. The student's chest and back muscles may collapse, revealing a posture which is unsupported by those muscles.)

b. Now videotape the student's breathing while he is *standing and reading a passage* (Handout A). Observe and take notes (using the chart in Assessment Form E) on the steadiness of the student's posture throughout the expansion of his chest and lower abdominal area, and his ability to manage his exhalation. (Pay attention to the speed of exhalation, rate of speech, and his ability to get through a sentence in one breath.)

6. **Assess volume modulation associated with situations.** Record your observations in Assessment Form F:

a. *Ambient noise:* Have the student read the passage in Handout B. During the student's recitation, as background, play a pre-recorded track of restaurant noise. Play the track at a volume level consistent with what one would hear in an actual restaurant. Assess his ability to increase his volume appropriately. Record the student in this exercise as a baseline.

b. *Distance:* This portion of the assessment will determine the student's ability to project his voice over a distance. Distance projection is measured by asking the student to speak the text in Handout B, loud enough to be heard from across the room, across the yard, or across the street.

c. *Social context:* Read the following situations to the student. Have the student demonstrate the appropriate volume for each situation. Note the student's performance of each:

   i.   You are discussing your day with your family at the dinner table, at home.

   ii. You and your young sister are on opposite sides of a busy street, when you see that your sister is getting ready to cross the street and you notice that she is unaware of a car that is rapidly coming towards her.

   iii. You and your father are seated in a crowded theatre at the local cinema. You are watching a movie and you ask your father to share his popcorn with you.

   iv. You and your family are out, seated at a table, at a crowded restaurant and your mom asks you, "How was your day?"

Reading Passage 1

When the newborn elephant appeared from behind his mother, he appeared lively and alert as he learned the walking stride of his family's small herd, but he seemed extremely distracted with another activity. He wasn't used to the strange appendage coming from his face. He shook his head and tried to fan away the thing with his ears, but he couldn't get rid of it, no matter how hard he tried. At times, he even tried to stomp it off with his small feet. He began to rotate his trunk rapidly like a propeller on an airplane. The rest of his family didn't really know what to do about it. Never had they observed a newborn bothered so much by this discovery. Eventually, the new and tiny family member began to touch other members, learning to smell and feel their skin with his trunk. When the herd finally began to move again, he was happy to discover that, even in the crowded herd, he was able to find his mother, and keep track of where she was going.

Reading Passage 2 (*to be read with a background of restaurant noise*)

Our little brother became a hero last week. It all started when our family decided to go to the cinema and watch a movie together. It would have to be appropriate for all family members. We decided to watch the latest release of *Star Wars*. We were all excited to finally see the new release and got in line for refreshments and snacks. We went to the theatre, and then it happened. Before we even had a chance to find our seats, my little brother asked my mother if she had turned off the burner on the stovetop. I guess he was thinking about food or something. We all looked at each other and said, as if in chorus, "Let's go now, c'mon." We hurried home, as we all imagined the worst. Getting closer, we were glad to not see the fire department at our house. Entering our house, we all ran to the kitchen, where we found a sizable flame coming out of the pan. We reacted quickly and put the fire out. We used our fire extinguisher. Afterwards we took my little brother to his choice of movies. The rest of the family was glad for him to see anything he wanted to see and we all stood in line for his favorite snack and drink. After all, he was the hero of the week.

Assessment Forms

A. Volume discrimination 1

		Volume change	Correct?
book	desk	Increase	
sky	boat	Decrease	
wall	shoe	Same	
car	tire	Increase	
chair	spin	Increase	
cup	phone	Same	
paper	apple	Decrease	
room	bed	Same	
hat	porch	Decrease	
head	think	Same	

B. Volume discrimination 2

Sentence	Volume change	Correct?
Stand closer to the desk.	Increase	
The sailboat is 42' in length.	Decrease	
His shoe size is 12.	Decrease	
Your tire looks flat to me.	Increase	
Please take me for a spin in your car.	Increase	
My phone was lost at the park.	Decrease	
She ate an apple for lunch.	Decrease	
It's time to go to bed.	Increase	
I love to relax in my porch swing.	Decrease	
Think about your assignment.	Decrease	

C. Production of volume 1

		Volume change	Correct?
book	desk	Increase	
sky	boat	Decrease	
wall	shoe	Same	
car	tire	Increase	
chair	spin	Increase	
cup	phone	Same	
paper	apple	Decrease	
room	bed	Same	
hat	porch	Decrease	
head	think	Same	

D. Production of volume 2

Sentence	Normal	Whisper	Outdoor	Emergency
Stand closer to the desk.				
The sailboat is 42' in length.				
His shoe size is 12.				
Your tire looks flat to me.				
Please take me for a spin in your car.				
My phone was lost at the park.				
She ate an apple for lunch.				
It's time to go to bed.				
I love to relax in my porch swing.				
Think about your assignment.				

E. Baseline video to anecdotally assess breath support

Part a – Observations while the student is breathing	Notes
Steady posture throughout?	
– Shoulders back?	
– Sternum up?	
– Is there a problem with the shoulders lifting when student breathes?	
– Is there a problem with the chest or back collapsing?	
Expansion of lower abdominals?	
– Is there a problem with the abdomen moving in or failing to expand when student breathes in?	

Part b – Observations while the student is speaking	Notes
Steady posture throughout?	
– Shoulders back?	
– Sternum up?	
– Is there a problem with the shoulders lifting when student breathes?	
– Is there a problem with the chest or back collapsing?	
Expansion of lower abdominals?	
– Is there a problem with the abdomen moving in or failing to expand when student breathes in?	
Modulation of exhalation	
– Speed of exhalation too short?	
– Speed of speech too fast?	
– Ability to get through a sentence in one breath?	

F. Assess volume modulation associated with situations

    a. Ambient noise: _____

    b. Distance: _____

    c. Social context:

        i. _____

        ii. _____

        iii. _____

        iv. _____

Section 2: Developing a more nasal timbre to increase volume

General goals

To develop the ability to auditorily discriminate oral and nasal timbre.

To develop the ability to produce nasal and oral sounds.

To: (a) understand the anatomic structures in the mouth and throat that are involved in directing the flow of air and sound to produce the preferred timbre; and (b) gain an understanding of how the tongue, lips, and soft palate are manipulated to produce a more nasal or a more oral sound ("anatomic gate").

To practice achieving a more nasal resonant timbre to increase the volume of the voice, even for the sounds which are naturally more oral.

Nasal timbre: Introduction to discrimination, production, and anatomy

Materials

Handout A: Oral and Nasal Sound Chart

Handout B: Anatomy of the Voice

Handout C: Diagram of Anatomical Structures Involved in the Creation of Nasal Timbre

Handout D: Diagram of Anatomical Structures Involved in the Creation of Oral Timbre

Appendix A: Sample of How to Fill Out Handout A

Appendix B: Guide for Coloring Anatomy

Mirror

Audio recording device

Pink and blue pencils

Flashlight

Goals

To practice auditory discrimination of oral versus nasal timbre.

To learn to produce and practice producing vowels and words which have nasal and oral timbres.

To learn about the anatomical structures in the mouth and throat that are involved in producing timbre and to gain a preliminary understanding of how the structures in the mouth are manipulated to produce a more nasal or a more oral sound.

Procedures

1. **Assess the student's ability to discriminate nasal from oral vocal sounds and teach the terminology "nasal" and "oral."** Say the same sentence twice, once with a pronounced hyper-nasal timbre and then again with a pronounced hyper-oral timbre:

   a. Ask the student if the two sentences are different and what he hears as different.

    b. Teach him the terminology, identifying one as "nasal" and the other as "oral."

2. **Practice discrimination.** Say a new sentence twice, once with a nasal timbre and once with an oral timbre, but this time make the contrast between the two smaller. Ask the student to identify which sentence sounds "nasal" and which sounds "oral." Repeat this procedure a few times, with new sentences, to make certain he can correctly use the labels associated with each timbre, each time.

3. **Understanding oral and nasal vowels.** Have the student write all of the vowels in the alphabet on a piece of paper. Read out loud each of the vowels the student wrote and have him imitate each vowel. Help him understand that some vowel sounds are naturally more nasal and some are more oral. Now help him enter the vowels into the chart in Handout A, writing each under the appropriate column, indicating which are nasal and which are oral. (Use Appendix A to guide you.)

4. **Discovering words that are nasal and oral.** Have the student come up with at least five words for each vowel sound and write them into the chart in the appropriate columns. Have him read out loud the words containing those vowels. Record him as he does this.

5. **Teach the student about the form and function of the vocal anatomy:**

    a. Give your student Handout B. Explain the anatomy depicted in the side view of the head and neck in the diagram: point out the lungs, trachea (windpipe), tongue, lips, and vocal cords. Label the nasal pharynx and the oral pharynx. Now explain the inserts, which show the trachea and vocal cords from the top. Explain how the cords open to breathe in, and come together before the onset of a vocalization, and vibrate rapidly, touching each other during vocalization. Explain that the vocal cords are the source of the sound. The throat, the oral pharynx, the nasal pharynx, the velum (soft palate), the tongue, and lips form the filter. By changing the shape of the filter, the sound generated at the source (cords) is modified. (To help with clarifying these concepts, have the student color specific parts of the anatomy diagram: lungs, trachea, diaphragm, vocal cords, soft palate, hard palate, lips, tongue, oral resonators, and nasal resonators.)

    b. Give the student Handouts C and D, which show the mouth, tongue, and throat; then explain and label the parts on each diagram. Color the velum (soft palate) and tongue pink. Make blue dots indicating the flow of air and sound. Label the diagrams according to whether the positioning of the anatomy produces a more oral or a more nasal sound (Handout C – nasal; Handout D – oral). Use Appendix B for this lesson as a guide for coloring.

6. **Model for the student with your own mouth how to produce oral and nasal sounds.** As you both look at the corresponding diagram for producing a nasal sound, shine a flashlight into your mouth and show

him how the back of your tongue is up and the soft palate is lowered to produce a nasal sound. In contrast, as you both look at the diagram illustrating the position of the anatomy associated with a more oral sound, show him how your entire tongue is relaxed and down with the tip of the tongue behind the lower teeth and the soft palate is up (yawn position) when you produce an oral sound.

7. **Now have the student imitate the positions for the production of oral sounds (vertical, oval) and for the production of nasal sounds (horizontal, smile, upper lip taut).**

8. **Homework:** In front of a mirror, practice saying nasal vowels from the chart and words containing them.

✓

Oral and Nasal Sound Chart

	Nasal timbre	Oral timbre
Target vowels		
Target consonants		
Anatomic gate (description)		

Anatomy of the Voice

Diagram of Anatomical Structures Involved in the Creation of Nasal Timbre

Diagram of Anatomical Structures
Involved in the Creation of Oral Timbre

Sample of How to Fill Out Handout A

	Nasal timbre	Oral timbre
Target vowels	ee – bee, tree ih – it, sit ay – say, may eh – egg, sled æ – cat, hat	ah – spot, drop uh – cup, mud awh – sought, caught oh – bone, phone ow – cow, now ooh – shoe, moose
Target consonants *Note:* Most voiced consonants are nasal in their pure form	M, N	P, T, K B, D, G F, S, H V, Z J, ch, sh W, L, R
Anatomic gate (description)	Tip of tongue lightly touching the back of the bottom front teeth Back of tongue buckled up and touching the upper molars on both sides Soft palate is at a neutral to lowered position	Entire tongue relaxed and lying in the bottom of the mouth, with the tip lightly touching the back of the bottom front teeth Soft palate is lifted to a high yawn position

Guide for Coloring Anatomy

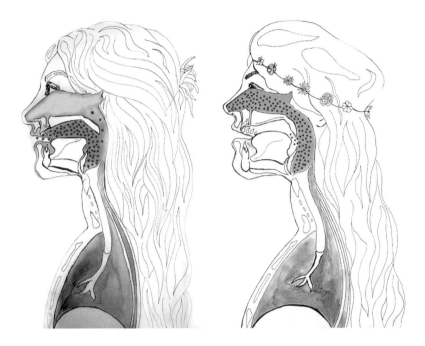

LESSON 2

Nasal timbre: Tongue position for vowels

Materials

Handout A from Lesson 1: Oral and Nasal Sound Chart
Handout C from Lesson 1: Anatomy diagram 1
Handout D from Lesson 1: Anatomy diagram 2
Appendix A from Lesson 1
Handout A: The Anatomic Gate
Handout B: Sneezing Mouth
Mirror
Audio recording device
Flashlight
Tongue depressors

Goals

To learn the anatomy of the mouth and nasal cavity and understand which parts of the anatomy are involved in producing different timbres.

To gain a preliminary understanding of how the anatomy of the mouth is manipulated to produce a more nasal timbre or a more oral timbre.

Procedures

1. **Review the homework from the last lesson.** Have the student produce all nasal vowel sounds and all words containing them that he practiced for homework. Give feedback.

2. **Explain the purpose of the lesson:** To learn the anatomy involved in producing oral and nasal timbres.

3. **Review the chart of oral and nasal vowel sounds from the last lesson together with the student, and ask him to produce all the sounds.** Have him produce those sounds in the way he does normally.

4. **Teach the student to produce the "Sneeze–Pause" position.** Ask the student to pretend that he is about to sneeze. The tip of his tongue should be lightly touching the back of the lower front teeth. The back of his tongue should raise up to touch his upper molars on both sides producing a trough down the length of his tongue. His soft palate should be lowered and touching the back of his tongue. This positioning of the vocal anatomy associated with the beginning of a sneeze is exactly the configuration to produce a nasal and projected sound. (*Note:* When the student has difficulty recognizing the sensation of

the back of his tongue touching his top molars, it may be useful to use a tongue depressor in order to help the student feel the points of his tongue that should be touching his molars.)

5. **Help the student to feel the difference in the sensations associated with nasal versus oral vocal production.** Demonstrate and have the student imitate the following sustained sounds, telling him which are oral and which are nasal:

   a. a briefly sustained nasal "ng" moving to a briefly sustained nasal "æ" (as in the word cat)

   b. a briefly sustained oral "ah" moving to a briefly sustained oral "oh"

   c. a briefly sustained oral "huh" moving to the nasal "ng"

   d. a briefly sustained nasal "hae" moving to the nasal "ng"

   e. a briefly sustained oral "hah," then moving back and ending with the nasal "ng."

6. **Talk about what he hears and notices.** As he moves between nasal and oral sounds he should feel the changes in the position of his tongue and velum (soft palate).

7. **Review the anatomy diagrams the student colored in Lesson 1.** Discuss the change in the position for the back of the tongue as the student produces oral versus nasal sounds. Now have him produce a sound, going back and forth from a sustained nasal "ng" to oral "ah." Have him notice and state when the back of his tongue touches his soft palate while producing these sounds. Review that, when the entire tongue is relaxed and down, the tip of the tongue is touching the back of the lower front teeth, and the soft palate is up, a more oral sound is produced. When the back of the tongue is up and the soft palate is low, air and sound travel through the nasal pharynx and a more nasal sound is produced.

8. **Discuss the "anatomic gate" (this is formed by the tongue and soft palate).** When the gate is closed by the tongue and the soft palate touching, or nearly touching, the sound is sent through the nasal pharynx. When the gate is opened by the tongue in a down position and soft palate in the up position, the sound is sent through the oral pharynx:

   a. Show and describe Handout A for this lesson.

   b. Add information to the chart (Handout A from Lesson 1) describing the anatomic gate. (Use Appendix A from Lesson 1 as an example.)

   c. Help your student feel the sensation of the position when the gate is closed (back of tongue up; soft palate down). Demonstrate a snoring sound. Now have him inhale and make a snoring sound to accentuate the feeling of the tongue and soft palate when they touch and vibrate. Also instruct him to use the consonants "k" and "ng" to help him feel this same sensation. (*Note:* Have him notice that ALL of these sounds put his tongue and soft palate in a position that will produce a nasal timbre.)

9. **Have the student practice producing a more nasal sound.** Shine the flashlight into your mouth and demonstrate what he will be doing. With the tip of your tongue lightly touching the back of your front lower teeth, you will raise the back of your tongue to touch your molars, and allow your soft palate to drop to a neutral position. Now have the student show you the same position. Look in the student's mouth with a flashlight to be certain this is happening:

   a. In this exercise you will take turns, saying the vowels in the chart from Lesson 1 with the student. You will say each of the "nasal" vowels and the accompanying words. The student will, in turn, breathe in calmly, form the "Sneeze–Pause" position, and imitate you after you speak all "nasal" vowels and words.

   b. Repeat this exercise until you are satisfied with the student's production of all the vowels in the chart.

   c. Now have the student imitate the vowel sounds and accompanying words that are categorized as naturally "oral." The student will now learn how to manipulate the vocal anatomy in order to produce oral sounds with a more nasal quality. Remind the student that:

   • the tip of the tongue will remain behind the lower front teeth

   • the back corners of his tongue will need to be up in the "Sneeze–Pause" position

   • the soft palate will be allowed to drop to a neutral position.

   d. You will say each of the "oral" vowels and words with a more nasal quality. The student will, in turn, breathe in calmly, form the "Sneeze–Pause" position, and imitate you after you speak all "oral" vowels and words, giving them all a more nasal quality.

10. **Teach the student to discriminate between phrases that contain oral or nasal vowels, by sound.** Fold a sheet of loose-leaf paper in half, vertically. Write the word "oral" at the top of one column and "nasal" at the top of the other. Have the student say the phrases below and decide which are oral and which are nasal. Now write the phrases that emphasize oral or nasal vowels under the appropriate column on the sheet. Have the student produce the phrases on his own; and then demonstrate and have him imitate you as you speak the phrases, using a more nasal quality:

    a. *Oral phrases:* box of socks; blue moon; blow the snow; cup of mud

    b. *Nasal phrases:* a red bed; a snack pack; bees in the trees; he's sneezing

11. **Homework:** Continue to practice speaking oral and nasal sounds on the chart (syllables and words) with a more nasal quality.

The Anatomic Gate

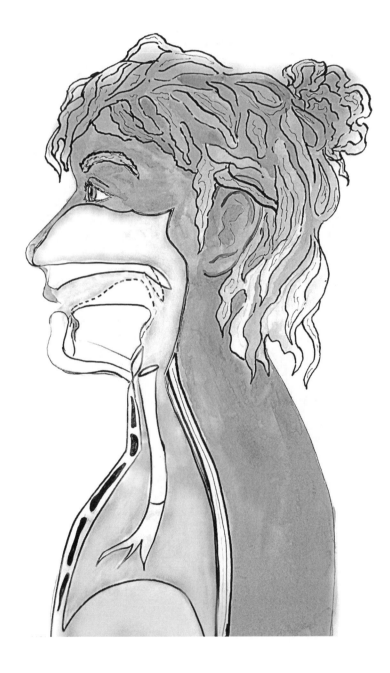

Sneezing Mouth

Nasal timbre: Tongue position – nasal and oral vowels

Materials

Handout C from Lesson 1: Anatomy diagram 1

Handout D from Lesson 1: Anatomy diagram 2

Handout A: Rules for Increasing the Volume of the Voice

Handout B: Homework

Appendix A: Pictures of Tongue Position for Vowels

Flashlight

Mirror

Goals

To practice producing nasal and oral vowels, with a more nasal quality.

To practice tongue position to produce a more nasal sound.

Procedures

1. **Review the homework from the last lesson.** Have the student produce the vowel sounds and words that he practiced, using a more nasal quality. Give feedback. Ask the student to explain to you where he thinks his tongue should be for these different sounds, and how he gets ready to produce a nasal quality (i.e., "Sneeze–Pause" position).

2. **Explain the purpose of the lesson:** To practice the tongue position for a nasal timbre and producing naturally oral vowels with a nasal quality.

3. **Introduce the Rules for Increasing the Volume of the Voice.** Give the student the chart in Handout A for this lesson, which lists cues for these rules:

   ✓ *Tongue* tip to a position behind the front lower teeth, *relaxed.*

   ✓ *"Sneeze–Pause" position:* Back corners of tongue up against upper molars.

   ✓ *Think* what you will say (like a goat would sound).

   ✓ *Speak* (maintaining "sneeze–pause"/goat position).

4. **Teach about airflow during oral and nasal sounds.** When the student produces a nasal sound, air and sound flow through the nasal pharynx and out of the nose. Make sure that this is the case as you complete the following activities:

   a. Allow the student to experience the sensation of airflow, associated with tone, in the nasal pharynx. Have the student keep his mouth closed and produce a "hum" while intermittently occluding the airflow from his nose by pinching his nostrils. (*Note:* The fact that the sound completely stops when he occludes his nose shows him that the sound is coming completely through his nose.)

   b. Now have the student continually pinch his nose while producing "ah." (*Note:* This shows him that the sound is coming completely through his mouth.)

   c. Next, have the student intermittently pinch his nostrils while producing the following contrasting sounds: "ng" and "ah." The "ng" engages the nasal resonators, while "ah" engages the oral resonators. Have him sustain each of these sounds while he intermittently pinches his nostrils. This gives the student a chance to experience the re-direction of airflow and the sensation within the resonators that are engaged (nasal and oral).

5. **Show the student how to apply the Rules for Increasing the Volume of the Voice.** Produce the following sentences, first with an oral sound. Look at Handout A together and articulate each step as you do it. "Who can say if I have been changed for the better? Because I knew you I have been changed for good." Have the student produce the sentences with a more nasal sound, applying the Rules for Increasing the Volume of the Voice (using the rules from step 3).

6. **Briefly review the pictures of anatomy that the student colored from Lesson 1 (Handouts B and C from that lesson).** Review the anatomic gate and the idea that oral sounds are produced with the tongue down and the soft palate up and nasal sounds with the back of the tongue high and the soft palate lowered.

7. **Teach the student how to discriminate between nasal versus oral vowels by sight.** Show the student the vowels and each associated picture of the mouth in Handout B for this lesson. Have him look at each of the pictures. Point out the dotted lines on some of the tongues. Explain that the dotted lines show the level of the middle of the tongue. The solid lines show the level of the sides of the tongue. Discuss the shape of the tongue and the position of the velum in each picture. Just by looking at the pictures, have your student tell you which mouths depict vowels that are naturally nasal and which are naturally oral, based on the position of the tongue and the velum in each of the pictures. Have him fill in the column where he is asked to write "nasal" or "oral."

8. **Continue to develop the sensations of nasal and oral production.** Demonstrate the following sound sequences and have the student repeat:

   a. Have the student produce the following words containing a nasal vowel and the nasal "ng": sing, king, ring.

   b. Have the student produce the following words containing an oral vowel and the nasal "ng": lung, hung, sung, tongue.

   c. Have the student alternate between ing and ung: ing-ung, ing-ung, ing-ung, each time sustaining the "ng" more than the vowel.

   The purpose of this exercise is to give the student a greater awareness of the sensations associated with producing a nasal quality, to achieve a more present sound, even when speaking words which contain naturally oral vowels.

9. **Making oral sounds more nasal.** Now shine a flashlight into your mouth so the student can see the position of your tongue:

   a. Have him watch the position of your tongue when you say "oh," "ow," "ooh," and "ah," "uh," and "awh." He should notice that the back of your tongue is down and relaxed, in the position used for an oral sound.

   b. Now have the student observe the position of the back of the tongue in each of the following sounds: "ohng-ahng," "ohng-ahng," "ohng-ahng." Talk about what he sees and hears. He should notice that the back of the tongue is higher now for the "oh" and "ah" vowels. This is because even though they are naturally oral vowels, they are being produced in a more nasal way because they occur in the context of "ng." Have the student write this concept in his notebook.

   c. Now use a hand mirror and have the student look in his own mouth and observe his tongue as he produces the following sounds: "oh," "ah," "ohng-ahng," "ohng-ahng," "ohng-ahng," so he can see the change in tongue position as he experiences the sensations.

10. **Homework:** Practice producing the sound "ah" to "ng" in front of a mirror. Practice all vowel sounds in your homework chart while in the "Sneeze–Pause" position. Record at least one practice session and bring the recording to your next lesson.

Rules for Increasing the Volume of the Voice

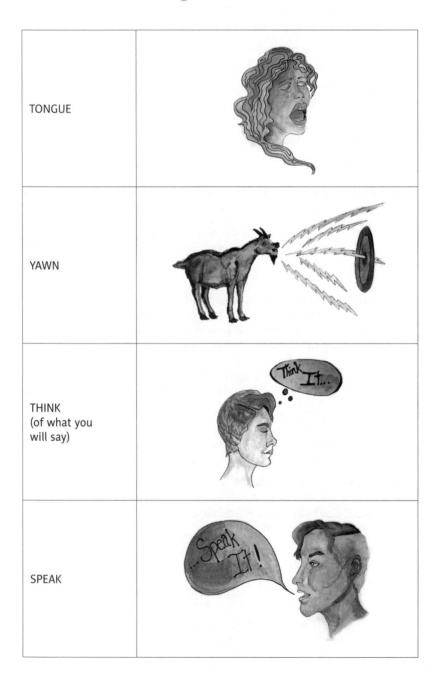

TONGUE	
YAWN	
THINK (of what you will say)	
SPEAK	

Homework

Remember the Rules for Increasing the Volume of the Voice:

- ✓ *Tongue* tip to a position behind the front lower teeth, *relaxed.*
- ✓ *"Sneeze–Pause" position:* Back corners of tongue up against upper molars.
- ✓ *Think* what you will say (like a goat would sound).
- ✓ *Speak* (maintaining "sneeze–pause"/goat position).

Practice the following sounds in front of a mirror.

Consonants	
ah to ng oh to ng	Ng to ah to ng Ng to oh to ng

Remember: Even for vowel sounds that are more naturally oral, use the rules for a more nasal sound.

Vowels	Word 1	Word 2	Word 3
ee (as in bee)			
ih (as in sit)			
ay (as in say)			
eh (as in egg)			
æ (as in cat)			
ah (as in mom)			
uh (as in cup)			
awh (as in saw)			
oh (as in low)			
ooh (as in shoe)			

Pictures of Tongue Position for Vowels

Vowels	Tongue position	Is the vowel naturally "nasal" or "oral"? (fill in below)
ee (as in bee)		
ih (as in sit)		
ay (as in say) eh (as in egg)		
æ (as in cat)		
ah (as in mom) uh (as in cup)		
awh (as in saw)		
oh (as in low) ooh (as in shoe)		

Nasal timbre: Tongue position for vowels, consonants, and words

Materials

Handout A from Lesson 1: Oral and Nasal Sound Chart

Handout A from Lesson 3: Rules for Increasing the Volume of the Voice

Handout B from Lesson 3: Homework

Appendix A from Lesson 3: Pictures of Tongue Position for Vowels

Flashlight

Mirror

Goals

To practice production of nasal and oral vowels, consonants, and words with a more nasal timbre.

To practice tongue position in order to produce a more nasal sound.

Procedures

1. **Review the homework from the last lesson.** Have your student say all vowel sounds on his homework chart with a nasal timbre.

2. **Explain the purpose of the lesson:** To practice production of nasal and oral vowels, consonants, and words with a more nasal timbre; and to practice tongue position in order to produce a more nasal sound.

3. **Review the chart of tongue positions for each vowel (Appendix A from Lesson 3).** Review the concepts of which positions make a more nasal or a more oral sound. Have your student repeat each of them after you while he looks in a mirror. Ask which are more nasal and which are more oral.

4. **Understanding the sensations associated with the tongue position for nasal and oral sounds:**

   a. Have your student repeat and practice transitioning from "ee" to "ooh" while looking in a mirror to check tongue positions. Have him repeat the sequence five times (EeOohEeOohEeOohEeOohEeOoh).

   b. Have him practice transitioning from "ng" to "ah" looking in a mirror to check tongue positions. Have him repeat the sequence five times (NgAhNgAhNgAhNgAhNgAh).

    c. Talk about what he notices. He should feel and see in both cases that at the beginning of each sequence the tongue starts high in the back, touching the soft palate, and the sound is more nasal. At the end the tongue drops, the soft palate lifts, and the sound is more oral.

5. **Review the Rules for Increasing the Volume of the Voice.** Have the student use a mirror to look at himself as he carries out each step:

    ✓ *Tongue* tip to a position behind the front lower teeth, *relaxed.*

    ✓ *"Sneeze–Pause" position:* Back corners of tongue up against upper molars.

    ✓ *Think* what you will say (like a goat would sound).

    ✓ *Speak* (maintaining "sneeze–pause"/goat position).

6. **Have the student write three words for each vowel into the homework chart (Handout A from Lesson 3: Homework) in the appropriate spaces.**

7. **Have the student say each of the words he wrote into his chart with a more nasal timbre.** Remind the student that he is aiming for a more nasal sound overall, even when he is pronouncing sounds that are naturally more oral. He will obtain this by starting in the "Sneeze–Pause" position.

8. **Introduce the concept that some consonants, like vowels, are naturally more or less nasal, too:**

    a. Say and have your student repeat the following nasal consonants: M, N.

    b. Now say and have your student repeat the following oral consonants: P, T, K, F, S, ch, sh.

    c. The student can tell which are oral consonants and which are nasal by pinching his nose as he says them. For M and N, occluding his nose will completely stop the sound because those consonants are produced by air and sound moving through the nasal pharynx. Occluding the nose does not affect the rest of the consonants because air and sound are moving through the oral pharynx as those consonants are produced.

9. **Homework:** Practice producing the sound "ng" to "ah" (as you did during the lesson) in front of a mirror. Practice all vowel sounds and words containing them, from your chart, using the "Sneeze–Pause" position. Record at least one practice session and bring the recording to your next lesson.

Nasal timbre: Learning the sensations associated with directing airflow and sound through the nasal pharynx: "ah," "uh," and "awh"

Materials

Handout A from Lesson 1: Oral and Nasal Sound Chart

Handout C from Lesson 1: Anatomy diagram 1

Handout D from Lesson 1: Anatomy diagram 2

Handout A: Homework

Fox in Socks by Dr. Seuss

Mirror

Audio recorder

Goals

To learn about and feel the sensations (vibrations of cartilage) associated with directing airflow and sound through the nasal pharynx, to create nasal timbre in speech production.

To produce the naturally oral vowels "ah," "uh," and "awh" with a more nasal quality.

To practice producing a more nasal and resonant timbre, in order to increase the volume of the voice.

Procedures

1. **Explain the purposes of the lesson:** To learn about and feel the sensations (vibrations of cartilage) associated with directing air and sound to flow mostly through the nasal pharynx or mostly through the oral pharynx. Review that directing most air and sound through the nasal pharynx creates a nasal timbre and that an increased nasal timbre makes the voice more audible. In this lesson the student will learn to produce the vowels "ah," "uh," and "awh" with a more nasal quality. He will learn to check whether he is effectively producing a vowel with a more nasal quality. He will do this by pinching his nose with his fingers to see if it is buzzing.

2. **Discuss with the student that until now he has been concentrating on producing a more nasal sound by positioning his tongue and his soft palate to send air and sound through the nasal pharynx.** Ask him to tell you how he does this (i.e., raise the back corners of the tongue against the upper molars, lower the soft palate). This lesson and the next concentrate on teaching him sensations which will confirm that he is in fact correctly directing more of the air and sound through his nasal pharynx and his nose. Use the vocal tract anatomy diagrams for an aid.

3. **Teach the student about the "mix" in producing a balanced timbre:**

    a. Explain that most vocal sounds, but not all, involve sending air and sound through both the oral and the nasal pharynx.

    b. The idea is to be certain that the sound is neither too oral nor too nasal. In the case of your student who speaks too quietly, his sound does not have enough nasal resonance and this is why you are working to make his sound more nasal.

    c. Explain that there are some vocal sounds that send air and sound only through the nasal pharynx. He will use these sounds in this exercise to get his tongue and velum set up in the right position to produce a more nasal timbre. These include sounds such as "hum," "m," "n," "ng," and "ny." Now have the student keep his mouth closed and produce a "hum" while intermittently occluding the airflow from his nose by pinching his nostrils. This stops the flow of air and tone, demonstrating to him that his sound is coming completely through his nose. Next, have the student pinch his nostrils during the production of the sounds "m," "n," "ng," and "ny." When he pinches his nose while trying to produce these sounds, all sound stops because this pinching does not allow any flow of air or sound through the nose. There is no oral resonance either. Pinching the nose eliminates nasal resonance. Use the vocal tract anatomy diagrams for an aid.

    d. Now have him pinch his nostrils when he pronounces "ah," "uh," and "awh." Ask what he notices. Pinching his nostrils will not affect the sound. These sounds have oral resonance. This time air and those oral sounds do not stop because the majority of the air and tone is coming through the mouth. The nasal resonator and these oral vowels can both still resonate even when the nose is pinched. Use the vocal tract anatomy diagrams for an aid.

4. **Explain to the student that he will now use sounds that only engage the nasal resonators to help make his vowels more nasal.** Have the student imitate the sound "Nyay." Tell him to think of this as being similar to the sound a goat makes. Have him repeat this sound three times, in sets of five (NyayNyayNyayNyayNyay). This sound maximally engages the nasal resonators. This important exercise will enable him to produce a more prominent, present, and assertive sound.

5. **Have the student use "ny" to make the vowels "ay," "ah," "uh," and "awh" more nasal.** He will start by producing the "Sneeze–Pause" position before saying each string of syllables. Have him repeat each of the following strings five times each:

   a. NyayNyayNyayNyayNyay

   b. NyahNyahNyahNyahNyah

   c. NyuhNyuhNyuhNyuhNyuh

   d. NyawhNyawhNyawhNyawhNyawh

6. **Use the sensation of a buzzing nose to feel and confirm that these oral sounds are becoming more nasal:**

   a. Have your student pronounce "ah" five times while pinching his nose. Ask him what he feels in his fingers while he is pinching his nose. Does he feel buzzing or not? Now have him say NyahNyahNyahNyahNyah. When he says this the fifth time, have him pinch his nose while sustaining the "ah." What does he feel now? The fingers that are pinching his nose should feel buzzing. Provide direction and corrections as needed.

   b. Have your student pronounce "uh" five times while pinching his nose. Ask him what he feels in his fingers while he is pinching his nose. He will probably not feel any buzzing because he is sending all of the air and tone through his mouth. Now have him say NyuhNyuhNyuhNyuhNyuh. When he says this the fifth time, have him pinch his nose while sustaining the "uh." He should feel buzzing now.

   c. Have your student pronounce "awh" five times while pinching his nose. Ask him what he feels in his fingers while he is pinching his nose. There is likely to be no buzzing. Now have him say NyawhNyawhNyawhNyawhNyawh. When he says this the fifth time, have him pinch his nose while sustaining the "awh." He should feel buzzing now. Remember, the "ny" will make the vowel attached to it more nasal.

7. **Have the student read passages from the Dr. Seuss book *Fox in Socks* while using a more nasal timbre.** Many of the words in this book are naturally more oral, so in reading this book the student can practice producing all words with a more nasal timbre.

8. **Homework:** Make a sentence using one of the words for each sound from your homework chart in Lesson 3. Practice saying these sentences with a nasal timbre, starting from the "Sneeze–Pause" position. In order to help set up the nasal placement, repeat the "Nyay" sound five times before you begin (NyayNyayNyayNyayNyay).

Homework

Remember the Rules for Increasing the Volume of the Voice:

- ✓ *Tongue* tip to a position behind the front lower teeth, *relaxed.*
- ✓ *"Sneeze–Pause" position:* Back corners of tongue up against upper molars.
- ✓ *Think* what you will say (like a goat would sound).
- ✓ *Speak* (maintaining "sneeze–pause"/goat position).

Vowels	Sentences
ee (as in bee)	
ih (as in sit)	
ay (as in say)	
eh (as in egg)	
æ (as in cat)	
ah (as in mom)	
uh (as in cup)	
awh (as in saw)	
oh (as in low)	
ooh (as in shoe)	

LESSON 6

Nasal timbre: Learning the sensations associated with directing airflow and sound through the nasal pharynx: "oh," "ow," and "ooh"

Materials

Handout A from Lesson 1: Oral and Nasal Sound Chart

Handout C from Lesson 1: Anatomy diagram 1

Handout D from Lesson 1: Anatomy diagram 2

Mirror

Audio recorder

Goals

To gain a better understanding of the sensations associated with directing airflow and sound through the nasal pharynx to create nasal timbre in speech production.

To produce the naturally oral vowels "oh," "ow," and "ooh" with a more nasal quality.

To practice producing a more nasal and resonant timbre, in order to increase the volume of the voice.

Procedures

1. **Review the homework from the last lesson.** Look at the sentences your student wrote for homework. Listen to him attempt to read them with a nasal timbre. Comment and make corrections as needed.

2. **Explain the purpose of the lesson:** To continue to develop an understanding of the physical sensations associated with directing air and sound to flow mostly through the nasal pharynx or mostly through the oral pharynx. Review that directing more air and sound through the nasal pharynx creates a nasal timbre and that an increased nasal timbre makes the voice more audible. In this lesson the student will learn to produce the vowels "oh," "ow," and "ooh" with a more nasal quality. He will again check whether he is effectively producing a vowel with a more nasal quality by feeling his nose with his fingers to see if it is buzzing.

3. **Review the concept of the "mix" in producing a balanced timbre:**

   a. Review that most vocal sounds, but not all, involve sending air and sound through both the oral and the nasal pharynx.

   b. The idea is to be certain that the sound is neither too oral nor too nasal. In the case of your student who speaks too quietly, his sound does not have enough nasal resonance and this is why you are working to make his sound more nasal.

   c. In the last lesson your student learned that there are some vocal sounds that send air and sound only through the nasal pharynx. Those considered in the last lesson were "hum," "m," "n," "n g," and "ny." He will again use "ny" in this exercise to get his tongue and velum set up in the right position to produce a more nasal timbre. Now have the student keep his mouth closed and produce "ny" while intermittently occluding the airflow from his nose by pinching his nostrils. This stops the flow of air and tone, demonstrating to him that his sound is coming completely through his nose. When he pinches his nose while trying to produce these sounds, all sound stops because this pinching does not allow any flow of air or sound through the nose. There is no oral resonance either. Pinching the nose eliminates nasal resonance. Use the vocal tract anatomy diagrams for an aid.

   d. Now have him pinch his nostrils when he pronounces "oh," "ow," and "ooh." Ask what he notices. Pinching his nostrils will not affect the sound. These sounds have oral resonance. This time air and those oral sounds do not stop because the majority of the air and tone is coming through the mouth. The nasal resonator and these oral vowels can both still resonate even when the nose is pinched. Use the vocal tract anatomy diagrams for an aid.

4. **Explain to the student that he will now use sounds that only engage the nasal resonators to help make his vowels more nasal:**

   a. Have the student imitate the sound "Nyay." Tell him to think of this as being similar to the sound a goat makes. Have him repeat this sound three times, in sets of five (NyayNyayNyayNyayNyay). This sound maximally engages the nasal resonators. This important exercise will enable him to produce a more prominent, present, and assertive sound.

   b. Have the student inhale and then speak NyaNyaNyaNyaNya (as in cat) five times. Think of a goat sound. This sound also sets up the positioning of his anatomy to produce a nasal timbre while speaking.

   If you feel that your student is not producing a noticeable amount of nasal quality, stop him and demonstrate for him. This exercise is intended to build stamina and coordinated muscle motor memory.

5. **Have the student use "y" to make the vowels "oh," "ow," and "ooh" more nasal.** He will start by producing the "Sneeze–Pause" position before saying each string of syllables. Have him repeat each of the following strings five times each:

   a. NyohNyohNyohNyohNyoh

   b. NyowNyowNyowNyowNyow

   c. NyoohNyoohNyoohNyoohNyooh

6. **Use the sensation of a buzzing nose to feel and confirm that the sound is becoming more nasal. Have the student set up in "Sneeze–Pause" position before he does each of the following exercises:**

   a. Have your student pronounce "oh" five times while pinching his nose. Ask him what he feels in his fingers while he is pinching his nose. Does he feel buzzing or not? Now have him say NyohNyohNyohNyohNyoh. When he says this the fifth time, have him pinch his nose while sustaining the "oh." What does he feel now? The fingers that are pinching his nose should feel buzzing. Provide direction and corrections as needed.

   b. Have your student pronounce "ow" five times while pinching his nose. Ask him what he feels in his fingers while he is pinching his nose. He will probably not feel any buzzing, because he is sending all of the air and tone through his mouth. Now have him say NyowNyowNyowNyowNyow. When he says this the fifth time, have him pinch his nose while sustaining the "ow." He should feel buzzing now.

   c. Have your student pronounce "ooh" five times while pinching his nose. Ask him what he feels in his fingers while he is pinching his nose. There is likely to be no buzzing. Now have him say NyoohNyoohNyoohNyoohNyooh. When he says this the fifth time, have him pinch his nose while sustaining the "ooh." He should feel buzzing now. Remember, the "ny" will make the vowel that is attached to it more nasal.

7. **Now, while looking at the picture depicting the "Sneeze–Pause" have the student form the "Sneeze–Pause" position and then say all six oral vowels "ah," "uh," "awh," "oh," "ow," and "ooh."** Make sure that these oral vowels now have a more nasal quality. Have him repeat them five times, alternating among the six vowels. Tell him he can pinch his nose while he pronounces these sounds to be certain he is pronouncing them with a more nasal quality.

8. **Voice projection exercises:**

   a. As you and your student pass a large rubber ball to each other, call out a single word on each pass, using a nasal timbre. You will call out words in sets of six. The first six will be "ah" words (e.g., hoe, show).

The next six will be "uh" words. You should continue in this way for the vowels "awh," "oh," "ooh," and "ow." He will pass the ball to you without a bounce. He must visualize throwing his voice with the same energy as when he throws the ball to you. A distance of six to eight feet will be appropriate and effective for the adolescent student. This distance may shorten for younger or smaller students. The difficulty of this exercise may be increased by completing it in the outdoors where more ambient noises may be present. If outside, you both will need to increase volume for the situation.

b. Now have the student pick a more distant target (50 feet away) and project his voice past that target. This exercise forces the student to use a more nasal timbre to project his voice past that target. For this step, have him produce the words and sentences he generated for the last lesson's homework.

9. **Homework:** Write 25 directive sentences (giving orders to someone). Practice these sentences with a nasal quality.

Section 3: Developing breath support to increase volume

General goals

To increase the volume of any vocal sound, tone, word, or phrase through effective breath support.

To increase lung expansion through an effective breathing posture and prevent collapse.

To develop lower expanded abdominal breathing to support the production of sound.

To develop an understanding of anatomic sensations associated with maintaining expansion to increase the length of time in which the student is able to sustain any vocalized sound, tone, word, or phrase at an appropriate volume.

To develop the ability to manage breath release through such techniques as Breath–Pause and phrase arcing.

To improve vocal issues related to difficulty producing an adequate volume, which are generated at the "source" (vocal cords) (e.g., creaky voice), through the Breath–Pause technique.

To develop mindfulness of how stress or excitement can negatively affect breathing and the need to calm before speaking.

Breath support: Posture and expansion

Materials

Handout A: Correct Expansion

Flat bench (preferred but not necessary)

*Optional: breath spirometer to measure sustained, deep inhalation

Goals

To increase lung expansion through an effective breathing posture and prevent collapse.

To build strength to maintain an effective breathing posture.

Procedures

1. **Explain the purpose of the lesson:** To learn the feeling of lung expansion and maintenance and an effective breathing posture.

2. **Expansion: increase lung expansion through an effective breathing posture:**

   a. Have the student stand and place both shoulders and back against a wall or door. This will increase the vertical alignment of the student's standing posture, by lengthening, straightening, and stretching the student's spinal column and inter-costal and abdominal muscles. This will help the student to obtain a more expansive lung capacity. The student is asked to breathe normally and, at the same time, strictly maintain the expanded vertical alignment. You should see an expansion in the ribcage, in the abdominal area below the sternum, and in the lower back. The student's shoulders should not rise during inhalation. If they do, place your hands on his shoulders to remind him that he should not raise his shoulders when he takes a full, low breath.

   b. Explain and demonstrate the expansion that should occur at the ribcage, the sternum, lower back muscles, and in the abdominal area. Show your student Handout A, which displays the correct expansion. This expansion happens when a person takes a *full* breath. Now, while still standing against the wall, have the student take a full, low breath.

   c. Now tell the student to let his posture collapse, with shoulder falling forward. Tell him to take a full breath now. Discuss the difference between breathing with an extended posture and breathing when collapsed.

d. Have the student go back to the wall and stand against it the same way he did in a. above. Now tell him to take a couple of steps forward and stand a few feet away from the wall, keeping the same posture. Observe whether he can maintain the same posture. If so, have him take three full breaths while strictly maintaining the expanded vertical alignment. If he loses the vertical alignment, send him back to the wall. Discuss the sensations the student experiences.

3. **Discuss Posture Rules for Effective Breathing.** Have your student write these in his notebook:

✓ Align the back muscles and spinal column symmetrically.

✓ Shoulders back.

✓ Point the sternum upward (never allowing it to collapse).

4. **Strength: muscle development to support and maintain an effective posture.** Remind the student of the benefits of an extended posture while breathing, the greatest of which is greater lung capacity. Discuss with the student that it is therefore beneficial to strengthen the muscles involved in maintaining an extended vertical posture:

a. Work with the student on the following exercise to increase the strength of his lower back muscles (to support his extended vertical posture). The student lies on his stomach on the floor or body-length bench (approx. 12" wide). With his arms out to his sides (at a 90 degree angle, like an airplane) he will lift his upper body, arms, and head off of the floor, keeping his legs and feet on the floor. He will hold this position for a count of two and lower his upper body, slowly, back to the floor. He should breathe in as he is coming up and breathe out as he returns to the floor. The student should do this for six sets of five. On the fifth repetition of each set, he should hold the raised position, breathe in, and say "ah" (sustained for two seconds) before lowering back to the floor.

b. The student should now return to the wall and stand, placing both shoulders and back flat against the wall. He should then breathe in, establishing and maintaining the same amount of chest expansion achieved in the previous sustained "airplane" step; and then sustain the same "ah" sound. The student should do this for six sets of five. It is important to make sure the student focuses on and monitors his breathing posture and that he also notices the expansion of his abdominal muscles. (*Note:* To test his expansion and provide the student with a visual image of the steadiness and depth of his inhalation and therefore degree of expansion, you may have him do the last set of five while breathing in using a spirometer. Time and keep a record of the number of seconds he keeps the balls in the spirometer up as he inhales. This will allow you to periodically assess your student's progress in lung expansion when he inhales.)

c. Now have the student stand away from the wall, maintaining the same posture. He should then breathe in, establishing and maintaining the same amount of expansion achieved in the previous step. He should then produce the same "ah" sound for six sets of five. If he loses the vertical alignment, send him back to the wall. (*Note:* Again, you may have him do the last set of five while breathing in using the spirometer. Time and record the number of seconds he keeps the balls in the spirometer up as he breathes.)

d. Now have the student maintain the same posture while sitting in a chair. Again, he should breathe in, establishing and maintaining the same amount of expansion achieved in the previous step, and then produce the same "ah" sound for six sets of five. If, while seated, he loses the vertical alignment, send him back to the wall. (*Note:* Then while your student is seated you may have him do the last set of five while breathing in using the spirometer. Time and record the number of seconds he keeps the balls in the spirometer up as he breathes.)

5. **Now have the student walk in a circle, around the perimeter of the room, maintaining the same effective posture while taking regular breaths.** If he loses his alignment, send him back to the wall to regain the sensation of what the vertical alignment feels like. As the student walks, remind him to relax his limbs and face, while also reminding him that he is still working to maintain the extended posture. His arms should swing in a relaxed manner, in opposition to his stride.

6. **Homework:** Practice the exercises you learned in today's lesson, to increase the strength of your lower back muscles (to support an effective breathing posture):

a. Lie on your stomach, on the floor or on a bench, with your arms out to your sides (at a 90 degree angle, like an airplane); lift your upper body, arms, and head off of the floor, keeping your legs and feet on the floor. Hold this position for a count of two and then lower your upper body back to the floor. Breathe in as you come up and breathe out as you return to the floor. Do this for six sets of five. On the fifth repetition of each set, hold the raised position, breathe in, and say the sound "ah" (sustained for two seconds) before lowering back to the floor.

b. For the second exercise, begin by standing with your back against the wall as you learned during the lesson. Then *walk* in a circle around the perimeter of the room while maintaining the same posture, taking regular breaths. As you walk, remember to relax your limbs and face, while maintaining the effective breathing posture. Your arms should swing in a relaxed manner, in opposition to your stride.

Correct Expansion

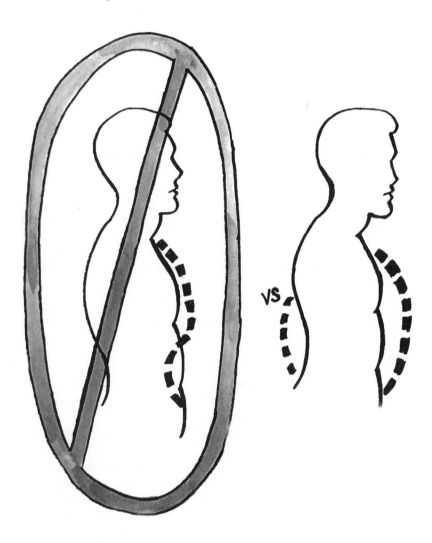

Breath support: Optimal expansion and maintaining expansion

Materials

Handout A: Rules for Optimal Breathing Expansion

Handout B: Reading Passage

Video recording device

*Optional: breath spirometer to measure sustained, deep inhalation

Goals

To develop a lower and more expanded breathing to support the production of vocal sound with adequate volume.

To begin to develop an understanding of the sensations associated with maintaining expansion so that the student can produce sustained speech while maintaining adequate volume.

To develop mindfulness of how stress or excitement can negatively affect breathing and the need to calm before speaking.

Procedures

1. **Review the homework from the last lesson.** Have the student demonstrate the "airplane" exercise and standing, walking, and breathing, all with an effective posture.

2. **Explain the purpose of the lesson:** One purpose of this lesson is to develop lower expanded breathing and to maintain expansion so the student can produce sustained speech with an adequate volume. Another purpose of the lesson is to understand how strong emotions negatively affect breathing and the need to achieve a calm baseline before speaking. *Note: This lesson should be used until the student demonstrates an understanding and becomes proficient with this breathing technique.*

3. **Diaphragmatic breathing technique:**

   a. Give the student Handout A: Rules for Optimal Breathing Expansion. Read and discuss the rules.

   b. Have the student stand with the effective breathing posture he learned in the last lesson. Have him slowly breathe in and out. Observe the expansion of the abdominal area below the ribcage and of the lower back muscles, which is associated with low diaphragmatic breathing. Videotape your student, in profile, as he does this. Review the video with him. Discuss observations of and corrections to the movements associated with the student's breathing. You should be able to see, and the student should be able to feel: (i) the maintenance of the effective breathing posture; (ii) the lower abdominal area, the sternum, upper ribcage, and the lower back muscles expanding with each inhalation; (iii) the sternum, upper ribcage, and shoulders stable, neither rising nor falling.

c. Have the student stand and read the attached passage (Handout B). Videotape him, in profile, as he does this. Make certain that he maintains the effective breathing posture he learned in the last lesson. Observe the expansion of the abdominal area (below the ribcage), which is associated with low diaphragmatic breathing, while he reads the passage. Encourage him to take full breaths whenever he breathes. Review the video with him. Discuss your observations of the movements associated with the student's breathing. Again, you should be able to see: (i) the maintenance of the effective breathing posture; (ii) the lower abdominal area and lower back expanding with each inhalation; (iii) the sternum, upper ribcage, and shoulders stable, neither rising nor falling.

4. **Abdominal expansion exercise: using lower expanded breathing to support the projection of sound.** In this exercise the student will begin to learn bodily sensations associated with maintaining expansion in order to support and sustain appropriate volume in connected speech: You have taught the student about an effective breathing posture and worked on strengthening his muscles to maintain that posture. Now you will teach him about maintaining optimal expansion. Have him do the following:

• Breathe out normally.

• Breathe in, dropping the lower abdominal musculature. Dropping means to suddenly completely relax those muscles. At this point emphasize that the muscles below the ribs and sternum must relax and drop to allow the organs below the diaphragm to drop. This gives the diaphragm more room to expand downward as a full, deep breath is taken. All of this allows the lungs to reach full capacity with inhalation. As the student breathes in he should feel like an expanding balloon, expanding downward. The upper anatomy (the sternum and upper ribcage) should be stable, neither rising nor falling.

• To maintain this achieved full expansion, tell him to firmly engage the abdominal muscles, as if he was going to get hit in the stomach with a hard ball. (You may use a large, firm ball and push it in quickly towards the student's abdominals but without releasing it and hitting him.) This will help him to experience the sensations involved as he is tightening and engaging the abdominal muscles involved in breath support.

- Now have the student read a few sentences from a written passage while maintaining this achieved full expansion. Tell him to firmly engage the abdominal muscles (call this his "support") as he works to stabilize his ribcage. The student should breathe whenever he needs to, then re-engage his "support" each time he breathes. (Remind him that it will be easier to re-engage his "support" if he pretends that he is going to be hit in the stomach by that large, hard ball each time he fills with breath.)

- Demonstrate and then have him stand against a wall with the effective breathing posture as he practices the same sequence four times. Pay careful attention as he moves through these steps and make corrections as needed. Have the student carry out the sequence one more time, while standing against a wall, with the effective breathing posture, but this time he should breathe in, using the *spirometer*, before reading *each sentence* from the passage. Time and record the number of seconds he is able to float the ball(s) in the spirometer as he inhales.

5. **Discuss the expansion rules (during breathing).** Have your student write them in his notebook:

   ✓ Set up and maintain the effective breathing posture, as prescribed above.

   ✓ Fill the lungs with the necessary amount of air. (Expand the lower abdominal area, the sternum, upper ribcage, and the lower back muscles with each inhalation.)

   ✓ The entire ribcage, front and back, must expand and maintain expansion.

6. **Mindfulness of stress and its effect on breathing.** Discuss emotional stress and excitement and how they make the muscles tense, which restricts airflow in both directions. Also explain how oxygen is used up more quickly by the body when a person is experiencing emotional stress or excitement. The oxygen is converted more quickly to CO_2, so even though the lungs may feel full, the person will feel like they need more air.

   a. Do the following exercise with the student to illustrate these sensations. Have the student breathe deeply and hold it for as long as he can. Time the length and record the time. Then have the student do 30 jumping jacks. Now have him take another deep breath and hold it for as long as he can. Discuss that even though he has taken in the same amount of breath (and oxygen) both times, he can't hold his breath for as long after the jumping jacks. Explain that when the body is stressed it uses more oxygen and it feels like there is less air in the lungs. Therefore, it is essential to stay calm while speaking, especially when trying to project the voice. Have the student recall the calming techniques he learned in Chapter 2.

b. Do a mindfulness exercise where the student practices self-calming, being mindful of (paying attention to) his bodily cues, such as rate and depth of his breathing. (Remind the student of the concepts of mindfulness discussed in Chapter 2; discuss what mindfulness is and that being mindful of one's body and slowing one's breathing helps one to calm and focus.)

- Have the student sit in a chair in a relaxed position. Tell him to relax, including having a relaxed jaw, mouth, tongue, and neck. Now tell the student that for three minutes both of you will concentrate only on your own breathing. Instruct him to feel the sensations of the breath going in and out; to feel the expansion and contraction of the chest and abdominal cavities. Instruct him to focus on being calm and slowing his heart rate and breathing rate. After the three minutes, each of you describe what you observed about your own breathing and the focus of your attention.

- Then have him stand in the effective breathing posture and read the passage from Handout B, following the steps in the expansion exercise above. Instruct him to focus on remaining calm. Videotape him doing this. Review the video with the student. Discuss.

7. **Homework:** Practice reading the passage from this lesson (Handout B), using diaphragmatic breathing and your "support." Also do the "airplane" exercise a few times this week to strengthen your muscles.

Rules for Optimal Breathing Expansion

✓ Set up and maintain the effective breathing posture.

✓ Fill the lungs with the necessary amount of air. (Expand the lower abdominal area, the sternum, upper ribcage, and the lower back muscles with each inhalation.)

✓ The entire ribcage, front and back, must expand and maintain expansion.

Reading Passage

It was a very stormy night. I was lying in my bed but having trouble sleeping. It was raining very hard and the wind was whistling and shaking my windows. A branch from the dogwood tree close to my window kept hitting the house. As I started to finally drift off to sleep, I was roused by a new louder sound. There was a persistent scratching coming up from the kitchen. I looked for my dog Max and saw that he was in his bed, sleeping. Early that night, at the first clap of thunder, he had come running into the kitchen through the doggy door. Since Max was not alarmed, I tried to go back to sleep. It was then that I heard a big crash. The sound definitely came from my kitchen. It sounded like metal hitting the tile floor. Max sat up and started to bark. I picked up the walking stick that was leaning against my bedroom wall and slowly, quietly walked down the steps and turned towards the kitchen. I flicked on the kitchen light, to find a family of waterlogged racoons feasting on my trash.

LESSON 9

Modulating breath release: Learning the relationship between the speed of airflow and volume

Materials

Kickball, volleyball, or basketball

Smart phone or computer application which measures and displays sound pressure waveforms

Goals

To learn how a louder volume is produced by moving air more quickly through the vocal folds; and that moving air more slowly will produce less volume.

To learn how to control the rate of outward flow of breath to produce sounds of differing volumes.

Procedures

1. **Explain the purpose of the lesson:** To teach the student how vocal volume increases when he moves his breath through his vocal folds faster, and how volume decreases when he moves his breath slowly.

2. **Show the student the instrument (smart phone, computer) you will use to measure the volume level of his voice.** Explain and demonstrate how the application works. Make sure he is able to see and understand that a louder sound (greater amplitude) will increase the height of the sound signal on your device.

3. **Begin by having the student take a full breath and then, as he begins to exhale, have him say the sounds listed below, as he bends forward at the waist as far as he can without falling.** Explain to him that, by bending over, his abdominal area is being compressed by his legs, forcing air from his lungs. The speed of this movement will determine the volume of his speech. In this exercise we are helping the student understand that, by moving breath faster (emptying the lungs faster), sound is projected with a greater volume. Record the following exercises with the sound pressure waveform application:

   a. Have the student bend forward at the waist *slowly* (which will move air out of his lungs slowly) and produce each of the following sounds, in turn:

- "Shhhhhhh"
- "Uhhhhhhh"
- "Ahhhhhhh"
- "Run"
- "Sun"
- "I will run"
- "In the sun"

b. Have the student bend forward at the waist *quickly* (which will move air out of his lungs quickly) and produce each of the following sounds, in turn:

- "Shhhhhhh"
- "Uhhhhhhh"
- "Ahhhhhhh"
- "Run"
- "Sun"
- "I will run"
- "In the sun"

4. **Notice the difference in vocal volume in the two exercises.** Look at the sound pressure waveforms you recorded. Point out that the sounds he produces when he bends quickly are louder, because the air is moving from the lungs at a faster rate. This is seen in the greater amplitude of the sound pressure waveforms when he bends quickly.

5. **Help your student experience the sensation of diaphragmatic support for faster breath release in order to produce sound at a higher volume.** Have the student hold a fully inflated kickball, volleyball, or basketball on his navel, just below his sternum, and walk up to a wall or closed door and lean in on the ball against the stable surface, holding the ball in place with his body weight. Have him remain in this position throughout the following exercise:

a. Demonstrate the first string of sounds in the table (TchoohTchooh TchoohTchoohTchooh) at the three indicated volume levels, with the specified volume change. Produce each of the sounds, in the strings of five, separately, as a quick burst, and spacing them about one second apart.

b. Have your student imitate you as you speak the sounds, in the strings of five, again, with the specified volume changes, as directed (separately, as a quick burst, and spacing them about one second apart).

Sounds	Normal	Loud	Soft
TchoohTchoohTchoohTchooh			
TchohTchohTchohTchoh			
TchahTchahTchahTchah			
TchehTchehTchehTcheh			
TchayTchayTchayTchay			
TcheeTcheeTcheeTchee			

c. Have the student imitate your production of all strings of sounds in the table (according to the procedure above). Each string of sounds will be spoken as quick bursts for a total of four times at each volume level indicated.

d. Discuss the physical sensations the student encountered as he produced the syllables at different volumes. Each time he said a syllable he should have noticed his body moving briefly and quickly away from the wall. This is due to the quick upward movement of the diaphragm, forcing a quick burst of air. The louder he spoke the syllables, the greater the movement of the diaphragm and the further his abdominal muscles pushed him away from the wall.

Review the recording and the amplitude of the sound pressure waveforms (indicating volume) with the student.

6. **Homework:** Choose a passage and practice reading it at a quiet volume level and at a loud volume level. Write down all the sensations you notice. Be ready to read the passage next time. Be ready to discuss the sensations you noticed.

Modulating breath release: Maintaining an expanded chest

Materials

Two one-inch-thick books or a pillow

Stack of books weighing about 20 lbs (about 9 kg)

Goal

To learn to maintain an expanded chest cavity while breathing out.

Procedures

1. **Explain the purpose of the lesson:** The student is to learn to manage the release of his breath as he speaks by maintaining an expanded chest.

2. **Review the homework from the last lesson.** Have him read the passage he chose at a quiet volume and at a loud volume. Discuss the sensations he feels. Provide feedback.

3. **Remind the student of the introduction to the bodily sensations of maintaining expansion, which he worked on in Lesson 8.** This is where your student was asked to pretend that he was about to be hit in the stomach by a ball. This made him react and engage (tighten) his abdominal, chest, and ribcage muscles as he managed to hold his chest in an expanded position.

4. **Ribcage musculature resistance exercises.** In these exercises, the student will control the release of air from his lungs while maintaining an expanded chest, recognizing and effectively engaging the inter-costal muscles surrounding and supporting the ribcage. This ability is necessary so that his supply of air is not immediately diminished when he begins to speak. It allows him to maintain a reservoir of air that can be moved through the vocal folds at the speed required to produce the desired volume. This exercise will engage and strengthen the inter-costal muscles, which support and maintain a fully expanded chest cavity. When the student is proficient with these exercises, he will be in control of his ribcage and his abdominal muscles.

   a. Have the student lie flat on his back, on the floor or a flat bench. Two one-inch-thick books or a pillow should be placed under the student's head. This will help the student correctly maintain his back and spinal alignment, and his muscles, flat against the floor/bench to avoid discomfort or injury. The teacher will then put books weighing approximately, and no more than, 20 lbs (about 9 kg) on top of the student's abdomen. They should be centered over the student's belly button. Now have the student take a full and deep breath and hold it in, keeping his ribcage from collapsing. He should see the books rise and remain up while he holds back his breath. Instruct the student to slowly release the breath after five to ten seconds.

b. Next, with the books still on his abdomen, have the student take a full, deep breath and hold it for two seconds while he forms the lips, tongue, and teeth to make a "tch" sound. Make sure his mouth, tongue, teeth, and lips form a very small opening (aperture). (If he cannot produce this sound right away, stop the exercise and teach him before you go on.) Then he will release the breath slowly, maintaining chest expansion (keeping the books up), while producing a sustained "tch" sound. The student should keep his ribcage expanded and the books raised up until the very end of his breath. He must fight gravity to keep his ribcage expanded and the books raised up. Have the student repeat this exercise five times.

c. Take a break and discuss the reason you asked your student to release the air from his lungs using this mouth position. Explain to your student that this mouth position produces a small space through which the breath flows. Therefore, the release of air is controlled (making it easier for the student to maintain an expanded ribcage during exhalation). The next exercise will not be as easy.

d. Have the student lie on the floor with the books on his abdomen again. You will now have him read sentences out loud while maintaining the expanded chest until he finishes each sentence. This is a difficult exercise. Begin this exercise with small sentences or phrases. As the student's strength increases (with practicing this exercise at home), you will increase the length of passages. Normal speech, as in reading a passage or conversing, will require the student to work even harder to control the airflow by keeping his chest expanded. Make sure he knows exactly what he will read before he begins this exercise. Have him take a deep breath. Watch for the books to rise. Do not let him read until he has properly expanded his ribcage. As he reads, he must maintain ribcage expansion until he is finished with a sentence. He will take a new breath before each sentence or phrase, making the books rise. He will hold the breath momentarily and then begin to speak, again keeping his chest expanded until he is finished speaking the sentence. Have him read one paragraph at a time. Pause for two to three minutes between each paragraph to give the student and his muscles time to recover and rest. During this time out, discuss your observations and remind him of the various sensations associated with this process.

5. **Homework:** Practice reading a passage while lying on your back with a couple of books stacked on your abdomen (over your belly button). Maintain expansion throughout each sentence. After each sentence, take another breath to prepare for the next sentence (as you did during the lesson). Take breaks between paragraphs. The more you practice, the stronger you will get. This will give you the ability to produce more volume when you speak.

Modulating breath release: Using the vocal cords as a valve

Materials

Kickball, volleyball, or basketball

Smart phone or computer application which measures and displays sound pressure waveforms

Goal

To learn to use the Breath–Pause technique to set up breath support for sustaining sounds at appropriate volumes.

Procedures

1. **Explain the purpose of the lesson:** To learn to manage the speed and amount of breath released, while using the Breath–Pause technique.

2. **Review the homework from the last lesson.** Have the student lie on the floor with a pillow under his head and books on his abdomen. Have him read the passage he chose for homework. Watch for the rising of the books as he breathes in before each sentence. See that he maintains ribcage expansion. Watch that the books do not instantly sink as he begins to speak. Listen to the quality of his speech. Discuss your observations and give feedback.

3. **Review the breath management concepts your student has mastered up to this point.** These include the effective breathing posture, relaxing the muscles below the ribcage while breathing for full expansion, engaging the abdominal muscles, maintaining rib expansion, and understanding the relationship between volume and the speed with which the breath is expelled.

4. **Explain to your student that in addition to maintaining chest expansion, the release of air from the lungs is managed by the opening and closing of the vocal cords.** Teach the student how the vocal folds are used as the aperture/valve to regulate breath release. By holding back air after a breath is taken or between words or phrases, air is conserved and a sound with more volume can be created. Teach the Rules for the Breath–Pause Technique and have him try the technique. The Rules for the Breath–Pause Technique are:

   ✓ BREATHE – Full breath.

✓ PAUSE – Immediately stop the outward flow of breath by closing the vocal cords completely (this allows air pressure to build up below the vocal cords and produces a sensation like the act of lifting a heavy object).

5. **Have the student apply the Breath–Pause technique.** Tell the student to do the following:

- Take a full breath.

- Pause: hold back the breath.

- Speak the word "Attaboy" during breath release.

Repeat this sequence five times, getting louder each time.

6. **Voice projection exercises using Breath–Pause:**

   a. *Bounce–pass exercise.* Now stand across the room from the student. Bounce–pass the ball to the student, shouting "Ay!" (as in "say") for each pass. The student will pass the ball back in the same manner. Remind the student to expand his ribcage when he breathes in, use the Breath–Pause technique before he passes, and to expel the air on the "Ay!" as he passes the ball. (*Note:* This exercise is intended to give the student a visual image, and a physical connection to the core muscles associated with sound projection. In this exercise the emphasis is on moving energy and air forward.)

   b. In this exercise the student is to pick a distant target, somewhere behind his listener, and project his voice to that target. The student will pretend to "pass the ball" to the target while shouting "Ay!" for each pass. Explain to your student that he must visualize throwing his voice in the same way that he throws the ball. Remind the student to expand his ribcage when he breathes in, use the Breath–Pause technique before he passes, and to expel the air on the "Ay!" as he passes the ball. This exercise forces the student to use the muscles necessary for projecting his voice to that target.

   c. Have your student repeat the exercise in a safe outdoor setting where ambient and competing noises will create a greater challenge.

7. **Help your student learn to recognize the feeling of back pressure when Breath–Pause is used correctly.** (Record your student during this exercise with the sound pressure waveform application.) Have the student stand facing a wall with a fully inflated 13 to 15 inch rubber kickball between the student's belly button and the wall. The student holds the ball in place against the wall by leaning into the ball using his body weight. Discuss the physical sensations the student encountered the last time he did a similar exercise. Each time he said a syllable he noticed his body moving briefly and away from the wall. This is due to the upward movement of the diaphragm as breath is released. As he produced syllables at different volumes, he noticed that the louder he

spoke the syllables, the greater the movement of the diaphragm and the further his abdominal muscles pushed him away from the wall. This time he should notice those sensations as well as the sensation of back pressure in his lungs produced by holding back the breath with closed vocal cords.

Have the student imitate you as you say each string of sounds in the table below in the following way:

a. Take a deep breath.

b. Use the Breath–Pause technique after your inhalation at the beginning of the string and then stop the flow of breath after each sound.

c. Make each sound last for one second, pausing for one second between each individual sound in the string.

d. Produce each of the sound strings at a normal volume and then according to the volume instructions in the rest of the table.

e. Repeat the entire exercise, producing the sounds in unison with the student.

f. Have the student produce the string of sounds, solo.

Demonstrate these patterns	Normal	Loud to soft	Soft to loud	Soft–loud–soft
ooh ooh ooh ooh ...				
oh oh oh oh ...				
a a a a ...				
ah ah ah ah ...				
eh eh eh eh ...				
ay ay ay ay ...				
ee ee ee ee ...				

8. **Review the recording.** Discuss your observations of each waveform's volume.

9. **Homework:** Practice reading a written passage out loud while lying on your back with a couple of books stacked on your abdomen (over your belly button). After you breathe in at the beginning of each sentence and you feel the books rise, use the Breath–Pause technique. Be sure to maintain expansion throughout each sentence from the reading you chose.

LESSON 12

Modulating breath release: Regulating the volume of sustained sounds

Materials

Handout A: Diaphragmatic Breathing

Handout B: Homework: Volume Practice Exercises

Video recording device

Smart phone or computer application which measures and displays sound pressure waveforms

Goals

To develop breath support.

To increase the length of time for which the student is able to sustain vocalizations at an appropriate volume.

To manage the volume (dynamics) of sustained vocalizations.

Procedures

1. **Explain the purpose of the lesson:** To continue to develop your student's breath support and to increase the duration of sustained vocalizations with an appropriate volume.

2. **Work with your student on developing more effective breathing for increased volume and vocal dynamics.** Have him do the following exercise five times:

   - Breathe in. With inhalation, the muscles below the ribs must relax to allow the organs below the diaphragm to drop, giving the diaphragm more room to expand downward as breath is taken in. All of this allows the lungs to reach full capacity with inhalation.

   - Show the student Handout A, explaining how the diaphragm expands down as he breathes in, and contracts up as he breathes out.

   - He should hold back the breath (Breath–Pause).

   - Then he should engage the lower abdominal muscles (as if he is going to be hit in the stomach by a ball).

   - Now the student should hold his breath, with his abdominal muscles engaged, for a count of five.

- Then, while maintaining the firm engagement of the abdominal muscles and a stable ribcage, the student should expel the breath. (*Note:* The lower abdominals do not push the air out; rather, the fully engaged lower abdominal muscles follow the upward movement of the diaphragm as the air is expelled from the lungs.)

3. **Teach your student to maintain and modulate the volume of sustained vocalization.** Tell the student that, up until now, he has been working on bursts of sound. The idea of those exercises was to teach him that increased speed of airflow is associated with louder sound. Now he will learn to maintain and modulate the volume of sustained speech. This will develop better control of the muscles to keep the chest cavity expanded for a longer period of time. Record each of the following exercises with a program that generates images of the sound pressure waveforms, so that you and the student can visually observe the amplitude of the waveforms (indicating the volume of the sound).

   a. *Maintaining chest expansion during the production of sustained sounds:* Have the student stand against a wall in the effective breathing posture. Tell him to breathe in, being sure to relax the muscles below the ribs to allow his lungs to fully expand. He should then hold back the breath (Breath–Pause). Then while maintaining firm engagement of the abdominal muscles and a stable, expanded ribcage, he will breathe out for a slow count of ten, on ahhhhhhhhh. His ribcage must not collapse and the volume of his production must remain constant. Have him repeat this sequence five times; that is, five sets for a slow count to ten.

   b. *Maintaining chest expansion while stopping and starting the breath during the production of sustained sounds:* Now have the student stand away from the wall with the same effective breathing posture. Have him take a low and expanded breath (relaxing all muscles beneath the ribcage to make more room). He should then hold back the breath (Breath–Pause). He should be reminded to firmly engage the abdominal muscles. Have him breathe out on ahhhhhhhhh, but this time have him intermittently stop the flow of breath (using the Breath–Pause technique) every second during exhalation and then continue with ahhhhhhhhh, still firmly engaging the lower abdominal musculature and maintaining ribcage expansion, until all his breath is expelled. His ribcage must not collapse and the volume of his production must remain constant. This will teach him to maintain firm abdominal muscles and chest expansion while controlling the breath. Have him repeat this sequence five times.

   c. *Re-engaging and then maintaining chest expansion after taking a new breath during the production of sustained sounds:* Now have the student stand away from the wall with the same effective breathing posture. Have him take a low and expanded breath (relaxing all muscles beneath the ribcage). He should then hold back the breath (Breath–Pause). He should be reminded to firmly engage the abdominal muscles and maintain rib expansion. Have him breathe out on ahhhhhhhhh for five seconds, but this time have him intermittently stop, then breathe out the remaining breath, and then re-engage support using the Breath–Pause technique. And then continue by producing another ahhhhhhhhh for five seconds. His ribcage will collapse when he lets out the breath after he says "ah," but as he is saying "ah," he is required to maintain firm abdominal muscles and chest expansion. The volume of each "ah" must be consistent with the preceding "ah." Have him repeat this sequence five times.

d. *Maintaining chest expansion while modulating the volume of a sustained sound.* (You should record the student during the next two exercises with your sound pressure waveform application, so that you have a visual referent for judging the change in your student's volume during these exercises.) Have the student stand against a wall in the effective breathing posture. Make sure he always starts by breathing in, being sure to relax the muscles below the ribs to allow his lungs to fully expand. He should then hold back the breath (Breath–Pause). Then, while maintaining a firm engagement of the abdominal muscles and a stable, expanded ribcage, have the student produce the sustained sound "ah," modulating volume in the following ways (you should demonstrate each first):

   i.   Begin moderately quietly and maintain level (on one breath).

   ii. Begin loudly and maintain level (on one breath).

   iii. Start moderately quietly, then increase slowly to loud and maintain for as long as possible (on one breath).

   iv. Start quietly, steadily increase to loud, then steadily decrease to quiet again (on one breath).

   v.   Start loud, steadily decrease to quiet, then steadily increase to loud again (on one breath).

   vi. Start quietly, steadily increase to loud, stop and let out the rest of your breath, breathe–pause, start loud, and then steadily decrease to quiet again.

   vii. Start loud, steadily decrease to quiet, stop and let out the rest of your breath, breathe–pause, start quiet, and then steadily increase to loud again.

e. *Maintaining chest expansion while modulating the volume of a sustained word:* Have the student stand against a wall in the effective breathing posture. Make sure he always starts by breathing in, being sure to relax the muscles below the ribs to allow his lungs to fully expand. He should then hold back the breath (Breath–Pause). Then, while maintaining a firm engagement of the abdominal muscles and a stable, expanded ribcage, have the student produce a single word containing an open vowel sound (e.g., dog, frog, sock, cop, job) (you demonstrate first):

i. Begin moderately quietly and maintain level (on one breath).

ii. Begin loudly and maintain level (on one breath).

iii. Start moderately quietly, then increase slowly to loud and maintain for as long as possible (on one breath).

iv. Start quietly, steadily increase to loud, then steadily decrease to quiet again (on one breath).

v. Start loud, steadily decrease to quiet, then steadily increase to loud again (on one breath).

vi. Start quietly, steadily increase to loud, stop and let out the rest of your breath, breathe–pause, continue the word by starting loudly, and then steadily decrease to quiet again.

vii. Start loud, steadily decrease to quiet, stop and let out the rest of your breath, breathe–pause, continue the word by starting quietly, and then steadily increase to loud again.

4. **Review the recordings you made during the last two exercises with the student.** Examine the sound pressure waveforms to evaluate how effectively your student modulated his volume during these activities.

5. **Homework:** Develop the strength of your abdominal muscles and ability to maintain abdominal expansion: (1) Lie flat on the floor with a pillow under your head; this will help to make sure that your back and spinal muscles are entirely flat against the floor. Place books weighing approximately 2 lbs on top of your belly button. Now take a full breath with the books rising. Maintain rib and abdominal expansion (do not collapse) and then release the air slowly (lowering the books slowly), while saying a sustained "ah." This exercise will strengthen the intercostal muscles to support/maintain a full and expanded chest cavity, thus allowing a release of air/sound that is both controlled and supported. (2) Practice the exercises from the lesson (Handout B).

Diaphragmatic Breathing

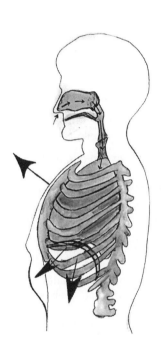
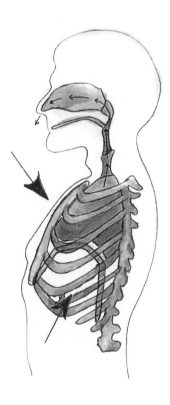

✓

Homework: Volume Practice Exercises

- Stand against a wall in the effective breathing posture.

- Start by breathing in, being sure to relax the muscles below the ribs to allow your lungs to fully expand.

- Hold back the breath (Breath–Pause).

- Maintain a firm engagement of the abdominal muscles and an expanded ribcage.

Produce a sustained "ah," modulating volume in the following ways:

i.   Begin moderately quietly and maintain level (on one breath).
ii. Begin loudly and maintain level (on one breath).
iii. Start moderately quietly, then increase slowly to loud and maintain for as long as possible (on one breath).
iv. Start quietly, steadily increase to loud, then steadily decrease to quiet again (on one breath).
v.   Start loud, steadily decrease to quiet, then steadily increase to loud again (on one breath).
vi. Start quietly, steadily increase to loud, stop and let out the rest of your breath, breathe–pause, start loud, and then steadily decrease to quiet again.
vii. Start loud, steadily decrease to quiet, stop and let out the rest of your breath, breathe–pause, start quiet, and then steadily increase to loud again.

Produce a single word containing an open vowel sound (e.g., dog, frog, sock, cop, job) in the following ways:

i.   Begin moderately quietly and maintain level (on one breath).
ii. Begin loudly and maintain level (on one breath).
iii. Start moderately quietly, then increase slowly to loud and maintain for as long as possible (on one breath).
iv. Start quietly, steadily increase to loud, then steadily decrease to quiet again (on one breath).
v.   Start loud, steadily decrease to quiet, then steadily increase to loud again (on one breath).
vi. Start quietly, steadily increase to loud, stop and let out the rest of your breath, breathe–pause, continue the word by starting loudly, and then steadily decrease to quiet again.
vii. Start loud, steadily decrease to quiet, stop and let out the rest of your breath, breathe–pause, continue the word by starting quietly, and then steadily increase to loud again.

LESSON 13

Modulating release and increasing volume: Combining the Breath–Pause technique with nasal timbre

Materials

Handout A: Rules for the Breath–Pause Technique

Handout B: Practice Sentences

Goals

To review the Breath–Pause technique and the functions of the anatomy involved so that the student can: (a) use his vocal cords as a valve to stop and start the flow of air, to conserve his breath so that there is enough to project his sound (with more volume); and (b) use the Breath–Pause technique to release breath in such a way that the onset of vocalization is clean, clear, and more precise.

To learn to combine the techniques for Breath–Pause and nasal timbre.

Procedures

1. **Explain the purpose of the lesson:** To review the Breath–Pause technique so that the student does not release all of his air too quickly in connected speech. A sustained air supply is needed to produce a sound with adequate volume. The Breath–Pause technique is used to reserve air. It also releases air in such a way that the quality of the sound of his speech is clearer and more assertive. Another purpose of this lesson is for the student to learn to combine the techniques for Breath–Pause and nasal timbre.

2. **Review the Breath–Pause technique with the student.** To carry out this technique, one breathes in and immediately holds back the breath. At this point, the cords are closed. As one begins to speak, the air is released by the cords in a controlled and calm manner. This technique allows the individual to regulate the release of his breath and improves phonation, so that word(s), phrase(s), and sentence(s) are expressed with more presence and volume.

3. **Review the Rules for the Breath–Pause Technique:**

   ✓ BREATHE – Full breath.

   ✓ PAUSE – Immediately stop the outward flow of breath by closing the vocal cords completely (this allows air pressure to build up below the vocal cords and produces a sensation like the act of lifting a heavy object).

Also:

- *Think* what you will say as you hold the breath back.

- Release the air in a controlled way as you speak.

4. **Solidify for the student the sensation of holding his breath back.** The student must understand that he is not simply just holding his breath. The air in his lungs will create back pressure below his vocal cords. To help your student experience this correct sensation, have him place his hands under the chair on which he is sitting, and have him try to lift the chair and himself off the floor. This same sensation is experienced when lifting or pushing something heavy.

5. **Have the student practice the Breath–Pause technique.** For the beginner, it is necessary to have him make a clear, audible sound as he stops his breath (like the sound one makes during a Karate chop: "Ha!"). Have him repeat, breathing in and stopping the breath, while producing the sound, five times (breathe "Ha!"/breathe "Ha!"/breathe "Ha!"/breathe "Ha!"/breathe "Ha!"). Have him read the sentences in Handout B, using an audible breath and pause before each sentence.

6. **Have the student practice the Breath–Pause technique with a quieter sound when stopping the breath.** Eventually the student will be able to use the Breath–Pause technique with no sound (stealth). However, at this point, an audible sound when he stops his breath will confirm for you that he is using the technique correctly. Have him repeat, breathing in and stopping the breath, while producing the "ha" sound, five times, but this time much more quietly (breathe "ha"/breathe "ha"/breathe "ha"/breathe "ha"/breathe "ha"). Have the student read the sentences in Handout B again, using an audible but much quieter "ha" at the beginning of each sentence.

7. **Teach the student to combine the Breath–Pause technique with a more nasal timbre.** Remind the student of the cues for a more nasal timbre:

   ✓ *Tongue* tip to a position behind the front lower teeth, *relaxed.*

   ✓ *"Sneeze–Pause" position:* Back corners of tongue up against upper molars.

   ✓ *Think* what you will say (like a goat would sound).

   ✓ *Speak* (maintaining "sneeze–pause"/goat position).

8. **Explain that "Sneeze–Pause" is a form of "Breath–Pause," which has the added benefit of creating a position of the tongue and velum that results in a more nasal timbre.** Refine your student's "Sneeze–Pause" position by taking him through the following steps:

   ✓ *Tongue* tip behind the front lower teeth, *relaxed.*

✓ BREATHE – Full breath in *sneeze* position (back corners of tongue up against upper molars).

✓ PAUSE – Immediately stop the outward flow of breath by closing the vocal cords completely.

✓ *Think* what you will say (like a goat would sound).

✓ Release the air in a controlled way as you speak.

9. **Now have the student practice the sequence above prior to saying the word "Action."** Have him repeat the word "Action" ten times. Discuss how combining a nasal timbre with the Breath–Pause technique produces a louder and more present sound.

10. **Homework:** Practice using the "Sneeze–Pause" technique to increase the volume of your speech while saying the words listed below. Do this exercise two times a day. Use the "Sneeze–Pause" technique and then say each word on the list. Repeat the "Sneeze–Pause" before saying each word: big, little, house, funny, pretty, jump, skip, run, monkey, tree.

Rules for the Breath–Pause Technique

✓ BREATHE – Full breath.

✓ PAUSE – Immediately stop the outward flow of breath by closing the vocal cords completely (this allows air pressure to build up below the vocal cords and produces a sensation like the act of lifting a heavy object).

Also:

- *Think* what you will say as you hold the breath back.

- Release the air in a controlled way as you speak.

Practice Sentences

I like ice cream.

We go out for pizza every Friday.

That little boy loves to swim.

Kick the ball to me!

Jerry is such a nice person!

Regulating breath release: Mindfulness of sensations associated with Breath–Pause

Materials

Handout A from Lesson 13: Rules for the Breath–Pause Technique

Goal

To develop mindfulness of physical sensations connected to the use of the Breath–Pause technique and to use those sensations to enhance the student's application of the "Breath–Pause."

Procedures

1. **Review the homework from the last lesson.** Listen to your student say each of the words from the list in his homework, using the "Sneeze–Pause" technique (this is the nasal form of Breath–Pause) before saying each word.

2. **Explain the purpose of the lesson:** To teach the student to be mindful of the sensations connected to the use of the Breath–Pause technique.

3. **Review the Rules for the Breath–Pause Technique.** Look at Handout A from Lesson 13 together, and discuss the rules. Practice implementing the Rules for the Breath–Pause Technique. Tell your student that as he is holding back his breath he should think that he will say, "This is a great day!" Then he should say it. Have him do this three times, calmly using the technique each time.

4. **Mindfulness of sensations connected to "Breath–Pause."** Remind the student that mindfulness means fully concentrating his focus where he needs to, while at the same time noticing other things that come to his attention but setting them aside, to re-fix his attention where it needs to be. Tell the student that during the next task he will focus on the physical sensations associated with the use of the Breath–Pause technique only, and set aside distracting thoughts. Instruct the student that, for a period of two minutes, you will both repeat the following sequence multiple times:

   a. Breathe in, pause the breath, and feel the sensation of back pressure from the air in the lungs.

   b. Hold your breath for a count of five.

   c. Slowly breathe out, completely.

   d. Take in another breath and repeat the process.

   e. Demonstrate the sequence and then have your student do it.

   f. Tell your student that during the next two minutes he will work to be completely mindful of the sensations associated with Breath–Pause: the expanded chest, abdomen, and lower back, keeping the vocal cords closed to hold back the breath, the back pressure in his lungs, and then the opening of the cords as the breath is slowly released.

   g. Begin the mindfulness exercise.

After two minutes have elapsed, discuss the sensations you both experienced while being mindful of the Breath–Pause technique. Discuss any distracting thoughts that came into his mind as he performed the exercise.

5. **Review "Sneeze–Pause."** "Sneeze–Pause" is a form of "Breath–Pause," which has the added benefit of creating a more closed position between the tongue and velum that results in a more nasal timbre. Practice implementing the "Sneeze–Pause" position. Tell your student that as he is holding back his breath he should think that he will say "This is a great day!" with a nasal quality (like a goat). Then he should say it. Have him do this three times, calmly using the technique each time.

   ✓ *Tongue* tip behind the front lower teeth, *relaxed.*

   ✓ Breathe in *"Sneeze–Pause" position* (back corners of tongue up against upper molars).

   ✓ Momentarily stop the breath (this allows air pressure to build up below the vocal cords and produces a sensation like the act of lifting a heavy object).

   ✓ *Think* what you will say (like a goat would sound).

   ✓ Release the air as you speak.

6. **Mindfulness of sensations connected to "Breath–Pause".** Tell the student that during the next task he will focus on the physical sensations associated with the use of "Sneeze–Pause" (a variation of the Breath–Pause technique that produces a nasal timbre), and set aside distracting thoughts. Instruct the student that, for a period of two minutes, you will both repeat the following sequence in unison multiple times:

   a. Breathe, in sneeze position, pause the breath, and feel the sensation of back pressure from the air in the lungs.

   b. Hold your breath for a count of ten.

   c. Say "Have a great day!" loudly, then expel the rest of your breath completely.

   d. Take in another breath in sneeze position and repeat the process.

e. Demonstrate the sequence and then have your student do it.

f. Tell your student that during the next two minutes he will work to be completely mindful of the sensations associated with sneeze–pause: the expanded chest, abdomen, and lower back, keeping the vocal cords closed to hold back the breath, the back pressure in his lungs, the back corners of the tongue up against the upper molars, the tip of the tongue behind the lower front teeth, and then the opening of the cords as speech begins.

g. Begin the mindfulness exercise.

After two minutes have elapsed, discuss the sensations you both experienced while being mindful of the "Sneeze–Pause." Discuss any distracting thoughts that came into his mind as he performed the exercise.

7. **Homework:** Practice using the "Sneeze–Pause" (a nasal form of Breath–Pause) to increase the volume of your speech while saying the following words: book, candy, orange, penny, dog, ice cream, mop, test, friend, drink. As you do this activity, be mindful of the sensations associated with "Breath–Pause." Breathe in and pause the breath. Hold your breath for a count of five. Feel your expanded chest, abdomen, and lower back, your closed vocal cords as the breath is held back, and the back pressure from the air in your lungs. As you begin to speak, feel the opening of the cords as the breath is slowly released. Do this exercise two times a day.

Modulating breath release: Learn the Breath–Pause notation to practice management of breath release

Materials

Handout A: Applying the Breath–Pause Technique to a Sound Conversation

Handout B: Applying the Breath–Pause Technique to a Scripted Conversation

Handout C: Sentences to Notate

Handout D: Paragraph to Notate

Goals

To learn to apply the Breath–Pause technique silently (stealth).

To learn and use the notation for the Breath–Pause technique, so that it can be applied to connected speech, to regulate the release of breath and improve phonation, and to increase volume.

Procedures

1. **Review the homework from the last lesson.** Listen to your student say each of the words from the list in his homework, using "Sneeze–Pause" (a nasal form of Breath–Pause), breathing in and pausing the breath for a count of five before saying each word. Give feedback and correction as needed. As he does this activity, tell him to be mindful of the sensations associated with "Breath–Pause." He should feel his expanded chest, abdomen, and lower back, his closed vocal cords as the breath is held back, and the back pressure from the air in his lungs. As he begins to speak, he should feel the opening of the cords as the breath is slowly released. Discuss these sensations.

2. **Explain the purpose of the lesson:** To learn to apply the Breath–Pause technique without making any sound (stealth) and to learn to use the Breath–Pause technique in connected speech by applying Breath–Pause notation to written text.

3. **Teach your student to use the Breath–Pause technique with no sound (stealth).** When your student first learned the Breath–Pause technique, he made an audible sound when he stopped his breath. Now he will work on breathing in and then stopping the breath in the same way, but

without a sound. Have him repeat breathing in and stopping the breath five times, making no sound. He should still feel his expanded chest, abdomen, and lower back, his closed vocal cords as the breath is held back, and the back pressure from the air in his lungs when he pauses.

4. **Teach the student the Breath–Pause notation:**

   a. Explain to the student that the V indicates the time to breathe.

   b. The x indicates the time to hold the breath back, as a pause (Breath–Pause).

   c. When both are together, as in the **V**ˣ combination, the instruction is to take a breath and immediately interrupt the breath release with a pause by closing the vocal cords.

5. **Read the Breath–Pause notation:**

   a. Give your student Handout A: Applying the Breath–Pause Technique to a Sound Conversation. Model the entire dialogue for the student, following the Breath–Pause notation. Then try the dialogue with the student, each reading your own part. Stop the student and provide feedback and correction as needed.

   b. Give the student Handout B: Applying the Breath–Pause Technique to a Scripted Conversation. Model the entire dialogue for the student, following the Breath–Pause notation. Then try the dialogue with the student, each reading your own part. Stop the student and provide feedback and correction as needed.

6. **Write the Breath–Pause notation:**

   a. Give the student Handout C: Sentences to Notate. Have the student read these sentences out loud. Then help him insert the Breath–Pause notation. Have him read the sentences again, following the notation. Encourage him to avoid speaking word to word. Rather, his breath should continue and carry him through each phrase from one pause (ˣ) to the next.

   b. Give the student Handout D: Paragraph to Notate. Have the student read the paragraph out loud. Then help him insert the Breath–Pause notation. Have him read the paragraph again, following the notation. Again, encourage him to avoid speaking word to word. Rather, his breath should continue and carry him through each phrase from one pause (ˣ) to the next.

7. **Homework:** Practice the Breath–Pause exercises on Handouts A and B at home with a partner. Create your own brief dialogue with the Breath–Pause notation.

Applying the Breath–Pause Technique to a Sound Conversation

Therapist: **V**^{x} ah ah ah ah ah ah ah ah ah **V**^{x}

Student: ah ah ah ah ah ah **V**^{x} ah ah **V**^{x}

Therapist: **V**^{x} ah ah ah ah ah ah ah **V**^{x} ah ah ah **V**^{x}

Student: **V**^{x} ah ah ah **V**^{x} ah ah ah ^{x} ah ah ah **V**^{x}

Therapist: **V**^{x} ah ah ah ah **V**^{x}

Student: **V**^{x} ah ah ah ^{x} ah ^{x} ah ah ^{x} ah **V**^{x} ah ah ah **V**^{x}

Applying the Breath–Pause Technique to a Scripted Conversation

Therapist: **V**ˣ How are you? ˣ OK? **V**ˣ

Student: **V**ˣ I'm feeling fine. **V**ˣ ... what about you? **V**ˣ

Therapist: **V**ˣ Well, let me tell you something! **V**ˣ I wrote a five-page essay. ˣ It took me all day yesterday. **V**ˣ I had it on the car dashboard **V**ˣ and it flew out of the car window. **V**ˣ There were no other copies of it. **V**ˣ

Student: **V**ˣ Whoa!ˣ That sounds awful. **V**ˣ

Therapist: **V**ˣ Oh, it's OK ˣ I can redo it. **V**ˣ

Student: **V**ˣ Well ˣ it seems like so much work. **V**ˣ I am sorry ˣ that this happened to you.

Sentences to Notate

As I walked through the yard, I saw how green and healthy it was.

This movie will increase her chances for an Oscar.

The students worked very hard and made a lot of progress this year.

Although she was only three years old, she could read very well.

Jenny is smart, pretty, and kind.

Paragraph to Notate

I love vacationing on Martha's Vineyard. Taking the ferry across to the island is fun. The seagulls swoop down and hover close to the boat to take bread right from my hands. I ride my bicycle everywhere on the island. I swim and play in the surf all day long. My very favorite time on the beach, though, is between sunset and dusk, after everyone has gone home. It is cool and breezy. Sitting quietly on the sand wrapped up in my blanket listening to the roar of the waves crashing on the shore is so relaxing.

LESSON 16

Modulating breath release: Using the Breath–Pause technique and arc phrasing to increase volume in spontaneous connected speech

Materials

Markers (red, green)

Two passages at an appropriate reading level, selected by the therapist in advance (*e.g., human interest stories found online*)

Goals

To apply the Breath–Pause technique to spontaneous conversation, promoting adequate volume throughout.

To apply arc phrasing (i.e., to plan to release air smoothly through an entire spoken phrase).

Procedures

1. **Explain the purpose of the lesson:** To learn to apply the Breath–Pause technique and arc phrasing to written text and spontaneous conversation.

2. **Help the student apply the Breath–Pause notation to a couple of paragraphs from a pre-chosen text of your choice.** Breaths with a pause (V^x) should occur at the very beginning, between sentences, and at some clause boundaries. Pauses without taking a breath (^x) should occur at clause boundaries and after words to be emphasized. It is helpful if the (V) is written in green and the (^x) is written in red. Have the student read the notated paragraphs, employing the Breath–Pause technique as he reads, trying to use a volume which is audible from across the room. Make certain he follows the notation correctly. If he has difficulty, stop him and provide feedback and instruction.

3. **Work on your student's use of the phrasing arc in managing his release of breath and tone.** Explain to your student that to produce greater volume he must sustain his breath in speaking each phrase, which occurs between pauses. His speech should not sound choppy, as if he were speaking a string of single words. His breath should continue and carry him through the entire phrase. Speaking word to word makes increasing volume very difficult. This kind of speech is associated with muscle tension in the tongue and jaw. In addition, because the person is constantly stopping and starting the breath, he does not use enough

breath to support a present sound. When a person speaks an entire phrase on the breath, the phrase has a shape such that the pitch contour starts lower, rises, and then returns to the baseline lower pitch (unless it is a question). People who speak word by word generally do not have this pitch contour.

4. **Discuss the Rules for Managing the Release of Breath/Tone:**

   ✓ Release the cords to release breath.

   ✓ Maintain an expanded chest cavity throughout release.

   ✓ Arc phrasing – plan to release air smoothly through the entire spoken phrase.

   ✓ Volume level must not diminish, unless required by your surroundings.

   ✓ Completely empty the air in your lungs as needed (expel excess air regularly).

5. **Have the student read a text, applying the Breath–Pause notation and the Rules for Managing the Release of Breath/Tone.** Have the student read the notated pages, employing the Breath–Pause technique as he reads, trying to use a volume which is audible from across the room. Observe him to see if he is maintaining chest expansion, using arc phrasing, and maintaining a consistent volume as he speaks. If he has difficulty, stop him and provide feedback, instruction, and practice.

6. **Help the student make a Web Graphic Organizer outlining a description of an event in his life (e.g., his school day, last weekend, family gathering).** His Graphic Organizer must have a main topic and at least two subtopics. He will use this Graphic Organizer to structure his discussion of the topic. Tell him that he must begin with a topic sentence about the main topic and then talk about each subtopic in turn. Tell him that as he talks you will ask him questions. Remind him, before he begins, that he will use the Breath–Pause technique between sentences and at clause boundaries to reset his breath support. Make sure that he applies arc phrasing. This will help him to produce adequate volume throughout the conversation.

7. **Homework:** Find online a speech by a famous person or an article of interest to you. Print it out. Notate breaths (green V) and pauses (red ˣ) on the speech and then practice reading it.

Section 4: Developing a more open passage to increase volume

General goals

To release tension in the jaw, tongue, and throat in order to produce a more projected sound.

To combine an open vocal passage with a nasal timbre and appropriate breath support in order to increase volume of voice.

<u>LESSON 17</u>

Open passage: Releasing tension in the jaw

Materials

Video camera

A tube made of paper or oak-tag paper 2.5" in diameter

A small piece of cloth

Goal

To develop a relaxed jaw position, which will help to produce optimal vocal projection.

Procedures

1. **Explain the purpose of the lesson:** To develop a relaxed jaw position for optimal vocal projection.

2. **Discuss that when anything blocks a sound it reduces the volume of that sound.** Tell your student that this is especially true when the object blocking the sound is soft-textured and absorbs sound. Talk to your student as you normally would. Then talk to your student through the paper tube. Then stuff the tube with the piece of cloth and talk to him through the tube again. Ask him to describe what happened to the sound of your voice when you talked through the empty tube and then what happened when you talked through the stuffed tube. Explain that a person's throat and mouth are like a tube. That tube can be kept open by the person or it can be closed off by obstructions (tongue, soft palate, teeth). When that tube is closed off, volume is decreased.

3. **Show your student how the dropped jaw position enhances vocal resonance and projection by repositioning the potential obstructions (back of the tongue, soft palate, teeth).** You will demonstrate each of the following exercises first with a relaxed jaw (unobstructed tube) and then with a clenched jaw (obstructed tube). Then ask the student which sound is louder. Then have him do the exercises with a clenched jaw and with a relaxed jaw:

   a. Produce the "ah" sound with a clenched jaw position and then with a dropped jaw position, helping the student to observe and understand that volume increases with the dropping of the jaw.

   b. Now, breathe in with a yawn position, and produce the "ah" sound in both the dropped jaw position and the clenched jaw position.

    c. Now do the same (with a dropped jaw and then a clenched jaw) while producing the "ae" sound, as in cat (like a sneezing goat).

    d. Finally, produce the sound of a crying baby, "whae" (as in cat), in the same two positions (with a dropped jaw and then a clenched jaw).

Have a discussion with your student about his observations and conclusion. He should conclude that having a relaxed jaw is necessary for producing a sound with more volume.

4. **Determining the optimal amount to open the mouth – Method 1:**

    a. Have the student position his right and left index fingertips into the indentation at the joint of the jaw on both sides of the face. To find the space on each side of his jaw where the joint pivots open, follow the base of the cheekbones with the fingertips towards the back of your head. At the back of the cheekbone you will find the indentations.

    b. Discuss the sensation he feels when he opens his mouth, as in a relaxed yawn position. The mouth should neither close tight nor open too far. He will feel the muscles at the jaw hinge protruding if he clenches or opens too much. If the muscles protrude, the way he is opening his mouth is wrong. In the correct position, he should feel a slight indentation on both sides, at the pivot point, when the jaw is dropped.

5. **Have the student speak with his mouth opened the optimal amount.** Have the student keep his fingers at the points on each side of his head where the jaw pivots open. He should open his mouth to the optimal position and keep his movements within the boundaries between clenched and open too much (where the muscles do not protrude). Have him recite the alphabet with his mouth in this position. Video the student during this exercise. Then review the video with the student. Observe whether the mouth is continually and consistently relaxed open, to the optimal degree or not, throughout. Discuss what you notice about the sound of his voice when he does this.

6. **Determining the optimal amount to open the mouth – Method 2.** The student should leave only one finger in place on one side of his head, and place the index and middle fingers of the other hand into his mouth. The palm of this hand should be placed facing to the side, at the center of his open mouth, with his index finger on the bottom and middle finger on the top. The index and middle fingers must be in a vertical position, one on top of the other. These fingertips should only make contact by barely touching the biting edge of the front teeth. This is another method by which the student can gauge that his mouth is open to an optimal position.

7. **Have the student speak again using these cues to determine that his mouth is open an optimal amount.** Have the student recite the alphabet with fingers in place at the jaw joint and teeth. Video the student during this exercise. Watch and discuss the video with the student.

8. **Explain the Rules for a Relaxed Jaw.** Tell the student that for his mouth to be open to the optimal degree during speaking, he simply must relax his jaw. Have the student write the following rules in his notebook:

   ✓ The jaw drops directly below the upper teeth without jutting his chin forward.

   ✓ The lowered chin is also on an even plane with the Adam's apple, when dropped.

   ✓ The tip of the tongue must remain relaxed, touching the lower front teeth.

9. **Explain that if the jaw is relaxed the student's mouth will be open enough for optimal volume as he speaks.** Have the student say the alphabet again, without fingers in his mouth or at the hinge of his jaw. Video the student during this exercise. Observe that the mouth should be continually and consistently dropped open to the optimal position throughout.

10. **Homework:** Recite the alphabet while maintaining an open oral pharynx. Do this while keeping your fingertips of both index fingers in the indentations on both sides of the head at the joint of the jaw. Use the depth of the indentation to make sure the space in the back of the mouth is optimal for maximum voice projection. Repeat the alphabet five times in this way. Try having a conversation with someone in your family while using this technique. Practice as much as you can to become very familiar with the feeling of a relaxed jaw.

Open passage: Releasing tension in the jaw and tongue

Materials

Handout A: Practice Words and Sentences

Handout B: Rules for Maintaining Tongue and Jaw Relaxation

Mirror

Goals

To develop an optimally open position of the mouth and a relaxed tongue to reduce obstructions, which negatively impact volume.

To combine the techniques involved in creating an open passage and a nasal timbre.

Procedures

1. **Review the homework from the last lesson.** Have your student say the alphabet with a relaxed jaw. Give feedback and correction as needed. If he begins to clench his jaw, have him place the tips of his index fingers in the jaw joint on both sides of his head and feel for whether the muscles are protruding or not. He should make certain that those muscles never protrude as he speaks.

2. **Explain the purpose of the lesson:** By relaxing the tongue and jaw the student can open the passageway for the sound of his voice and thereby increase the volume of his voice.

3. **Begin with two simple mindfulness exercises.** Remind the student that being mindful means fully concentrating his focus where he needs to, while at the same time noticing other things that come to his attention but setting them aside to re-fix his attention where it needs to be. Now do the following mindfulness exercises with your student to work on developing a more relaxed jaw and tongue:

   a. You and your student will simply sit quietly and be mindful of your jaw and tongue as you take slow, deep breaths through your nose. During this exercise you will both keep the tip of the tongue behind and touching the lower front teeth. This will keep the tongue relaxed. You will both keep your lips closed but the teeth will be opened within the mouth. Do this for three minutes. Afterwards discuss both of your observations. Was it easy to keep the tongue and jaw relaxed? Did you notice movement and tension?

b. Now do a mindfulness exercise monitoring the state of the jaw muscles at the hinge. Both of you should place your fingertips in the indentation at the jaw hinge (as in the last lesson). Sit like this for three minutes being mindful of what those muscles feel like and do. Be mindful of the sensations when still, when swallowing, and when biting down. After three minutes you should both describe those sensations. Concentrate your discussion on the sensations associated with those muscles tightening and relaxing. Again explain why a relaxed jaw is necessary for producing adequate volume. If one's jaw is tight and the mouth is mostly closed, the sound stays inside your head instead of going out into the world.

4. **Practice speaking with a relaxed jaw and tongue.** Tell the student to produce the relaxed tongue and jaw position he maintained during the mindfulness exercises and say the words and sentences on Handout A.

5. **Combining an open passage with a nasal timbre.** Explain to your student that he will need to combine all the techniques he has learned (nasal timbre, breath support, including expansion and regulating release of air, and open passage) in order to optimize the volume of his speech. Two of the trickiest techniques to combine are creating a nasal timbre and maintaining an open, relaxed passage. This can be difficult because the tongue position involved in creating a nasal timbre promotes tension in the tongue and jaw.

Explain to the student that there are three Rules for Maintaining Tongue and Jaw Relaxation when producing a vocal sound with such a nasal quality (Handout B):

✓ Keep an optimally open mouth position (with no clenching).

✓ The tip of the tongue must always return quickly to its relaxed spot, touching the lower front teeth.

✓ When the tongue is raised in the back, it is the back corners of the tongue which come up to touch the upper molars. There is a trough down the middle of the tongue.

6. **Exercises to combine an open passage with a nasal timbre.** Explain that these exercises create a more present sound by setting up the positions of the anatomic structures so that the student is able to create a more nasal timbre, while at the same time maintaining an open, relaxed passage. The high position of the back of the tongue directs more of the tone vertically, into the nasal resonators. Yet, since the student maintains a relaxed, optimally opened jaw and the position for the tip of the tongue behind the lower front teeth produces a relaxed, lowered shape, the passage is open. This combination creates volume with more presence.

a. *Exercise 1:* In this exercise, the student maintains a relaxed jaw and relaxed tongue position, with the tip of the tongue touching the back of the lower front teeth, while pronouncing the initial consonant cluster "ng" followed by the vowel "æ" (as in the word "cat"). In this exercise the tongue will be high in the back. This tongue position should produce a timbre like the sound a goat makes. Have the student repeat the "ng...æ" sound sequence ten times, being certain to follow the Rules for Maintaining Tongue and Jaw Relaxation.

b. *Exercise 2:* Now as the student maintains a relaxed jaw and relaxed tongue, with the tip of the tongue still touching the back of the lower front teeth, he will produce the initial consonant cluster "ng" followed by the vowel "ah" (as in the word "hot"). Again the "ng" sound sets up the anatomy so that the sound and tone are directed through the nasal pharynx and resonators for both the "ah" sound and the "ng" sound. Remind the student of the increased buzzing which happens in the nose when an oral vowel like "ah" becomes more nasal in quality. As he learned in Lesson 5, this increased buzzing is evidence that more sound and air are moving through the nasal pharynx and nose. Discuss the student's observations. He should find that it is possible to maintain jaw and tongue relaxation while increasing the nasal quality of all vocal sounds.

7. **Homework:** Practice saying the words and sentences from this lesson (Handout A) twice a day, in front of a mirror, being certain to maintain a relaxed jaw and tongue throughout. Use the technique of monitoring the indentations at the pivot joint of your jaw, on both sides of your head, to make certain your jaw is relaxed. Return the tip of your tongue to its relaxed position, behind the front lower teeth, prior to each word or sentence.

✓

Practice Words and Sentences

drop	jaw	my	sound	lions
are	tired	cows	walked	I
plowed	try	find	for	moo

Dropping my jaw will open up my sound.

Lions are always tired.

The cows walked where I plowed.

Lions try to find lambs.

Cows moo for their food.

Rules for Maintaining Tongue and Jaw Relaxation

✓ Keep an optimally open mouth position (with no clenching).

✓ The tip of the tongue must always return quickly to its relaxed spot, touching the lower front teeth.

✓ When the tongue is raised in the back, it is the back corners of the tongue which come up to touch the upper molars. There is a trough down the middle of the tongue.

Section 5: Putting it all together

General goals

To combine an open vocal passage with a nasal timbre and appropriate breath support in order to increase volume of voice.

To appropriately modulate volume of voice given differing environmental situations including differences in ambient noise and social context.

LESSON 19

Putting it all together: Sound production with an open passage, in combination with nasal timbre and appropriate breath support 1

Materials

Handout A: All Individual Rules for Improving Vocal Projection

Goals

To review the rules for producing a more nasal/projected timbre.

To review the breath support rules, including: posture, expansion, Breath–Pause technique, and regulating release (including phrasing).

To review how to produce an open passage.

To combine nasal timbre and breath support techniques with an open passage.

Procedures

1. **Explain the purpose of the lesson:** The student to put all of the techniques he has learned to increasing the volume of his voice together. This includes rules about using an open passage, in combination with nasal timbre and appropriate breath support.

2. **Discuss that there are three techniques to combine in working to produce greater volume and a more projected sound when one speaks:**

   • Nasal timbre

   • Breath support (posture, expansion, Breath–Pause technique, regulating release)

   • Open passage: relaxed lips, tongue, and jaw.

3. **Review the form and function of the anatomy for creating a nasal and projected timbre (Handout C from Lesson 1).** Discuss how the tongue is up in the back, its back corners touching the molars, with a trough down the middle.

4. **Review the breath support techniques, including: posture, expansion, Breath–Pause position, and regulating release.**

   a. **Posture rules**

      • Align the back muscles and spinal column symmetrically.

- Shoulders back.

- Point sternum upward (never allowing it to collapse).

b. **Expansion rules (during breathing)**

- Set up and maintain posture, as prescribed above.

- Fill lungs with the necessary amount of air.

- The entire ribcage, front and back, must expand and maintain expansion.

c. **Rules for the Breath–Pause Technique**

✓ BREATHE – Full breath.

✓ PAUSE – Immediately stop the outward flow of breath by closing the vocal cords completely (this allows air pressure to build up below the vocal cords and produces a sensation like the act of lifting a heavy object).

d. **Rules for Managing the Release of Breath/Tone**

✓ Release the cords to release breath.

✓ Maintain an expanded chest cavity throughout the release.

✓ Arc phrasing – plan to release air smoothly through the entire spoken phrase.

✓ Volume level must not diminish, unless required by your surroundings.

✓ Completely empty the air in your lungs as needed (expel excess air regularly).

5. **Now review how to maintain an open oral pharynx.** Do this by keeping your fingers in the indentations on both sides of the head at the pivot joint of the jaw. Use the depth of the indentation to make sure the space in the back of the mouth is optimal for maximum voice projection. If the muscles protrude at those points, this means the mouth is either too open or too closed. Remember to keep the lips and tongue relaxed, the tip of the tongue always returning to its relaxed position behind the front lower teeth.

6. **Have your student perform the following exercises to demonstrate proficiency with volume for communication:**

a. Check posture.

b. Practice inhaling as if surprised, setting up an open throat position (five times).

c. Repeat step "b," but this time maintain that open throat position while breathing in, expanding the chest to its fullest capacity (five times).

d. Repeat step "c," but this time form tongue and mouth, creating a "nasal timbre" with the "Sneeze–Pause" position (sides of the back of the tongue touching the upper molars with a trough down the middle of the tongue) (five times).

e. Repeat step "d," but this time after each inhalation the breath is stopped before exhaling, using the Breath–Pause technique to regulate release by the vocal cords (five times).

f. Repeat step "e," but this time have the student loudly speak the word "Attaboy" on the exhalation (five times), being sure to maintain an expanded ribcage and "sneezing goat" position during the release of sound.

7. **Homework:** In front of a mirror, practice reading any passage from a newspaper or periodical, twice a day, being certain to maintain a relaxed jaw and tongue.

All Individual Rules for Improving Vocal Projection

Nasal timbre

a. **Nasal Timbre Rules**
   - ✓ Tip of the tongue behind the lower front teeth.
   - ✓ Sides of the back of the tongue touching the upper molars with a trough down the middle of the tongue.

Breath support

b. **Posture Rules**
   - ✓ Align the back muscles and spinal column symmetrically.
   - ✓ Shoulders back.
   - ✓ Point sternum upward (never allowing it to collapse).

c. **Expansion Rules (During Breathing)**
   - ✓ Set up and maintain posture, as prescribed above.
   - ✓ Fill lungs with the necessary amount of air.
   - ✓ The entire ribcage, front and back, must expand and maintain expansion.

d. **Rules for the Breath–Pause Technique**
   - ✓ BREATHE – Full breath.
   - ✓ PAUSE – Immediately stop the outward flow of breath by closing the vocal cords completely (this allows air pressure to build up below the vocal cords and produces a sensation like the act of lifting a heavy object).

e. **Rules for Managing the Release of Breath/Tone**
   - ✓ Release the cords to release breath.
   - ✓ Maintain an expanded chest cavity throughout the release.
   - ✓ Arc phrasing – plan to release air smoothly through the entire spoken phrase.
   - ✓ Volume level must not diminish, unless required by your surroundings.
   - ✓ Completely empty the air in your lungs as needed (expel excess air regularly).

Open passage

f. **Open Passage Rules**
   - ✓ Relaxed lips, tongue, and jaw.

Putting it all together: Sound production with an open passage, in combination with nasal timbre and appropriate breath support 2

Materials

Handout A from Lesson 19: All Individual Rules for Improving Vocal Projection

Handout A: Combined Rules for Increasing the Volume of the Voice

Goals

To review the rules for producing a more nasal/projected timbre.

To review the breath support rules, including: posture, expansion, Breath–Pause technique, and regulating release (including phrasing).

To review how to produce an open passage.

To combine nasal timbre and breath support techniques with an open passage.

Procedures

1. **Explain the purpose of the lesson:** To put together some of the things you have taught the student about volume production, including rules about using an open passage, in combination with nasal timbre and appropriate breath support.

2. **Review that there are three techniques to combine in working to produce greater volume and a more present sound when one speaks:**

   • Nasal timbre

   • Breath support (posture, expansion, Breath–Pause technique, regulating release)

   • Open passage: relaxed lips, tongue, and jaw.

3. **Review All Individual Rules for Improving Vocal Projection (Handout A from Lesson 19) regarding nasal timbre, breath support (posture, expansion, Breath–Pause technique, regulating release), and open passage.**

4. **Explain that all of these rules can be combined into one set of rules.** Give the student Handout A for this lesson. Tell the student that now that he is relatively proficient in using each of the individual rules for

producing greater volume and a more present voice, all of the individual rules are now combined into this one set of rules, which remind him to maintain an open passage, use breath support, including management of breath release, and nasal timbre. He has seen these rules before, but now can understand them and use them in a more sophisticated way.

5. **Review the Rules for Increasing the Volume of the Voice.** Explain how they are used to remind him to maintain an open passage, use breath support, including management of breath release, and nasal timbre:

   a. **Tongue.** Relaxing the tongue and keeping its tip behind the lower front teeth produces a sensation associated with a relaxed jaw. The two sensations work together to help maintain an *open passage* for the desired sound.

   b. **Sneeze–pause:**

      i. Just before a sneeze, a person fills with air and *expands* the chest cavity.

      ii. The mouth and throat position associated with a sneeze is precisely the position which produces a *nasal timbre* to the voice. The soft palate in its natural state will be in a position to lightly touch the back corners of the tongue as they push up against the upper molars. This merge between the two articulators produces a "joining together" sensation. This, in turn, creates a clear track directing breath and sound through the nasal pharynx. At the same time, the trough down the middle of the length of the tongue directs some of the breath and sound though the oral pharynx as well. The physical sensation experienced in the back of the mouth helps the student to produce the desired combination of nasal and oral resonance, which has volume and presence.

      iii. The "pause" part of "Sneeze–Pause" is a form of Breath–Pause and involves managing the release of air. The student stops and holds back the release of air at the vocal cords. The momentary pause and hesitation of breath at the cords helps to propel and define the initial phonation of the student's vocalization, as the airflow speed is increased by the momentary burst of air that is naturally held back by the cords.

   c. **Think goat...and of what you will say.** The third step requires the student to think of the sound a goat makes. This maintains the sneeze position and gets the student ready to produce the desired *nasal timbre* and speed and duration of airflow (*managing the release of air*) as the student simply tries to emulate the timbre of a goat. This, in coordination with the propelled air from the expanded lungs as the breath is released, will create the preferred assertive and appropriate vocal volume.

d. **Speak.** Finally, the student speaks in phrases, *managing the release of air*, while maintaining the position established in the three steps above.

6. **At this time, repeat the assessment (all but Step 6) carried out in the Baseline Assessment to evaluate your student's progress.**

7. **Homework:** Practice reading any passage from a newspaper or magazine twice a day, in front of a mirror, using the Combined Rules for Increasing the Volume of the Voice.

Combined Rules for Increasing the Volume of the Voice

TONGUE	
SNEEZE–PAUSE POSITION	
THINK (of what you will say)	
SPEAK	

Modulation of volume: Adjusting to situation

Materials

Handout A from Lesson 20: Combined Rules for Increasing the Volume of the Voice

Handout A: Reading Passage 1: The Curious Seagull

Handout B: Reading Passage 2: My Lost Frog

Previously recorded background restaurant noise

Device to play the recording

Kickball

Goals

To understand the appropriate speaking volume given ambient noise in various environments.

To appropriately modulate vocal volume, given the situation.

Procedures

1. **Explain the purpose of the lesson:** To understand the changes in vocal volume necessary in different situations and to be able to modulate volume given the context.

2. **Review the concepts of timbre, breath support, and open passage related to voice projection and volume using Handout A from Lesson 20.**

3. **Have the student read the passage in Handout A for this lesson.** Now play a pre-recorded track of restaurant background noise and have the student read the passage again.

4. **Discuss his ability to increase his volume with this background noise.** If he does not increase his volume with an increase in background noise, discuss the need to do so and produce a more present, assertive sound so that he can effectively communicate in a loud environment. Work on increasing nasality, expanding fully when breathing before speaking, using the Breath–Pause technique and an open passage. He needs to make certain to use the Combined Rules for Increasing the Volume of the Voice (Handout A from Lesson 20). Have him read each passage again, one sentence at a time. Prior to beginning each sentence, have him "set up" using the first three rules of Handout A from Lesson 20 before he speaks.

5. **Explain to the student that the same concept is applied when a person is outdoors in a busy street where there is lots of ambient noise.** Have the student read a new passage at a volume that is appropriate for your quiet office or classroom. Then take the student outdoors and have him read the passage again at a volume that can be heard over the ambient noise. Ask the student to explain the difference between an increased vocal projection (required for the outside) and vocal projection for the inside. Talk about what he changes in a louder environment with respect to nasal timbre and breath support, including the Breath–Pause technique and an open passage.

6. **Pass a ball to each other by kicking it.** Before one person passes to another he must say the name of the person to whom he is passing. Increase or decrease the distance between you and the student during this game, so that you close or broaden the space between you and your passing partner. The passer's voice should increase in volume to reflect an increase in distance. A decrease in distance should be associated with a decrease in volume of speech. Again he needs to make certain to use the Combined Rules for Increasing the Volume of the Voice (Handout A from Lesson 20).

7. **Role-play the following scenarios with your student, using an appropriate volume:**

   a. You and your little brother are attending your favorite sporting event. You are very involved in the action and don't want to miss any of it. The refreshment vendor appears in your seating section. You would like to order a snack and drink from the vendor before he moves away from the section.

   b. You are in your classroom where your mid-term exam is taking place. You have to go and visit the restroom, so you approach your professor's desk and ask to be excused.

   c. You're helping your mom unload groceries from her car and you see your friends walking by on the other side of the street and you want them to cross over to your side so you can tell them something important.

   d. You are attending a basketball game and cheering for your favorite team.

   e. You are seated in your classroom. You drop your pencil. It is out of your reach, on the floor, and you ask the student next to you to hand you the pencil.

   f. While riding with your family in the car, you notice that your little sister has dropped her pacifier on the floorboard of the car and you want to inform your mom about this as your sister is crying.

g. While attending summer camp, you are wading along in the lake when you feel a sharp object with your foot in the mud of the swimming area. You want to warn nearby swimmers.

8. **Homework:** Write down two situations for the week where you needed and then used a louder/more assertive tone when speaking to others (due to increased ambient noise or other characteristics of the social situation).

Reading Passage 1: The Curious Seagull

We watched the seagulls as they hovered near the fishing boat's stern. The boat had finished its morning run and now the deck hands were dumping the remains of the bait into the water. It was breakfast time for the gulls as they took turns swooping down to grab tidbits from the chum before it sank down to the crabs below. Just to our right, a single gull seemed to be patiently waiting for a bite of *our* breakfast. We had only just finished our bagels when the large bird hopped up on our table. We were so impressed by his curiosity that we didn't notice at first when he snatched my wife's purse. After noticing the purse in the struggling bird's beak, we tried for about 15 minutes to catch him as he hopped around the deck. Finally, we decided to sit back and relax since we knew the bag was too heavy for him to carry out to sea. When we were served another round of coffee and bagels, he immediately flew over, dropped the purse, took a bagel, and flew off.

Reading Passage 2: My Lost Frog

My little green water frog, Sam, had stayed in my aquarium for six years. He was very easy to care for, and for some reason his tank never needed cleaning. It seemed that the quiet little guy was a very busy fellow at night when no one was watching. One day my best friend, Tony, came over to play outside with me. We made our plans to climb up to our tree house and hide out until lunchtime, doing what best friends do (cards, spying on my sister, spitting at bugs). Of course we took our canteens with us, full of Kool-Aid, just in case we got thirsty. At about 2:30, Tony had to take a bathroom break. He must have been gone for about two hours because I had fallen asleep due to boredom. All of a sudden I heard him calling out to me. He sounded upset. I climbed down and went to the back door and into the kitchen.

My mom and Tony were waiting there to give me the bad news. My mom told me that my frog, Sam, was missing and that they had been looking for him. She said, "Tony was getting some crackers to bring out to me and decided to give Sam a bite of a cracker." Going on, she said, "Sam seemed to be waiting, ready to spring, because just as Tony opened the aquarium lid, Sam jumped out," and "it happened so quick that Tony couldn't even see where Sam landed." Before I could become upset or sad I noticed a tiny little green frog finger sticking out from under Tony's collar. I felt so relieved that something in my brain told me to make a joke out of the situation. I pretended to be upset for a moment, and as they began to say they were so sorry, I reached over and took Sam from under Tony's collar. We all laughed with relief.

CHAPTER 5

Rhythm of Speech

Introduction: Fluency and rate

Most verbal individuals with Autism Spectrum Disorders have difficulty with the rhythm of their speech. Some are hyper-verbal, speaking too rapidly, and fail to pause at the ends of sentences and clause boundaries, making them difficult to understand. Many with ASD are dysfluent when expressing their ideas in speech. It is difficult for them to convert ideas into words. Their oral expression is halting, marked by false starts (where the first sound, word, or words in a phrase are repeated over and over before the person completes the utterance) and hesitations (e.g., um, ah). In either case, the rhythm of speech must improve. In order to do this, the student needs to learn how to produce pauses in their speech. The Breath–Pause technique teaches the speaker to produce pauses at the ends of sentences and at clause boundaries for this purpose. The Breath–Pause technique also helps the student regulate his emotional state when he verbally expresses himself, because he is breathing and stopping with regularity.

Our method not only instructs students about when to pause and formulate speech, it also provides a physical sensation for them to attend to. The monitoring and use of this sensation helps to reinforce "motor patterns," which can improve formulation of expressive language.

The term Breath–Pause describes a technique in which, in breathing, there is a designated moment of interruption or "pause" just as exhalation begins. The physical sensation created by the Breath–Pause technique is experienced at the base of the throat. It is the sensation one feels in trying to lift something heavy, when exhalation is stopped, by the closing of the cords.

In this chapter, to improve rhythm and fluency you will be teaching the physical sensation associated with the Breath–Pause technique. You will teach your student to apply the Breath–Pause technique at the ends of all sentences and at clause boundaries. Sometimes, at the very beginning of an utterance, you will instruct your student to inhale and immediately stop the breath at the beginning of the exhalation, before he speaks. At other times, usually at clause boundaries, you will have him simply pause, by having him just stop the outward movement of his breath.

First, you will teach the sensation associated with Breath–Pause in isolation. Later, you will teach the timing for using the technique during his verbal expression. Prior to vocal onset at the beginning of a phrase, the student will learn to "pause" his exhalation for a moment. This may be a brief moment, which simply marks a clause boundary for speaker and listener, or it may be a longer pause, allowing time for the speaker to formulate what he will say before he speaks it. You will also instruct the student to practice the technique in various settings: in front of a mirror, in session, and at home, as part of his homework. (*Note:* Use of the Breath–Pause technique has the added benefit of improving phonation, thereby enhancing the sound of the speaker's utterances, making them more "present.")

Initially in the lessons, you will require that your student's breaths and pauses be audible. As he advances, you will teach him to use a "stealth" (silent) quality when implementing the Breath–Pause technique. You will begin with written text, notating where each breath and pause will occur. The use of written text removes the demand for formulation, so that the student can concentrate on developing technique. This also emphasizes the relative strength in concrete, visual processing which the majority of individuals with ASD possess. Once the technique is established, the student will apply it to his spontaneous speech.

Rhythm plays a significant role in conveying meaning in conversation. Pauses at the ends of sentences and clause boundaries in connected speech allow time for the listener to process meaning. They emphasize the immediately preceding information. They can make the student's expression more fluent, because they give him time to choose the ideas he wants to express and to put his ideas into words.

In addition to teaching "Breath–Pause," you will use Graphic Organizers to help the student formulate his ideas for expression. A Graphic Organizer is a concrete, visual representation of the organization of language. It establishes the hierarchy of main topic, subtopics, and details. Graphic Organizers are used in many of the lessons to help improve fluency. They also help the student to maintain the topic and to be more responsive to the topics of others.

To firmly establish the motor patterns and cognitive skills associated with this new way of speaking requires a significant amount of practice. This practice is accomplished during the lessons themselves, enforced with direction and feedback from the therapist, and through homework assignments (which generalize the skills to the rest of life). Practice serves to automate the newly acquired motor skills, which then allows the student to allocate more of his attentional resources to what he wants to say rather than to the technique. The student will keep copies of all handouts, homework, and notes in a three-ring binder, which he can refer to at home to practice and must bring to all lessons. The lessons are developmentally ordered. Later lessons refer back to concepts in earlier ones and make repeated use of materials from earlier lessons to solidify the concepts as the student develops the skills.

Fluency assessment

Materials

Handout A: Fluency Assessment Data Sheet

Audio recording device

Goal

To assess the student's fluency in connected spontaneous speech.

Procedures

1. **Collect a spontaneous speech sample.** You have established through anecdotal evidence (in Chapter 1) that the student has an impairment in fluency or rate of speech. Now carry out the following formal detailed baseline assessment. Be sure to audio record this. Ask the student to do one of the following, making sure not to speak until your student is finished telling his entire story:

   a. Tell me a story about your last birthday.

   b. Tell me a story about your favorite thing to do.

   c. Small talk conversation: e.g., tell me about your day, including your favorite part.

2. **Assess fluency by collecting the following data from the language sample:**

   a. *FS: the total number of false starts.* A false start is when the child begins an utterance and repeats the first word or words over and over, including the initial word/words.

   b. *HES: the total number of hesitations.* A hesitation is something that is not a word, such as um, ah, or uh, that comes before an utterance.

   c. *TOTAL WORD COUNT.* The total number of words (including words which are false starts).

   d. *TIME.* The length, in minutes, of the language sample.

3. **Calculate the number of false starts, hesitations, and words per minute to establish the baseline for fluency and rate.**

4. **As you listen to the language sample, qualitatively assess for misarticulations.** These can include sound substitutions; but more commonly in this group of individuals, in their great effort to formulate their ideas into words or to get their ideas out as quickly as possible, the jaw, lips, and tongue become very tight. When this happens,

consonants and vowels are misarticulated and are often elided in such a way that words become unintelligible. When these individuals take their time to formulate their expression and to speak, they can pronounce all consonants and vowels, and sequence them correctly. This aspect of dysfluency is addressed throughout the lessons in this chapter by teaching the student to pause between sentences and at clause boundaries and through the use of "shadow vowels" (Lesson 8). Beginning in this assessment and throughout the coming lessons, keep an inventory of your student's misarticulations in his spontaneous speech.

5. **Explain to the student that this data will be compared with his data at the end of the intervention where he will be working to improve his fluency.**

Fluency Assessment Data Sheet

Name		Time	
Age		VIQ	
Gender		PIQ	
Date		Language score	

Fluency	Number	Sample (minutes)	Rate per minute
False starts			
Hesitations			
Total words			
Total sentences			

Does the student often fail to pause at the ends of sentences or clause boundaries?

Notes:

<u>LESSON 1</u>

Introducing the Breath–Pause technique for improving fluency and rate

Materials

Handout A: Anatomy Diagram Breath–Pause

Handout B: Breath–Pause Technique Description

Handout C: Rules for Fluency

Handout D: Breath–Pause Practice with Vowels

Handout E: Breath–Pause Practice with Words

Handout F: Breath–Pause Practice with a Conversation Script

Handout G: Sentences: Practice Applying Breath–Pause Notation

A small, lightweight, and fluffy feather

Goals

To learn the Breath–Pause technique, how to use it, and how it improves airflow and fluency in speech.

To identify the physical sensations involved with the technique.

Procedures

1. **Explain to your student your observations of his speech and how the skills taught in this chapter will help him to communicate more effectively.** If he is dysfluent and his speech is halting and marked by false starts and hesitations, explain how slowing down and learning to pause before he starts to speak, between sentences, and at clause boundaries ("commas") gives him time to formulate his thoughts before he speaks, making him more fluent. For the student who speaks too rapidly, explain that slowing down and learning to pause before he starts to speak, between sentences, and at clause boundaries produces a more effective rhythm for communicating with others. In doing this he can think more clearly about his ideas and others have time to process the meaning of what he said and contribute to a reciprocal conversation. Explain to your student that he will be taught a special method of pausing during connected speech (called Breath–Pause) and how to self-calm. These techniques are very useful for both types of rhythmic issues in speech.

2. **Explain the anatomy involved in the Breath–Pause technique.** With your student, look at the diagram of the anatomy of the vocal mechanism (Handout A). The human vocal mechanism is made up of many parts,

which are moved and positioned to produce many different sounds, and to affect fluency in connected speech.

Explain the anatomy depicted in the side, cutout view of the head and neck in the diagram: point out the lungs, trachea (windpipe), tongue, lips, and vocal cords. Label the nasal pharynx and the oral pharynx. Now explain the insert, which shows the trachea and vocal cords from the top. Explain how the cords open to breathe, close before the onset of a vocalization, and vibrate rapidly very close to each other during vocalization. Explain that the vocal cords are the source of the sound. The throat, the oral pharynx, the nasal pharynx, the velum (soft palate), the tongue, and lips form the filter. By changing the shape of the filter, the sound generated at the source (cords) is modified.

Tell the student that during these lessons he will focusing on breathing and control of the source of the sound.

3. **Teach your student the Breath–Pause technique.** Demonstrate the Breath–Pause technique: tell the student to breathe in (small arrows), expanding his chest (large arrows), as in Handout, and then immediately stop the breath, by closing his cords, holding back the breath for a moment. To teach how this feels, have him use the image of a weight-lifter lifting a heavy weight, or a karate chop. Another way to help him to understand is to have him put his hands under the chair he is sitting in, take a deep breath, and then pull up on the chair as if he were trying to lift it. Each of these ideas and activities will close the vocal cords and stop the breath from leaving his lungs. Some back pressure beneath the cords will be created. He should be able to feel this pressure as he holds his breath.

Encourage your student initially to produce the audible sound associated with stopping the breath. It will sound similar to a weight-lifter as he/she begins to lift; or the sound someone makes with a karate chop ("ha").

Explain that, in a few more lessons, when the student begins to master this technique, the weight-lifter grunting sound will go away, so that stopping the breath for that moment just before he speaks will be a stealth act and no one will hear the breath being stopped. No one will know the technique is being used.

4. **Practice the Breath–Pause technique.** Use the feather for this breathing exercise (holding the feather in front of the student's mouth). This will give you and the student a visual aid to help monitor the student's new ability to close and open his vocal cords as he regulates his airflow. You will demonstrate and help the student to practice.

   a. Start by having the student simply breathe in and out. He should take a deep breath and let it out, sometimes stopping the airflow, as you both monitor the movement of the feather. Practice this ten times.

   b. Then instruct the student to use the Breath–Pause technique. He will practice breathing in (the way he does when preparing to speak).

Then, just as he begins the flow of his breath, stop immediately, closing his cords and stopping the airflow. Now do this ten more times with him breathing in and stopping the exhalation on the sound "ha." The student must practice this technique so that he develops a strong awareness of those physical sensations created by the technique.

c. Now have him imitate you as you demonstrate five to ten Breath–Pauses. Remember to stop the outward flow of breath immediately.

5. **Explain, demonstrate, and have the student follow the Rules for Fluency (Handout C), where he will employ Breath–Pause to aid fluency.** The Rules for Fluency are:

✓ Calming breath.

✓ Use the Breath–Pause technique (like lifting a heavy weight).

✓ Think of your next sentence in your head, as you hold back your breath.

✓ Then speak the sentence you hear in your head, using the breath you were holding.

Explain the importance of always beginning with a calming breath. Both of you should practice taking a calming breath. Make sure your student understands that calming must happen first, in order to learn and implement the strategies effectively.

6. **Explain breathing and Breath–Pause notation to your student while looking at Handout C.** The diamond symbol indicates a deep and calming breath. The V symbol designates a breath before speaking, and the X designates a pause.

7. **Practice applying the Breath–Pause technique and notation:**

a. Read the pattern of "ahs" with the student while using the Breath–Pause technique as notated (Handout D).

b. Read the words and scripted conversation in Handouts E and F out loud with your student. You and your student will take turns as speaker 1 and 2 reading the conversation in Handout F, following the Breath–Pause notation.

c. Together, use the Breath–Pause notation to notate the sentences in Handout G. Have the student imitate you as you read the text as notated. Discuss his and your observations.

8. **Homework:** Practice the Breath–Pause technique using your handouts from today's lesson.

Anatomy Diagram Breath–Pause

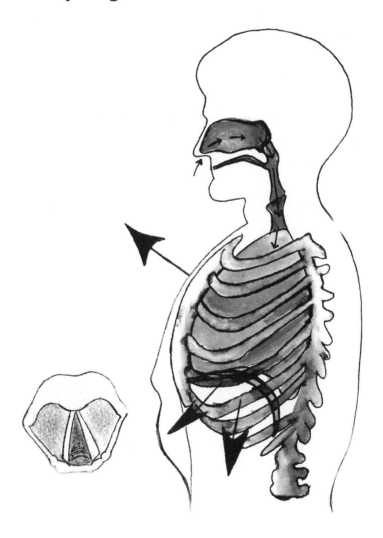

Breath–Pause Technique Description

When you are ready to speak:

1. BREATH – Breathe in.

2. PAUSE – Immediately stop the outward flow of breath by closing the vocal cords completely. (When first learning the technique, this sounds and feels like a weight-lifter lifting a heavy weight or a karate chop.)

Note: When proficiency at the technique is achieved, the pause becomes stealth/silent.

Rules for Fluency

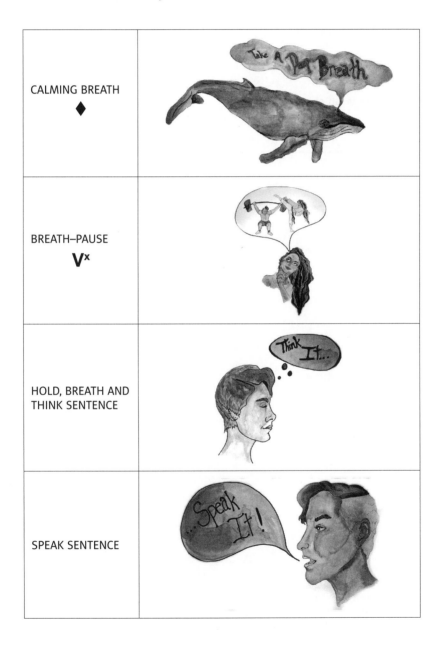

CALMING BREATH ♦	
BREATH–PAUSE **V**ˣ	
HOLD, BREATH AND THINK SENTENCE	
SPEAK SENTENCE	

Breath–Pause Practice with Vowels

V^x ah ^{x} ah

V^x ah ah ah **V**^{x} ah ah

V^x ah ^{x} ah ^{x} ah **V**^{x} ah

Breath–Pause Practice with Words

V^x cat ^{x} dog

V^x bean ^{x} hair **V**^{x} run ^{x} play

V^x tail ^{x} wake ^{x} yes **V**^{x} train

V^x mow jump **V**^{x} egg ^{x} ice

V^x food ^{x} loop **V**^{x} goat not

V^x rake sun oak **V**^{x} van

Breath–Pause Practice with a Conversation Script

Speaker 1: **V**ˣ Hi ˣ How are you?

Speaker 2: **V**ˣ I'm fine thanks. **V**ˣ What are you doing today?

Speaker 1: **V**ˣ I'm going shopping ˣ to buy shoes. **V**ˣ What are you doing today?

Speaker 2: **V**ˣ I'm washing the car ˣ with my dad. **V**ˣ Then we are going to lunch ˣ at my favorite place.

Sentences: Practice Applying Breath–Pause Notation

As I walked through the yard, I observed how beautiful, green, and healthy it was.

The movie will increase her chances for an Oscar.

The students made a lot of progress this year.

Breath control associated with the Breath–Pause technique

Materials

Handout A from Lesson 1: Anatomy Diagram Breath–Pause

Handout C from Lesson 1: Rules for Fluency

Handout D from Lesson 1: Breath–Pause Practice with Vowels

Handout E from Lesson 1: Breath–Pause Practice with Words

Handout F from Lesson 1: Breath–Pause Practice with a Conversation Script

A small, lightweight, and fluffy feather

A large bouncy ball

Goals

To learn the Breath–Pause technique, how to use it, and how it improves airflow and fluency in speech.

To review the physical sensations involved with the technique and how to apply it before speaking single spontaneously formulated words.

Procedures

1. **Review the anatomy of the human vocal mechanism, especially the function of the cords and the sensations associated with opening, closing, holding breath back, and the vibration during phonation** (Handout A from Lesson 1).

2. **Practice Breath–Pause technique review.** Breathe in and then immediately stop the outward flow of breath by closing the vocal cords completely. Use Handouts D, E, and F from Lesson 1 to practice.

3. **Review the Rules for Fluency (Handout C from Lesson 1):**

   ✓ Calming breath.

   ✓ Use the Breath–Pause technique (like lifting a heavy weight).

   ✓ Think of your next sentence in your head, as you hold back your breath.

   ✓ Then speak the sentence you hear in your head, using the breath you were holding.

Emphasize the importance of a calming breath so that the student can focus on using the sensations, associated with the technique, while in a calm state.

4. **Practice answering questions in single words using the Breath–Pause technique.** Now tell the student that you're going to ask him a series of "Yes/No" questions. These questions are to be answered with just a "yes" or a "no" using the Breath–Pause technique (the student breathes in, holds his breath while he thinks of "yes" or "no," and then he answers).

    Here are some examples:

    - Are your clothes made of metal?

    - Do you always wear shoes?

    - Do you feel hot?

    - Do you feel cold?

    - Do you like to draw?

    - Do you like outdoor activities?

    - Have you ever gone fishing?

    - Have you ever ridden a horse?

    - Do you like the zoo?

    - Do you have any siblings?

5. **Practice Breath–Pause with spontaneous single words.** Explain and play the *Bouncing Word Game*. The purpose of this game is to practice the Breath–Pause technique, immediately followed by spontaneously generated individual words. This is accomplished by passing a ball, with one bounce, back and forth to each other, at a distance of about eight feet. Before the ball is passed, the Breath–Pause technique is used. The player breathes in and holds his breath and the ball until he thinks of a word. Then the player says the single word, on the pass. Producing the word on the pass helps the student to release and move his breath as he speaks. The game continues until each player successfully completes a list of ten different spontaneous words. Discuss your and your student's observations.

6. **Learn to use the Breath–Pause technique in a stealth way, so that only the student knows he is using it.** In this lesson, give your student the choice of trying to make the Breath–Pause technique more silent – "stealth." (*Important:* In trying to make his pauses silent, the technique itself may be compromised. Any time this happens, the student must make his use of the technique audible.)

7. **Homework:** Practice with your vowel, word, and scripted conversation sheets from Lesson 1 (Handouts D, E, and F from that lesson).

<u>LESSON 3</u>

Using the Breath–Pause technique with spontaneous single words and pre-formulated connected speech

Materials

Handout C from Lesson 1: Rules for Fluency

Handout A: The Gettysburg Address

A large bouncy ball

Goal

To learn to apply the Breath–Pause technique to spontaneously generated single words and pre-formulated connected speech.

Procedures

1. **Review the Rules for Fluency (Handout C from Lesson 1), focusing on stopping the breath while formulating what he will say.** Review the following concept: "stop and hold your breath as you prepare your thought, then speak it."

2. **Explain the benefit of using the Rules for Fluency:**

   a. In students with halting speech, following the rules reduces the number of false starts and hesitations in speech. Define these terms for your student and have him write the definitions in his notebook. A false start is when the student begins an utterance and repeats the first word or words over and over before completing the utterance. A hesitation is sound that is not a word, such as um, ah, or uh, that comes before an utterance begins. Tell the student he is learning to substitute Breath–Pause for false starts and hesitations.

   b. In students with an overly rapid rate of speech, the rules help the student to slow down and insert pauses between sentences, at clause boundaries, and after words or phrases they want to emphasize (stress).

3. **Use the Breath–Pause technique prior to spontaneously generated single words.** Play the *Bouncing Word Game*:

   a. Play this game as you did in the last lesson. (In this activity do not use the stealth version of the technique.) Pass the ball, one bounce only, back and forth to each other, at a distance of about eight feet.

Before the ball is passed, the Breath–Pause technique is used. The player breathes in and then holds his breath and the ball while he thinks of a word. Then the player says the single word, on the pass. The game continues until each player successfully completes a list of ten different spontaneous words. Discuss observations made by both partners. Give feedback and corrections as needed.

b. Play the game again until each player successfully completes a list of ten different spontaneous words, again discussing what each other observed about the use of the Breath–Pause technique.

c. Continue to play the game, this time creating simple spontaneous single sentences before passing the ball. Discuss observations made by both partners. Give feedback and corrections as needed.

4. **Using the Breath–Pause notation with written sentences:**

a. Have the student generate five sentences and write them down.

b. Next tell the student to notate these sentences with the Breath–Pause notation.

c. Have him speak these sentences out loud, using the Breath–Pause technique, as notated (the player breathes in and holds his breath, where marked).

d. Now ask him a few questions about the sentences. Have the student work at using the Breath–Pause technique in his spontaneously generated answers. Point out the fluency differences in his spontaneously generated sentences and his notated/planned sentences. Discuss and write the observations in his notebook.

5. **Using the Breath–Pause notation with a written text:**

a. Have the student read the first six lines of the Gettysburg Address (Handout A) without the Breath–Pause notation (record this activity).

b. Insert the Breath–Pause notation into that same six lines of the Gettysburg Address and have him read it again (record this activity).

c. Listen to both recordings. Compare and discuss.

d. Insert the Breath–Pause notation into the remainder of the Gettysburg Address and practice reading it using the notation.

6. **Have the student read the sentences below, using the Rules for "Breath–Pause."** Have him try and create his own pattern of Breath–Pauses in the sentences without notating them. Make sure he thinks the sentence in his head before he speaks and repeats how he hears it in his head.

a. Even though it is early spring, many plants are growing in my garden.

b. This year I will go to Australia to see marsupials in the wild.

    c. The players worked hard all season, and their team won the championship.

7. **Have the student notate and speak these sentences with the Breath–Pause notation.**

8. **Ask him something about those sentences, looking for spontaneous answers.** Have the student use the Breath–Pause technique in his spontaneously generated answers (record this activity). Listen to the exchange and point out the differences between his spontaneously generated answers and the pre-notated sentences. Discuss and note his observations in his notebook.

9. **Homework:** Practice speaking the Gettysburg Address from your notated version. Do this in front of your mirror (recording yourself).

The Gettysburg Address

Four score and seven years ago our fathers brought forth on this continent a new nation, conceived in liberty, and dedicated to the proposition that all men are created equal.

Now we are engaged in a great civil war, testing whether that nation, or any nation so conceived and so dedicated, can long endure. We are met on a great battlefield of that war. We have come to dedicate a portion of that field, as a final resting place for those who here gave their lives that that nation might live. It is altogether fitting and proper that we should do this. But, in a larger sense, we cannot dedicate, we cannot consecrate, we cannot hallow this ground. The brave men, living and dead, who struggled here, have consecrated it, far above our poor power to add or detract. The world will little note, nor long remember what we say here, but it can never forget what they did here. It is for us the living, rather, to be dedicated here to the unfinished work which they who fought here have thus far so nobly advanced. It is rather for us to be here dedicated to the great task remaining before us – that from these honored dead we take increased devotion to that cause for which they gave the last full measure of devotion – that we here highly resolve that these dead shall not have died in vain – that this nation, under God, shall have a new birth of freedom – and that government of the people, by the people, for the people, shall not perish from the earth.

Lincoln, A. (1865) The Gettysburg Address.
www.abrahamlincolnonline.org/lincoln/speeches/gettysburg.htm

How calming positively influences fluency and rate of speech

Materials

Handout A: An article or book passage that you select in advance, which is about the student's favorite topic or preoccupation

Handout B: A second article or book passage that you select in advance, which is about the student's favorite topic or preoccupation

Goal

To teach the student to stay calm and use the Breath–Pause technique while reading about a favorite topic or obsession.

Procedures

1. **Review the Rules for Fluency (Handout C from Lesson 1).** Place a major emphasis on the student beginning with a calming breath. Explain that he must try to maintain a calm baseline when talking about any topic. If he cannot maintain calm he must use his rules from the Modulation chapter (Chapter 2) to regain calm.

2. **Briefly discuss the topic of the new pre-chosen written material with your student.** The piece used should be one to five paragraphs in length. Remind him that this topic will be exciting and interesting for him, and it could potentially cause over-excitement and perseveration. Tell him that over-excitement about a topic has a negative impact on fluency.

3. **Help your student establish a calm baseline.** Remind him to follow the calming exercises from the Modulation chapter.

4. **Help your student plan his coping strategies for dealing with being triggered by the topic.** You and the student will discuss and plan a strategy, including calming techniques, before he begins to read. This will include self-calming and his use of the Breath–Pause technique.

5. **Help your student notate and then read the pre-chosen passage in Handout A.** Tell the student to be mindful of his fluency. He must also be aware of anything else that may come into his mind, but set anything other than his fluency aside and bring his focus back to his fluency.

6. **Read the second pre-chosen, un-notated passage (Handout B) in unison with the student.** Tell the student to be mindful of your rhythm, stresses, and speed and follow you, while reading with you.

Spontaneously and intermittently speed up, slow down, and pause your speech at the ends of sentences and clause boundaries. This activity requires that the student listen carefully to follow your changing speed and rhythm. Doing this will help the student to monitor his own speech patterns and the speech patterns of others during conversation. Discuss your and his observations.

7. **Homework:** Look for a few passages about something you're interested in. Notate them with Breath–Pauses, then read them out loud to someone at home while using the Breath–Pause technique to aid with your fluency by reducing false starts and hesitations.

Staying calm and mindful to promote effective fluency through the Breath–Pause technique

Materials

Handout A: An article or book passage that you select in advance, which is about the student's favorite topic or preoccupation

Handout B: A second article or book passage that you select in advance, which is about the student's favorite topic or preoccupation

Goal

To practice staying calm and to use the Breath–Pause technique while reading about a favorite topic or obsession.

Procedures

1. **Review the Rules for Fluency and how to use the Breath–Pause technique in a stealth way, so that only the student knows he is using it.**

2. **Briefly discuss the topic of the new pre-chosen written material with your student.** The piece used should be between one and five paragraphs in length. Remind him that this topic will be exciting and interesting for him, and it could potentially cause over-excitement and perseveration. Tell him that over-excitement about a topic has a negative impact on fluency.

3. **Help your student establish a calm baseline.** Remind him to follow the calming exercises from the Modulation chapter (Chapter 2).

4. **Help your student plan his coping strategies for dealing with being triggered by the topic.** You and the student will discuss and plan a strategy, including calming techniques, before he begins to read. This will include self-calming and his use of the Breath–Pause technique.

5. **Help your student notate and then read the first two paragraphs of the pre-chosen passage in Handout A.** Tell the student to be mindful of his fluency. He must also be aware of anything else that may come into his mind, but set anything other than his fluency aside and bring his focus back to his fluency.

6. **Read the remainder of the un-notated, pre-chosen passage with the student sentence by sentence (Handout A).** Read the passage one sentence at a time. After each sentence stop and have your student

repeat the sentence. Between sentences, remind your student to use the Breath–Pause technique in his repetition. This helps the student maintain mindfulness of his stealth Breath–Pause technique.

7. **Read the second pre-chosen, un-notated passage (Handout B) in unison with the student.** Tell the student to be mindful of your rhythm, stresses, and speed and follow you, while reading with you. Spontaneously and intermittently speed up, slow down, and pause your speech at the ends of sentences and clause boundaries. This activity requires that the student listen carefully to follow your changing speed and rhythm. Doing this will help the student to monitor his own speech patterns and the speech patterns of others during conversation. Discuss your and his observations.

8. **Have the student read the same passage alone, using the Breath– Pause technique.** Before he starts, help him establish a calm baseline. If he starts to become over-excited, stop him and have him use the self-calming techniques from the Modulation chapter. When he is finished, discuss your and his observations.

9. **Homework:** Write out five sentences describing in detail your favorite activity of the week. Add the Breath–Pause notation. Speak them out loud, in front of your mirror, while using the Breath–Pause technique, as notated. Be prepared to repeat the sentences at your next lesson.

Using the Breath–Pause technique with spontaneous questions and sentences

Materials

Bouncy ball

Goal

To practice using the Breath–Pause technique (preferably stealth mode) when generating single-word responses to questions and single sentences.

Procedures

1. **Discuss the purpose of the lesson:** To help the student (whether dysfluent or a hyper-verbal/rapid speaker) develop the basic skills to produce a fluent rhythm in his spontaneous speech. This will be accomplished through applying the Breath–Pause technique before he begins speaking and between sentences.

2. **Review the Rules for Fluency and how to use the Breath–Pause technique in a stealth way, so that only the student knows he is using it.**

3. **Help the student establish a calm baseline.** This is very important. If he starts to get over-excited or stressed at any time during this activity, remind him to follow the calming exercises from the Modulation chapter (Chapter 2).

4. **Play Twenty Questions.** Specific instructions and examples are:

   a. First, have the student choose something in the room or outside to think of. Explain that he should not tell you what it is. He should just start with a hint: "I'm thinking of..." For example: "I'm thinking of...

      i.   ...something in this room."

      ii.   ...something you see in the sky."

      iii. ...something you see in the park."

      iv.   ...a place where you might hear music."

      v.   ...someone who helps you."

   b. You will ask him questions to try to figure out what it is.

   c. He should use the Breath–Pause technique when he answers your questions with a "yes" or "no." This will allow him to warm up before he needs to use Breath–Pause with spontaneous questions and sentences.

d. You will continue to inquire about the student's choice until you solve the riddle. Model using Breath–Pause each time you speak.

e. Once you have guessed what your student is thinking of, reverse roles. The student will now be the one asking the questions.

Note: The student must use the Breath–Pause technique each time he prepares to speak. If he does not, stop him and remind him to do so. If he gets stressed or over-excited, remind him to use self-calming techniques.

5. **Play the Bouncing Word Game.** Pass the ball, one bounce only, back and forth to each other, at a distance of about eight feet.

a. *First play this game with no words.* Each of you should produce a Breath–Pause just before bounce-passing the ball to the other. The person who will be passing the ball breathes in, holds his or her breath, pauses for a count of two, then passes the ball, simultaneously releasing his breath. When each of you holds back your breath, produce the sound associated with starting to breathe out and then quickly closing the vocal cords (i.e., "ha"). Practice this five times with no speaking, listening for the audible glottal sound. Discuss his and your observations. Did the Breath–Pause make him feel more air pressure in his chest? He should feel back pressure.

b. *Now each of you should produce a sentence on each pass.* Again each of you should produce a Breath–Pause (breathe in and then hold the breath back) before speaking and passing the ball. The sentences can be random or your sentences can be questions for your student to answer. The game continues until the student has successfully generated ten sentences each preceded by a "Breath–Pause." If he is not generating a Breath–Pause before each sentence and pass, then stop and correct him. When the game is finished, discuss his and your observations. How difficult was it? How can he improve next time?

6. **Discuss the benefit of Breath–Pause to your student.** If he talks too rapidly, explain that using Breath–Pause between his utterances slows down his speech and makes it easier for his conversational partner to process what he is saying. If he is dysfluent, remind him that the Breath–Pause buys him time to formulate his thoughts.

7. **Homework:** Write out five sentences describing in detail your favorite activity of the week. Add the Breath–Pause notation. Practice speaking the sentences, out loud, in front of your mirror, using the Breath–Pause technique, as you have notated.

<u>LESSON 7</u>

Using the Breath–Pause technique to speak spontaneous sentences fluently and at an appropriate rate

Materials

Handout B from Lesson 1: Breath–Pause Technique Description

Handout A: An Excerpt from Chaplin's "The Great Dictator's Speech"

A photograph

A picture of a painting

Pens or pencils (red, blue, green)

Goals

To apply a calming breath before speaking and Breath–Pause notation in reading a text.

To speak spontaneous single sentences fluently and at an appropriate rate.

Procedures

1. **Discuss the purpose of the lesson:** To review the Breath–Pause technique and notation with the student and to give him practice applying the Breath–Pause technique to written text and spontaneously generated sentences.

2. **Review how to use the Breath–Pause technique in a stealth way, so that only the student knows he is using it.** Make certain the student remembers that it is not necessary to breathe out and in at every pause. Sometimes he will simply stop the breath and his speech for a brief moment and then go on.

3. **Establish a calm baseline.** Follow the calming exercises from the Modulation chapter (Chapter 2).

4. **Have your student read the excerpt from the speech by Charlie Chaplin (Handout A).** He will read the excerpt first, without any notation. Tell him to try to apply the Breath–Pause technique as he does this. Give him feedback.

5. **Review the Breath–Pause notation.** A V^x means that he should breathe in and then hold the breath in his lungs by closing the cords. An ^{x} means he should simply pause (holding his breath for a moment) and then read on.

6. **Together, notate the speech by Charlie Chaplin:**

   a. Pauses (red ˣ), where he stops the flow of air without taking a breath and continues.

   b. "Breath–Pauses" (**Vˣ**), where he breathes in, stops the flow of air, and then continues to speak.

7. **Have your student read the notated speech.** Video-record him. Watch the video and discuss your observations. How calm is he? How well does he follow the notation? How well does he apply the Breath–Pause technique?

8. **Apply Rules for Fluency when generating spontaneous descriptive sentences about a picture:**

   a. Show a picture (painting, photograph).

   b. After you count down "3–2–1" out loud, the student immediately uses Breath–Pause and formulates and speaks a spontaneous sentence about the picture. (*Note:* His sentences do not have to form a logical paragraph. They can be disconnected from each other but they do have to be about the picture.)

   c. The student continues to generate as many spontaneous sentences as possible about the picture, one after another, using Breath–Pause before he begins each new sentence.

   d. When the student has exhausted his imagination, you will ask a few more questions regarding the picture for him to answer.

   e. He will answer, using Breath–Pause before each sentence.

   f. Discuss his observations, then yours.

9. **Now have your student talk about the Chaplin speech:**

   a. After you count down "3–2–1" out loud, the student immediately uses Breath–Pause and formulates and speaks a spontaneous sentence about the speech. (*Note:* His sentences do not have to form a logical paragraph. They can be disconnected from each other but they must be about the speech.)

   b. The student continues to generate as many spontaneous sentences about the speech as possible, one after another, using Breath–Pause before he begins each new sentence.

   c. When the student has exhausted his imagination, you will ask a few more questions regarding the speech for him to answer.

   d. He will answer, using Breath–Pause before each sentence.

   e. Discuss his observations, then yours.

10. **Homework:** Practice reading the speech by Charlie Chaplin out loud, first to yourself in front of a mirror, and then to someone at home, using the Breath–Pause technique, while strictly following your Breath–Pause notation.

An Excerpt from Chaplin's "The Great Dictator's Speech"

I'm sorry but I don't want to be an Emperor – that's not my business – I don't want to rule or conquer anyone. I should like to help everyone if possible, Jew, gentile, black man, white. We all want to help one another. Human beings are like that. We all want to live by each other's happiness, not by each other's misery. We don't want to hate and despise one another. In this world there is room for everyone and the earth is rich and can provide for everyone. The way of life can be free and beautiful. But we have lost the way. We think too much and feel too little: More than machinery we need humanity; More than cleverness we need kindness and gentleness. Without these qualities, life will be violent and all will be lost.

The airplane and the radio have brought us closer together. The very nature of these inventions cries out for the goodness in men, cries out for universal brotherhood for the unity of us all. Even now my voice is reaching millions throughout the world, millions of despairing men, women and little children, victims of a system that makes men torture and imprison innocent people. To those who can hear me, I say, "Do not despair."

Don't give yourselves to these unnatural men, machine men, with machine minds and machine hearts. You are not machines. You are not cattle. You are men. You have the love of humanity in your hearts. You don't hate. Only the unloved hate. Only the unloved and the unnatural hate. Soldiers, don't fight for slavery, fight for liberty.

Chaplin, C. (1918) The Great Dictator's Speech.
www.charliechaplin.com/en/synopsis/articles/29-
The-Great-Dictator-s-Speech

LESSON 8

Shadow Vowel technique: Addressing misarticulation produced by muscle tension resulting from overly rapid speech or anxiety/overexcitement

Materials

Handout A: An Excerpt from Chaplin's "The Great Dictator's Speech"

Handout B: A short story, written by you, that contains words in which your student makes articulation errors

Handout C: The same text as in Handout B, which you have prepared in advance by substituting words spelled out with "shadow vowels" for words that the student misarticulates

Goals

To decrease the rate of speech and create a more fluid rhythm by applying the Breath–Pause technique between sentences and at clause boundaries.

To learn the "Shadow Vowel" technique.

To improve articulation by applying the "Shadow Vowel" technique.

Procedures

1. **Explain the purpose of the lesson:** To improve the student's articulation. Explain to your student that since your baseline assessment you have been keeping an inventory of his misarticulations.

2. **Describe the specific articulation errors you hear in his speech.** Explain that when he speaks too quickly or feels anxious, stressed, or excited, the muscles in his jaw, lips, and tongue tighten and become inflexible. When this happens, consonants and vowels are misarticulated and are often elided (smudged) in such a way that words become unintelligible. By taking time when formulating connected speech and individual words, it becomes possible to relax these muscles, which are responsible for articulation. Then vowels and consonants are pronounced and sequenced correctly and speech can be understood well by others.

3. **Explain the two methods by which articulation will be addressed:**

   a. Breath–Pause technique. Tell your student that the Breath–Pause technique, which he has been working on for some time, helps him to slow his speech overall. It is the basis for a fluent rhythmic speech pattern, which allows time for the speaker to calmly formulate his ideas into words and for the listener to process what the speaker has said.

b. A second, new method will be introduced in this lesson. It is called the "Shadow Vowel" technique. It slows speech within words.

4. **Have the student apply the Breath–Pause technique between sentences and at clause boundaries ("commas") as he reads the text in Handout A.** Was he able to produce a fluent rhythmic pattern at a reasonable rate? If not, have the student notate the text.

5. **Review the Breath–Pause notation.** A V^x means that he should breathe in and then hold the breath in his lungs by closing the cords. An ^{x} means he should simply pause (holding his breath for a moment) and then read on.

6. **Together, notate the speech by Charlie Chaplin:**

a. Pauses (red ^{x}), where he stops the flow of air without taking a breath and continues.

b. "Breath–Pauses" (V^x), where he breathes in, stops the flow of air, and then continues to speak.

7. **Have your student read the notated speech.** Video-record his face as he does this. Watch the video, particularly his mouth, and discuss your observations. How calm is he? How relaxed are his jaw, tongue, and lips? How well does he apply the Breath–Pause technique? Did the notation produce a fluent rhythmic pattern at a reasonable rate?

8. **Now make a list of words in which your student makes articulation errors.** Point out the commonalities among these words. For many students, consonant clusters will be problematic.

9. **Teach the "Shadow Vowel" technique.** Show the student how to separate the consonant combinations with "shadow vowels." This is accomplished by inserting the shadow vowel "uh" (as in cup) after each consonant in a consonant cluster:

Target word: grow

- The student says: "gwoh."
- With shadow vowel: guh-ruh-oh, repeat five times, gradually getting faster.
- Repeat five times: guhrow, gradually getting faster.
- Eventually back to the original target word five times: grow.

Target word: grown

- The student says: "growuhn."

- With shadow vowel: guh-ruh-ohn, repeat five times, gradually getting faster.
- Repeat five times: guh-rohn, gradually getting faster.
- Repeat five times: guhrohn, gradually getting faster.
- Eventually back to the original target word five times: grown.

Target word: training

- The student says: "cheraining."
- With shadow vowel: tuh-ruh-ay-ning, repeat five times, gradually getting faster.
- Repeat five times: tuh-ruh-aining, gradually getting faster.
- Repeat five times: tuhraining, gradually getting faster.
- Eventually back to the original target word five times: training.

Target word: street

- The student says: "shreet."
- With shadow vowel: stuh-ruh-eeet, repeat five times, gradually getting faster.
- Repeat five times: stuh-reet, gradually getting faster.
- Repeat five times: struhreet, gradually getting faster.
- Eventually back to the original target word five times: street.

10. **Homework:** Practice the shadow vowel substitutions for all words in your problem words list. Also, practice the text used in the lesson, first with the shadow vowels written in (Handout C) and then with the plain text (Handout B).

✓

An Excerpt from Chaplin's "The Great Dictator's Speech"

You the people have the power, the power to create machines, the power to create happiness. You the people have the power to make life free and beautiful, to make this life a wonderful adventure. Then in the name of democracy let's use that power – let us all unite. Let us fight for a new world, a decent world that will give men a chance to work that will give you the future and old age and security. By the promise of these things, brutes have risen to power, but they lie. They do not fulfill their promise, they never will. Dictators free themselves but they enslave the people. Now let us fight to fulfill that promise. Let us fight to free the world, to do away with national barriers, do away with greed, with hate and intolerance. Let us fight for a world of reason, a world where science and progress will lead to all men's happiness.

Chaplin, C. (1918) The Great Dictator's Speech.
www.charliechaplin.com/en/synopsis/articles/29-
The-Great-Dictator-s-Speech

LESSON 9

Rules for answering others' questions about you

Materials

Handout A: Sequential Graphic Organizer: Small Talk – Example

Handout B: Sequential Graphic Organizer: Small Talk – Blank

Goals

To learn a formula for answering questions about oneself so that the answer is complete and interesting.

To apply the Rules for Fluency to formulating answers to questions about yourself.

Procedures

1. **Review the Rules for Fluency and how to use the Breath–Pause technique in a stealth way, so that only the students know they are using it.**

2. **Review the homework from the last lesson.** Listen to your student read sections of Chaplin's "The Great Dictator's Speech" according to the Breath–Pause notation. Provide feedback and correction as needed.

3. **Explain the purpose of the lesson:** To have a method for providing complete and interesting answers to questions about yourself and to apply the Rules for Fluency in formulating those answers.

4. **Discuss typical small-talk questions the student may be asked by others.** Explain that people will often ask how things are going in life. This is a very global topic question. Although one should not give an overabundance of detail in response (since a conversation with one other person should be about 50/50 with respect to the topic in focus), it *is* important to give enough information to keep the conversation interesting, so that it can continue.

5. **Teach the student that he must answer questions with full sentences, not single words.** When asked a question like "How was your day?" it is not enough to give one-word answers like "fine," "good," "bad," or "OK." Giving single-word responses ends a conversation quickly.

6. **Explain the concept of answering a question about yourself.** When someone asks a question such as "How was your morning? How was

your afternoon? How was your day? How was your weekend? How was your week?":

a. **First one needs to STOP and THINK.** "I am being asked a question about myself. I should give the other person enough information so he can stay interested and can continue the conversation."

b. **Then use the Rules for Answering a Question about Yourself.** Give your student Handout A and explain the rules:

   ✓ Respond with a general topic sentence (e.g., My day was fine).

   ✓ Add a topic sentence about a specific aspect related to the general response (e.g., My day was a little different because we had an assembly today).

   ✓ Then give two detail sentences (e.g., A group came into my school to teach us about comedy. It was really funny when they asked volunteers to come up on stage).

7. **Have your student practice applying the Rules for Answering a Question about Yourself:**

   a. Using Handout B as a guide, he should write out three different responses to the question, "How was your day?"

   b. He should then notate these sentences with the Breath–Pause notation.

   c. Then have him read the sentences out loud according to the Breath–Pause notation.

   d. Finally, he should speak the sentences without looking.

   e. Give feedback and correction as needed.

8. **Homework:** At least two times this week, answer the question "How was your day?" with a general response, a specific topic sentence, and at least two details about the specific topic. Be sure to listen to the response of others and answer others' questions about what you say using the Breath–Pause technique to aid in your fluency by reducing your false starts.

Sequential Graphic Organizer:
Small Talk – Example

"HOW WAS YOUR DAY?"

General Response

I had a very good day.

Specific Topic Sentence

I went to the amusement park.

Three Details

1. I stayed all day

2. I went with my family

3. I rode the roller coaster five times

Sequential Graphic Organizer:
Small Talk – Blank

"HOW WAS YOUR DAY?"

General Response

[ ]

↓

Specific Topic Sentence

[ ]

↓

Three Details

[ ]

LESSON 10

Graphic Organizer: Formulating a description of a person

Materials

Handout A: Description of a Person

Handout B: Sample Graphic Organizer – Description of a Person

Handout C: Blank Graphic Organizer – Self-Description

Goals

To learn to formulate a description of oneself using a Graphic Organizer.

To apply the Rules for Fluency to an oral description of oneself.

Procedures

1. **Explain the purpose of the lesson:** To learn to formulate an organized and fluent oral description of a person.

2. **Ask the student to describe himself to you.** Ask him to provide as many details as possible, in order for you to have as complete a description as possible. Do not provide any additional prompts. Record him. This will be compared with a description of himself with the support of a Graphic Organizer and Breath–Pause notation.

3. **Give the student Handout A: Description of a Person.** Have the student read through the written description of the person. Discuss anything that stands out about that person.

4. **Give the student Handout B: Sample Graphic Organizer – Description of a Person.** Explain to the student that Graphic Organizers begin with a main topic, in the center. A number of subtopics radiate out from the main topic, and the details about a particular subtopic are attached to their subtopic.

5. **Model how to use the sample Graphic Organizer to describe the person orally.** Begin with a main topic sentence about the person. Then provide a topic sentence about one of the subtopics, followed by that subtopic's associated details. Continue on to the next subtopic, and so on. Model the use of the Breath–Pause technique during your description. Instruct the student to ask you questions about the person you are describing. Answer them, demonstrating good use of the Rules for Fluency.

6. **Review with your student how to use the Breath–Pause technique in a stealth way.** Tell your student that he will now tell you about the person described in the Graphic Organizer. Make certain the student

knows he is expected to apply the Breath–Pause technique during all speech formulation activities in this lesson and try to apply it in a stealth quality.

7. **Speaking about a topic (someone else) based on a Graphic Organizer.** Now switch roles and have your student tell you about the same person. Have the student begin with one main topic sentence. He will then give a sentence about one of the subtopics. Follow that with detail sentences associated with that subtopic. Have him move on to the next subtopic, following the same formula (a subtopic sentence, followed with two detail sentences about that subtopic). Repeat this process until he has finished discussing all subtopics describing the person. The student should *not* skip around the Graphic Organizer as he describes, but rather use the Graphic Organizer in the way it is organized and in the direction indicated.

8. **Give the student Handout C: Blank Graphic Organizer – Self-Description.** Have the student fill in the Graphic Organizer with the main topic, subtopics, and details to outline the description of himself. Now, help him to number the subtopics in the order he will talk about them, before he begins to give his oral description.

9. **Have the student describe himself.** Have the student use the Graphic Organizer from the previous step for his description (as in step 7). Remind him to use the Breath–Pause technique throughout. Have him describe himself twice. The first time, provide feedback and correction, as needed. The second time, let him go through the entire description without stopping him. Record him on these two tries.

10. **Listen to the recordings from this lesson.** Listen to the first recording and then to the second and third. Ask the student for his observations regarding differences in his descriptions of himself. Make sure to comment on the organization of his accounts and his fluency, including the use of the Breath–Pause technique. (*Note:* The point in recording completely spontaneously generated speech, and then comparing it with speech outlined with a Graphic Organizer, is to demonstrate to the student that organization makes speech more fluent.)

11. **Explain the importance of using the Rules for Fluency and especially the Breath–Pause technique.** Tell him that starting with a calming breath and from a calm baseline will allow him to think more clearly because his short-term memory will be filled with his ideas rather than his anxiety. (Have him recall what he learned in the Modulation chapter.) Tell him that using Breath–Pause at the ends of sentences and clause boundaries gives him time to think of what he wants to say. His oral language then has a fluent rhythm and also gives time for his listener to process what he is saying. Have him write these concepts in his notebook.

12. **Homework:** On a sheet of paper, make and fill in another Graphic Organizer about someone else or something in your life. Practice speaking it, using the Breath–Pause technique to aid your fluency, reducing false starts and/or hesitations.

Description of a Person

John Bristol is an 18-year-old senior. He is in high school and looking forward to his future. He is excited and positive about his upcoming college years. Since he was in the tenth grade, he has excelled in his science classes. He is always interested in taking on new science projects. Science is the subject he feels the most excited about. He even won the school science award for his participation in the science department and the science club.

His goals are to study hard and get good grades and become a veterinarian back in his hometown. He has been offered a scholarship in Veterinarian Sciences in the School of Veterinary Medicine at Oklahoma State University. John plans on attending school at that university.

John's family consists of his two parents and four other siblings, all girls. His family also claims two dogs and four cats as part of their family. He is the youngest of the five children. He and his family enjoy golf and play as often as possible. They also enjoy hiking and rock climbing as a family. He and his family reside in White Plains, New York. There are many places to hike, rock climb, and play golf in that area.

John has many interests, but his favorites include science fiction movies and talking about politics. His family has had many interesting and heated discussions about politics. His favorite hobby is fishing. He loves any type of fishing, in any lake, river, or stream.

Sample Graphic Organizer – Description of a Person

- Golf
- Camping
- Fishing is my hobby
- Read science fiction
- Enjoy politics

- 4 siblings
- I am the youngest
- Home – White Plains, NY

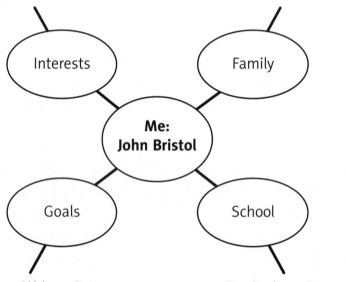

- College – Oklahoma State
- Good grades
- Career – Veterinarian

- Favorite class – Art
- Now in tenth grade
- My best grades – Science

Blank Graphic Organizer –
Self-Description

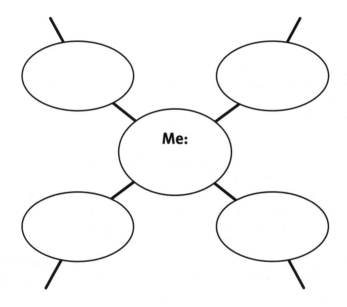

Me:

LESSON 11

Graphic Organizer: Using a book, periodical, or article

Materials

Handout A: Honey Badger Article 1

Handout B: Honey Badger Article 2

Handout C: Sample Graphic Organizer: Article Summary

Goal

To learn to formulate and summarize a book, a chapter in a book, a periodical, a magazine article, or an online article, using a Graphic Organizer.

Procedures

1. **Explain the purpose of the lesson:** To learn to formulate an organized, fluent oral summary of an article the student has read. These kinds of descriptions (critiques, reviews) will be used in conversation with other people. The student will learn to use a Graphic Organizer to organize information about an informational article and to apply the Rules of Fluency during his recounting of the information.

2. **Give an article about the honey badger to the student (Handout A or B, whichever is more appropriate for your student).** Have him read the article.

3. **Ask the student to tell you about the article he has just read.** Ask him to provide a complete description of the article, making sure he includes the point of the piece. Give no more instruction than this. Record him as he does this.

4. **Have the student make a Graphic Organizer based on the information in the Handout A or B honey badger article (whichever he read).** Remind the student that Graphic Organizers are comprised of a main topic in the center, its subtopics radiating from the main topic, and the details associated with those subtopics. Have him draw a Graphic Organizer with six subtopics. If he needs help, you can help him understand that his subtopics could be: appearance, diet, habitat, survival skills, special features, "so what?"/the point.

5. **Review how to use the Breath–Pause technique in a stealth way.** Tell your student that he will now recount the information he learned

in the article. Make certain the student knows he must apply the Breath–Pause technique as he does this. Remind the student that using Breath–Pause at the ends of sentences and clause boundaries gives him time to think of what he wants to say. His oral language then has a fluent rhythm and also gives time for his listener to process what he is saying.

6. **Summarize the article out loud, using the sample Graphic Organizer.** You should first model retelling the information from Handout C: Sample Graphic Organizer: Article Summary, making sure to use the Breath–Pause technique.

7. **Have the student summarize his outlined description of the article.** Have the student use his own Graphic Organizer for his own summary. Remind him to use the Breath–Pause technique throughout his description/summary. Have him tell about the article twice. The first time, provide feedback and correction as needed. The second time, let him go through the entire description without stopping him. Record him as he does this.

8. **Listen to the recordings from this lesson.** Listen to the first recording and then to the second. Ask the student for his observations regarding differences in his two accounts of the article. Make sure to comment on the organization of his accounts and his fluency, including the use of the Breath–Pause technique. (*Note:* The point in recording completely spontaneously generated speech and then comparing it to speech, outlined with a Graphic Organizer, is to demonstrate to the student that organization makes speech more fluent.)

9. **Homework:** Make your own Graphic Organizer about another article you find interesting or fun. Fill in your Graphic Organizer and practice speaking it, using the Breath–Pause technique to aid your fluency. This will help you reduce your false starts and hesitations.

The Honey Badger is a Fierce Hunter

Honey Badgers, which live in Asia and Africa, are extremely tough animals. They are so tough that military tanks in South Africa are named after them. Honey Badgers are remarkably intelligent problem solvers.

Honey Badgers have long black and white fur covering loose skin. They have sharp claws that are about an inch and a half long, which are used effectively for digging. They are great tunnel makers. Males are about 25 pounds. They are 3 feet long. Their range is huge, at about 200 square miles. Honey Badgers are fast, running up to 6 miles an hour. Females are about 15 pounds and their range is 50 square miles. They remain closer to their young. They do not give birth to litters but rather have one baby at a time. They care for the baby for more than 1 year. When cubs are tiny, mother Honey Badgers will carry them to new dens ever few nights. As the babies get older the pair will sleep in a new den every night, mostly to avoid predators. Half of all babies die. Their main predators are lions, leopards and humans. Honey Badgers are killed by honey producers because they raid and destroy their beehives.

Honey badgers eat tsama melon (about 90% liquid) to stay hydrated. They eat bees, rodents and reptiles, including highly poisonous snakes like Cape cobras and Puff adders. Although they find about ¾ of their food underground, they climb trees after a snake dinner. Honey Badgers are often struck by venomous snakes as they hunt, but they do not die. They collapse, sleep it off and then have their dinner. They are remarkable in that they have the ability to survive even the most potent venoms.

Reference

Begg, C. & Begg, K. (2004). The tough Kalahari honey badger reigns as one of the desert's fiercest hunters. National Geographic Magazine.

Biology Explains Why Honey Badger Don't Care

Honey Badgers are amazing animals that are unaffected by stinging bees, or even highly venomous snakes, including cobras. Danielle Drabeck, a University of Minnesota graduate student, wanted to understand why. She, along with her collaborators, biologist Sharon Jansa and biochemist Antony Dean obtained some precious Honey Badger blood samples to investigate the Honey Badger's resistance to venom on a molecular level. This could help in designing better anti-venoms for humans.

Resistance to venom puts the Honey Badger at a distinct advantage when it comes to obtaining food. Honey Badgers are omnivores whose diet is about 25% snakes. Being able to withstand venom means that they have little competition for one of their major food sources.

Typically snake venom can act to paralyze muscles, destroy body tissue and stop blood from clotting, causing bleeding to become uncontrollable. The researchers knew that snake venom has over 100 proteins and other substances that can poison a victim, but they guessed that the Honey Badger's molecular defence might be similar to other venom resistant animals, such as the mongoose, and so they focused on alpha-neurotoxins. These toxins paralyze the muscles involved in breathing by blocking receptors in cells so they cannot receive input from the nervous system and so they stop working. Honey Badgers have genetic mutations in the gene that determines how this particular receptor is built. As a result, cobra neurotoxin cannot fit into and block the receptors so it does not produce paralysis of the Honey Badger's breathing. Interestingly, there are 3 or more other species, including mongooses, hedgehogs, and pigs that had evolved molecular defence mechanisms against snake venom.

Reference

Cartwright, M., (2015). Biology Finally Explains Why Honey Badger Don't Care. Retrieved from: www.slate.com/blogs/wild_things/2015/06/16/honey_badger_venom_resistance_biologists_discover_the_secret.html

✓

Sample Graphic Organizer: Article Summary

• Fast and quick
• Fearless
• Anti-venom

• Africa
• Asia

Survival skills

Habitat

Honey Badger

Diet

Why so interesting?

Appearance

• Snake
• Reptiles
• Rodents

• Great tunnel maker
• Intelligence
• Problem solvers
• Survives poisonous snake bites

• Long hair
• Loose, tough skin
• 3ft. long
• Long, sharp claws
• Black and white

LESSON 12

Sequential Graphic Organizer: Giving step-by-step instructions 1

Materials

Audio recorder

Handout A: Sequential Graphic Organizer: Making a Peanut Butter and Jelly Sandwich

Goals

To teach the student how to use a Sequential Graphic Organizer to help him formulate and give his own step-by-step instructions (task analysis) for completing a task.

To apply the Rules for Fluency to his oral step-by-step instructions.

Procedures

1. **Explain the purpose of the lesson:** To learn to formulate and orally give organized instructions for how to carry out a task and to apply the Rules for Fluency when giving oral instructions to another person.

2. **Ask your student to tell you how to make a peanut butter and jelly sandwich.** Record this.

3. **Give your student Handout A: Making a Peanut Butter and Jelly Sandwich.** Read through the instructions together.

4. **Review the stealth Breath–Pause technique.** Remind the student that he will apply the stealth version of the Breath–Pause technique during the activities in this lesson.

5. **Have the student summarize the instructions out loud.** Have him use Handout A: Making a Peanut Butter and Jelly Sandwich to teach you. He will look at the instructions in the Sequential Graphic Organizer. Record him as he does this.

6. **Have the student summarize the instructions out loud a second time.** This time he will not use Handout A to give the instructions. Tell him to look once more at Handout A, and then put it down and give the instructions. Record him as he does this.

7. **Listen to the recordings from this lesson.** Listen to the first recording and then to the second. Ask the student for his observations. Make sure to comment on his organization, his fluency, and his use of the

stealth Breath–Pause technique. (Again, note that the point in recording completely spontaneously generated speech, and then comparing it with speech outlined with Graphic Organizers, is to demonstrate to the student that organization makes speech more fluent.)

8. **Homework:** Draw and fill in your own Sequential Graphic Organizer for how to complete a task that you find interesting or fun. Practice giving the instructions to someone (friend or family member), incorporating a stealth Breath–Pause technique to aid in your fluency and to help you reduce false starts and hesitations.

Sequential Graphic Organizer: Making a Peanut Butter and Jelly Sandwich

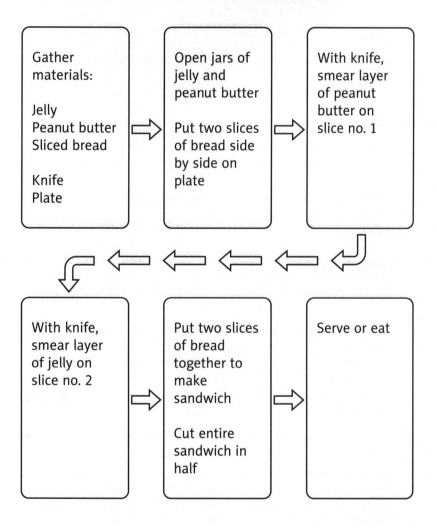

LESSON 13

Sequential Graphic Organizer: Giving step-by-step instructions 2

Materials

Handout A: Sequential Graphic Organizer: Do My Laundry

Audio recorder

Goals

To teach the student how to use a Sequential Graphic Organizer to help him formulate and give his own step-by-step instructions for completing a task.

To apply the Rules for Fluency to his oral step-by-step instructions.

Procedures

1. **Explain the purpose of the lesson:** To learn to formulate and orally provide complete and organized instructions for how to do a task and to apply the Rules for Fluency when giving oral instructions to another person.

2. **Review the homework from the last lesson.** Look at the Sequential Graphic Organizer your student generated. Give feedback and corrections. Have your student orally give the instructions in his organizer, making sure to apply the Rules for Fluency.

3. **Ask the student to tell you the step-by-step instructions for how to do the laundry.** Record him as he does this.

4. **Give Handout A: Do My Laundry to the student.** Read through the instructions.

5. **Review the stealth Breath–Pause technique.** Tell the student to be certain to apply the stealth version of the Breath–Pause technique during the activities in this lesson. Remind the student that using Breath–Pause at the ends of sentences and clause boundaries gives your student time to think of what he wants to say. His oral language then has a fluent rhythm and also gives time for his listener to process what he is saying.

6. **Ask the student to summarize the instructions out loud.** Ask him to use Handout A: Do My Laundry to instruct you. He will look at the instructions of the Sequential Graphic Organizer. Record him as he does this.

7. **Have the student summarize the instructions out loud a second time.** This time he will not use the handout. Tell him to look once more at Handout A and then put it down. He will not look at the handout while instructing you this time. Record him as he does this.

8. **Listen to the three recordings from this lesson.** Ask the student for his observations. Make sure to comment on his organization, his fluency, and his use of the stealth Breath–Pause technique.

9. **Homework:** Draw and fill in your own Sequential Graphic Organizer for how to complete a task that you find interesting or fun. Practice giving the instructions to someone (friend or family member), incorporating a stealth Breath–Pause technique to aid in your fluency and to help you reduce false starts and hesitations.

✓

Sequential Graphic Organizer: Do My Laundry

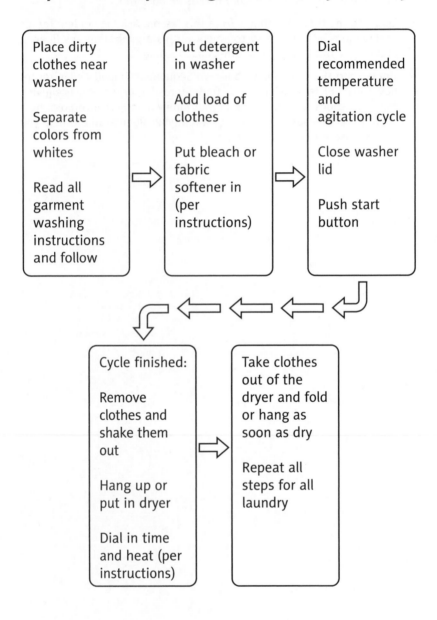

Place dirty clothes near washer

Separate colors from whites

Read all garment washing instructions and follow

Put detergent in washer

Add load of clothes

Put bleach or fabric softener in (per instructions)

Dial recommended temperature and agitation cycle

Close washer lid

Push start button

Cycle finished:

Remove clothes and shake them out

Hang up or put in dryer

Dial in time and heat (per instructions)

Take clothes out of the dryer and fold or hang as soon as dry

Repeat all steps for all laundry

Web Graphic Organizer: My best day ever

Materials

Handout A: Web Graphic Organizer: Joe's Best Day

Goals

To learn to formulate a description of a favorite event, using a Graphic Organizer.

To apply the Rules for Fluency to the oral description of a favorite event.

Procedures

1. **Explain the purpose of the lesson:** To help your student learn to formulate an organized description of one of his favorite memories (favorite day, weekend, vacation, trip, class, etc.), again using a Graphic Organizer to organize information about a topic (in this case, a favorite memory) and to apply the Rules for Fluency as he tells it.

2. **Using Handout A, describe Joe's best day.** Make sure to give a clear model of how to describe a favorite memory. Demonstrate proper use of the Web Graphic Organizer, with topic sentences for main topics and subtopics, before telling the details associated with each subtopic. Apply the stealth Breath–Pause technique.

3. **Review the Rules for Fluency.** Review the proper use of the stealth Breath–Pause technique, and emphasize for the student that pauses must be placed at the ends of sentences and at clause boundaries. Remind the student that using Breath–Pause at the ends of sentences and clause boundaries gives him time to think of what he wants to say. His oral language then has a fluent rhythm and also gives time for his listener to process what he is saying.

4. **Give the student Handout A: Joe's Best Day.** Have him look briefly at Handout A, then put it down and describe Joe's best day, without looking at the handout. Record him as he does this.

5. **Have the student draw and fill in his own Web Graphic Organizer about one of his own favorite memories.** He will use one of his own favorite days. Remind him of the *correct format* of a Web Graphic Organizer: a main topic, two to five subtopics, and two to three details for each subtopic. Also remind him to number the subtopics, to show the order in which he will talk about them.

6. **Have the student describe a favorite memory, using the Graphic Organizer.** Have him look at his Web Graphic Organizer when giving his description, this first time. Record him. After he tells you the description the first time, provide feedback and correction as needed. Now have him give his description again, but this time without looking at his Graphic Organizer. Let him go through the entire story, without stopping him. Record him again.

7. **Listen to the recordings from this lesson.** Listen to all three recordings (one recording of Handout A: Joe's Best Day and two recordings of his own favorite memory). Ask the student for his observations regarding differences in his descriptions. Make sure to comment on the organization of his accounts and his fluency, including the use of the Breath–Pause technique.

8. **Homework:** Draw and fill in another Web Graphic Organizer about another one of your own favorite memories (favorite day, weekend, vacation, trip, class, event, etc.). You should then practice speaking it, using the Breath–Pause technique to aid fluency and reduce false starts and/or hesitations.

Web Graphic Organizer: Joe's Best Day

- Celebrate graduation
- I love sailing
- Relaxing setting
- Helped me recharge

- Night sailing
- Dinner served
- Passenger with no duties

- Long-time friends
- Family members
- Close school mates

- Late summer
- NYC Harbor

LESSON 15

Web Graphic Organizer: Description of a vacation

Materials

Handout A: Web Graphic Organizer: My Favorite Vacation

Goals

To learn to formulate a description of an event using a Graphic Organizer, including the point of the description.

To apply the Rules for Fluency to the telling of a description.

Procedures

1. **Explain the purpose of the lesson:** To help your student learn to formulate an organized description of an event in his life, again using a Graphic Organizer to organize information about his topic and to apply the Rules for Fluency to his oral account.

2. **Orally give the description outlined in Handout A: My Favorite Vacation.** Make sure to give a clear model of how to describe an event. Demonstrate proper use of the Web Graphic Organizer and the stealth Breath–Pause technique.

3. **Review the Rules for Fluency.** Review the proper use of the stealth Breath–Pause technique. Remind the student that using Breath–Pause at the ends of sentences and clause boundaries gives him time to think of what he wants to say. His oral language then has a fluent rhythm and also gives time for his listener to process what he is saying.

4. **Give the student Handout A: My Favorite Vacation.** Have him look briefly at Handout A, then put it down and describe the vacation without looking at the handout. Record him as he does this. Provide corrections on his use of the Graphic Organizer if needed.

5. **Have the student construct his own Web Graphic Organizer about another one of his own favorite memories.** This could be his last vacation (or any other favorite day, weekend, class event, etc.). Give feedback on how his Graphic Organizer is organized and on the details provided. At this point help him to include details he finds interesting and he thinks will be interesting to others.

6. **Teach your student to make a point when he talks to another person.** To do this, add a new subtopic to his Graphic Organizer. The topic should

be labeled "So what?" or "Importance." The details for this subtopic could be about something he learned or why his description might be important to you. Now he should number the order in which he will talk about his subtopics.

7. **Again, remind the student to use the Breath–Pause technique, in a stealth way.**

8. **Remind the student that he will apply the stealth Breath–Pause technique while telling you his description.**

9. **Have the student relate his description of the event he chose.** Have the student use his Web Graphic Organizer when describing his event the first time. Record him. After the first time, provide feedback and correction as needed, especially about how he talks about the point of his description. Now have him give his description a second time, without the Graphic Organizer. Let him go through the entire description without stopping him. Record him again.

10. **Listen to the recordings from this lesson.** Listen to all three recordings (one recording of his description based on Handout A: My Favorite Vacation and two recordings of his description of his own event). Ask the student for his observations regarding differences in his descriptions. Make sure to comment on the organization of his accounts and his fluency, including the use of the Breath–Pause technique. Note improvements over the past few lessons. You may want to play a recording from a few lessons ago to let him hear just how much he has improved.

11. **Homework:** Draw and fill in a Web Graphic Organizer to describe another one of your favorite memories (favorite day, weekend, vacation, trip, class, etc.). One of your subtopics should be "So what?" (Importance). You should practice speaking your description, incorporating the appropriate Breath–Pause technique to improve fluency and reduce false starts and/or hesitations. You should tell your description to another person. Use the Rules for Fluency (including starting with a calming breath) to help you to communicate more effectively and help your listener process what you are saying.

Web Graphic Organizer: My Favorite Vacation

• Family bonding
• Try out new trails
• Spend time together

• Maine coastline
• Fall vacation

"So what?" Importance

When and where

My Favorite Vacation

Who brought what?

What did we do?

• Mom: packed lunch
• Dad: spare tubes
• Sister: tools
• Sister: water bottles
• Me: food bars

• Historical sites
• Bed and breakfast
• Cycled with family
• Colorful leaves

Plot Contour Graphic Organizer: Telling a good story

Materials

Handout A: Plot Contour Graphic Organizer: A Story Including My Family

Goals

To learn to formulate a story, or summary of a story, with background, rising action, a climax, and point, using a Plot Contour Graphic Organizer.

To apply the Rules for Fluency to the telling of a story.

Procedures

1. **Explain the purpose of the lesson:** To help your student learn to formulate a story, or summary of a story, with background, rising action, a climax, and point, using a Plot Contour Graphic Organizer; and to apply the Rules for Fluency to the telling of a story. Explain that this is the first time you are asking him to tell a real story. Prior to this he has been using Web Graphic Organizers to describe events. Explain how descriptions of events differ from stories. Stories have a definite shape, beginning with background and building to a climax.

2. **Review the homework from the last lesson.** Listen to your student give his description of an event. Give feedback and corrections as needed.

3. **Explain the form of the Plot Contour Graphic Organizer.** Using Handout A: A Story Including My Family, discuss how the Plot Contour Graphic Organizer is constructed and used, including all parts: background, rising action, climax, and "so what?" sections. Discuss how the Plot Contour Graphic Organizer will help him to tell interesting stories fluently. Also explain that a story must have a shape. It must get to a climax that is interesting or emotional in some way. Illustrate a flat story for your student (e.g., I got up, had breakfast, got dressed, and went to school). In the next step you will show him the difference between a flat story and one that has a plot contour.

4. **Using Handout A: A Story Including My Family, demonstrate proper use of the Plot Contour Graphic Organizer to tell an interesting story fluently.** Model use of a calming breath and the Breath–Pause technique. Also model building up to the climax with your voice.

5. **Give the student Handout A: A Story Including My Family.** Have your student look briefly at Handout A, then put it down and tell the story without looking at the handout. Record him.

6. **Now have the student outline a story by constructing a Plot Contour Graphic Organizer.** This may be a story with which he is familiar (e.g., a nursery rhyme, a favorite book, the story of a movie) or may be a story from his life or about another person's life. Discuss the format of a Plot Contour Graphic Organizer (background, rising action, climax, and "so what?" sections). Help him fill in his plot contour.

7. **Have the student tell his story using the Plot Contour Graphic Organizer.** Remind the student to take a calming breath and to use the stealth Breath–Pause technique while telling his story to you. Have him tell his story twice. The first time, provide feedback and correction as needed. Now have him tell his story a second time. This time, let him go through the entire story without stopping him. Record him.

8. **Listen to the recordings from this lesson.** Listen to the two recordings (one recording of his telling of the story outlined in Handout A: A Story Including My Family and one recording of his own story). Ask the student for his observations. Make sure to comment on the organization of his accounts and his fluency, including the use of the Breath–Pause technique and whether he had a calm baseline.

9. **Homework:** Fill in a Plot Contour Graphic Organizer to outline a story about your childhood. Ask your parents to help with ideas. Practice speaking the story. Incorporate the Breath–Pause technique for better fluency, and to reduce false starts and hesitations. Tell this story to a friend or family member.

Plot Contour Graphic Organizer:
A Story Including My Family

Climax

Rising Action

- Italian restaurant
- All agreed on salad and pizza
- Very tasty
- My vegan sister ate her pizza without cheese

- Big treat after dinner
- Surprised
- Dad took us to our favorite place – book store
- Whatever we wanted
- My book *History of Martial Arts*

Background

- Out to dinner
- My dad's idea
- Last Friday
- All were tired
- But hungry

Falling Action
"So what?"

- Great evening coming to an end
- Stayed till the store closed
- Loaded up the car
- Tried to read in car
- Up too late reading

LESSON 17

Web Graphic Organizer: Recounting what I learned from an article

Materials

Handout A: Birds Evolving Short Wingspans to Dodge Traffic

Handout B: Web Graphic Organizer: Recounting Information

Goals

To practice recounting factual information from television news or a periodical or book, from a prepared Graphic Organizer outline.

To apply the Rules for Fluency to an oral account of information.

Procedures

1. **Explain the purpose of the lesson:** To review the use of a Web Graphic Organizer to organize and outline information about a topic to aid in recounting that information to others; and to apply the Rules for Fluency to the oral account.

2. **Give Handout A: Birds Evolving Short Wingspans to Dodge Traffic to the student.** Read the article together, alternating paragraphs. Both of you should apply the appropriate stealth Breath–Pause technique. (*Note:* Any time your student fails to appropriately apply the technique, stop him and have him apply the technique as he did in the beginning with an audible sound, as when he momentarily holds back the air at his cords.)

3. **Have the student add additional information to Handout B: Recounting Information.** He may find additional information in the article interesting. Have him add this to the prepared Web Graphic Organizer outline. Make sure he writes these details as notes, not as full sentences.

4. **Ask the student to tell you about the article, using Handout B: Recounting Information.** Have the student orally summarize the article, using the Web Graphic Organizer to accomplish this. Record him.

5. **Have the student tell you about the article, without Handout B.** Have the student take a very brief look at the handout again and then put the handout down. Remind him to think of how the Web Graphic Organizer looked with its main topic in the middle, surrounded by subtopics and their details. Instruct him to think of its shape, form, and the article

details, as he provides you with a complete summary and description of the article. Remind him to use a calming breath whenever he needs it and to use the stealth Breath–Pause technique. Record him again.

6. **Listen to the recordings from this lesson.** Listen to the first recording and then to the second. Ask the student for his observations regarding differences in his two recordings. Make sure to comment on the organization of his accounts and his fluency, including the use of the stealth Breath–Pause technique.

7. **Homework:** Make and fill in a Web Graphic Organizer about another article you find interesting or fun. You should then practice speaking about the article, incorporating the stealth Breath–Pause technique to aid your fluency and reduce false starts and/or hesitations. You should then tell another person about this article.

Birds Evolving Short Wingspans to Dodge Traffic

Many cliff swallows make their homes under bridges and highway overpasses. This means that these birds feed near highways. Each year, close to 60 million birds are killed by motor vehicles in the United States. A group of researchers headed by Dr. Charles Brown from the University of Tulsa noted in a 30-year study that more and more cliff swallows living near highways were surviving over that time period. They also noted that the wing span of the cliff swallows studied, near those structures, had decreased. They hypothesized that the shorter wingspans were indeed responsible for the reduction in deaths. The shorter wingspan afforded the evolved birds an ability to have faster take-offs. They could gain altitude more quickly, rising above the oncoming vehicles to avoid disaster. Those with shorter wingspans were more agile and aerodynamic. The researchers studied dead swallows found on the ground, and discovered that those killed by motor vehicles were in fact birds with a longer wingspan. As human beings change the environment, animals will adapt their behavior by moving into human made structures. It also seems that natural selection can quickly promote the development of adaptive physical features which aid the survival of a species.

Reference

Gates, S. (2013) "Birds Evolving Short Wingspans to Dodge Traffic, Study Suggests." The Huffington Post. www.huffingtonpost. com/2013/03/19/birds-evolving-dodge-vehicles-traffic_n_2901431.htm

Web Graphic Organizer: Recounting Information

- Habitat
- Humans change environment
- Natural selection

- Short wings = survive
- Long wings = more often killed

- University of Tulsa
- Wing hypothesis

- Faster take-offs
- Gain altitude quicker
- More aerodynamic

Web Graphic Organizer: Recounting a fable and its significance

Materials

Handout A: The Bundle of Sticks

Handout B: Web Graphic Organizer: Recounting a Fable and Its Significance

Goals

To learn to formulate a summary of a fable, including the point of the piece, using a Graphic Organizer.

To apply the Rules for Fluency to a summary.

Procedures

1. **Explain the purpose of the lesson:** To review the use of a Web Graphic Organizer to formulate a summary of a story, including the point of the story; and to apply the Rules for Fluency to a summary.

2. **Review the homework from the last lesson.** Check the student's Web Graphic Organizer for completeness and make sure that he has written his topics, subtopics, and details as notes, not full sentences. Then listen to him as he tells his story. Give feedback and correction as needed.

3. **Remind the student of the Rules for Fluency (Handout C from Lesson 1):**

   ✓ Calming breath.

   ✓ Use the Breath–Pause technique (like lifting a heavy weight)

   ✓ Think of your next sentence in your head, as you hold back your breath.

   ✓ Then speak the sentence you hear in your head, using the breath you were holding.

4. **Give the student Handout A: The Bundle of Sticks.** Have him read the fable out loud, using the Breath–Pause technique.

5. **Have the student summarize the fable, using Handout B: Web Graphic Organizer: Recounting a Fable and Its Significance to accomplish this.** Be certain to point out that his summary will include talking about the point of the piece. Record him.

6. **Have the student tell you about the fable without Handout B.** Have the student take a very brief look at the handout and then put the handout down. Remind him to think of (visualize) how the Web Graphic Organizer looked with its main topic in the middle, surrounded by subtopics and their details. Instruct him to think of its shape, form, and the article details as he provides you with a complete summary and description of the fable, including the point of the piece. Also ask him to discuss how the point of the piece of the fable affected him. Remind him to use the stealth Breath–Pause technique as he summarizes his thoughts about the fable. Record him again.

7. **Listen to the recordings from this lesson.** Listen to the first recording and then to the second. Ask the student for his observations regarding differences in his two different accounts of the fable. Make sure to comment on the organization of each account and his fluency.

8. **Homework:** Make a Web Graphic Organizer to outline a story or fable you find interesting or funny. Practice telling your story, applying the Rules for Fluency.

The Bundle of Sticks

A father had a family of sons who were perpetually quarreling among themselves. When he failed to heal their disputes by his exhortations, he determined to give them a practical illustration of the evils of disunion; and for this purpose he one day told them to bring him a bundle of sticks.

When they had done so, he placed the bundle into the hands of each of them in succession, and ordered them to break it in pieces. They tried with all their strength, and were not able to do it.

He next opened the bundle, took the sticks separately, one by one, and again put them into his sons' hands, upon which they broke them easily.

He then addressed them in these words: "My sons, if you are of one mind, and unite to assist each other, you will be as this bundle, uninjured by all the attempts of your enemies; but if you are divided among yourselves, you will be broken as easily as these sticks."

Aesop, Winter, M. (1919) Aesop for Children. The Bundle of Sticks.
http://mythfolklore.net/aesopica/milowinter/13.htm

✓

Web Graphic Organizer: Recounting a Fable and Its Significance

- Lessons taught:
  1. Strength in unity
  2. If an impossible task:
     - Cooperate
     - Divide labor

- Old father
- 3 sons

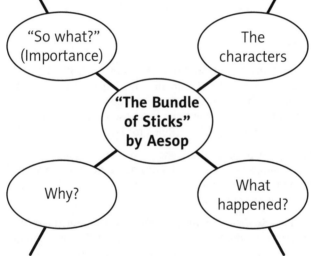

"So what?" (Importance)

The characters

"The Bundle of Sticks" by Aesop

Why?

What happened?

- Father is dying
- Passing on wisdom to sons

- Sticks presented
- "Break the bundle"
- Unable to break
- Bundle separated
- Each stick broke

LESSON 19

Learning to play the Conversation Game to develop fluency in conversation

Materials

Handout A: The Conversation Game: Topic Talk (two copies)

Goal

To learn to play the Conversation Game, applying the Rules for Fluency, to develop fluency in spontaneous conversation.

Procedures

1. **Review the homework from the last lesson.** Look at your student's Web Graphic Organizer. Make certain all of his ideas are written as notes and not as full sentences. Give feedback and correction as needed. Listen to your student talk about the topic he chose for homework. Comment on the content and his use of the Rules for Fluency when he is finished.

2. **Explain the purpose of the lesson:** To learn to play the Conversation Game, applying the Rules for Fluency as he does, to develop fluency in spontaneous conversation. Today you will construct the Conversation Game and teach your student how to play.

3. **Review how to use the Breath–Pause technique, in a stealth way.** Explain to the student that when the Breath–Pause technique is used in a stealth way, only the student will know he is using it. Tell the student that he will be applying the Breath–Pause technique to long and spontaneously generated language. Tell him to expect a difficult lesson, but that you will be helping him by giving him reminders throughout.

4. **Construct the *Conversation Game: Topic Talk*:**

   a. *Make TOPIC cards.* Make a set of index cards with single topics for getting to know someone (school, work, interests, family, friends) and subtopics within these main topics, written on each. There should be one topic to a card. Write the word "TOPIC" on the back of each card. You should make 50 TOPIC cards.

   b. *Make CONTINUE cards.* Take 24 index cards and write the word "CONTINUE" on the back of each. Now, write the word "Comment" on the other side of eight of those cards. Write "Add information" on the other side of eight more. Write "Ask" on the other side of the remaining eight.

5. **As you construct the game, teach your student about what it means to comment on, add information to, and ask questions about what someone says about a topic.** Practice if necessary.

6. **Teach the student how to play the game.** To play (rules for three or more players):

   a. Make two stacks of cards. The first pile should include all 50 TOPIC cards. Place them, face down, on the table. The second pile should include all 24 of the CONTINUE cards, shuffled.

   b. Player 1 chooses a TOPIC card. The other players will choose a card from the CONTINUE pile.

   c. Player 1 then formulates and gives one topic sentence and two supporting details about the topic on his card.

   d. The other players will respond by completing the actions on their individual CONTINUE cards.

   e. Player 1 responds to the statements or questions of the other players.

   f. Once player 1 has responded, all players discard their original cards.

   g. A new player then chooses a TOPIC card.

   h. The other players choose new CONTINUE cards, and the play continues.

7. **Remind and discuss with the student the definitions of false starts, hesitations, and an excessively rapid rate of speech (without pauses).** Tell him he will need to be mindful of all of these in his own speech while playing the game. Remind him to stop at the end of each and every sentence and to breathe at the end of each and every sentence. He must also pause at clause boundaries ("commas"), as he has learned in past lessons.

8. **Play the *Conversation Game: Topic Talk*.** Remind your student to be certain he uses the Breath–Pause technique throughout the game.

   You will need to use this modification of the game rules for only two players. In this version, set up the game in the same way as for standard play. Player 1 chooses a TOPIC card. Player 1 generates a topic sentence and two details. Player 2 chooses a CONTINUE card and does what it says on his card. Player 1 responds. Then Player 2 chooses another CONTINUE card and does what it says. Player 1 responds. Player 2 chooses a third CONTINUE card and does what it says. Player 1 responds. Then Player 2 picks up a TOPIC card and play continues as above. If your student does not use the Rules for Fluency, stop him and have him take a calming breath and start again.

9. **Make sure your student takes his Conversation Game cards home.**

10. **Homework:** Play the Conversation Game with your parents, family members, or friends during the week (three or more players). Make sure you take home the rules for how to play (Handout A) so that you have the instructions for the game and can show them to anyone who plays with you. Make sure to use the Rules for Fluency every time you play.

✓

The Conversation Game: Topic Talk

Materials

TOPIC cards: 50 TOPIC cards with a single topic written on each

CONTINUE cards: 24 CONTINUE cards – eight with the words "Add information" on the other side, eight with the word "Ask" on the other side, and eight with the word "Comment" on the other side

To play (for three or more players):

a. Make two stacks of cards. The first pile should include all 50 TOPIC cards. Place them, face down, on the table. The second pile should include all 24 of the CONTINUE cards, shuffled.

b. Player 1 chooses a TOPIC card. The other players will choose a card from the CONTINUE pile.

c. Player 1 then formulates and gives one topic sentence and two supporting details about the topic on his card.

d. The other players will respond by completing the actions on their individual CONTINUE cards.

e. Player 1 responds to the statements or questions of the other players.

f. Once Player 1 has responded, all players discard their original cards.

g. A new player then chooses a TOPIC card.

h. The other players choose new CONTINUE cards, and the play continues.

Note: Modification for just two players

In this version, set up the game in the same way as for standard play. Player 1 chooses a TOPIC card. Player 1 generates a topic sentence and two details. Player 2 chooses a CONTINUE card and does what it says on his card. Player 1 responds. Then Player 2 chooses another CONTINUE card and does what it says. Player 1 responds. Player 2 chooses a third CONTINUE card and does what it says. Player 1 responds. Then Player 2 picks up a TOPIC card and play continues as above. If your student does not use the Rules for Fluency, stop him and have him take a calming breath and start again.

Achieving fluency in spontaneously generated small talk

Materials

Handout A: Small-Talk Questions

Handout B: The Two-Question Rule

Handout B from Lesson 9: Sequential Graphic Organizer: Small Talk – Blank

Goals

To learn to formulate spontaneously generated small talk using the two-question rule, and applying the Rules for Fluency.

To practice asking and answering small-talk questions, and continuing a small-talk conversation by asking follow-up questions, adding information, and making comments (as in the Conversation Game), all while applying the Rules for Fluency.

Procedures

1. **Review the homework from the last lesson.** Discuss how your student did playing the Conversation Game with his family or friends. Play one round of the game with him according to the rules for just two players. Give feedback regarding his topic sentences, comments, questions, and additions of information as well as his application of the Rules for Fluency.

2. **Explain the purpose of this lesson:** To practice asking and answering small-talk questions, and continuing a small-talk conversation by asking follow-up questions, adding information, and making comments (as in the Conversation Game), all while applying the Rules for Fluency.

3. **Review the Rules for Fluency and how to use the Breath–Pause technique.** Explain to the student that when the Breath–Pause technique is used in a stealth way, only the student will know he is using it. Tell the student that he will be applying the Breath–Pause technique to spontaneously generated language. Tell him to expect a difficult lesson, but that you will be helping him by giving him reminders throughout.

4. **What to do when asked a small-talk question.** Give the student Handout A: Small-Talk Questions. Explain that when he is asked a small-talk question, he can give himself time to formulate an answer. This

can be achieved by employing Handout B: The Two-Question Rule. The two-question rule indicates that the person who is asked a small-talk question answers briefly and then reflects the first speaker's question back. Practice this with your student using the questions in Handout A, being certain to apply the Rules for Fluency.

5. **What to do to initiate a small-talk conversation.** Tell your student that he can initiate small talk by asking a small-talk question. Then he must listen carefully to the response. Have him ask you three of the small-talk questions in Handout A, applying the Rules for Fluency each time.

6. **How to continue a small-talk conversation.** If after answering a small-talk question or getting an answer to his question there is time, and the other person seems interested in continuing the conversation, he can continue the conversation in the ways he learned in the Conversation Game. Ask him to tell you the three ways to continue a conversation (i.e., follow-up questions, adding information, and making comments). Explain that small talk can also make a bridge between the greeting and the main point of the conversation. Small-talk topics are always very general and can be discussed by anyone.

7. **Now the student should choose and ask a small-talk question.** Based on your response he should ask a follow-up question. After each answer you give, he should formulate another follow-up question for a total of three to five. Make certain he uses the Breath–Pause technique appropriately.

8. **Now you will ask a small-talk question.** He should answer your question and *not* reflect back. Instead he should give a complete response as in Lesson 9, which includes a general response to the topic, a specific topic sentence, and two details. (Give him a copy of Handout B from Lesson 9 to guide him.) You should listen and ask a follow-up question. As the student continues to talk, ask more follow-up questions (three to five). Make certain you both use the Breath–Pause technique appropriately.

9. **Homework:** (a) Make a list of additional topics for small talk. In your notebook, write more questions that can be used to start small talk (e.g., "Will you go away on vacation this summer? Did you hear about [*recent current event*]?"). (b) Play the Conversation Game at home with your parents, a family member, or friend during the week. Make sure to use the Breath–Pause technique to improve fluency.

Small-Talk Questions

How are you?

Have you been doing anything interesting lately?

How was your day?

Did you have a nice weekend?

What are you going to do this weekend?

What did you think of [the test, math, the ballgame last night, etc.]?

Did you see anything good on TV last night?

The Two-Question Rule

1. First person: How are you?

2. Second person: I am fine. *How are you?*

3. First person: I'm doing great, today.

Baker, J.E. (2003) *Social Skills Training for Children and Adolescents with Asperger's Syndrome and Related Social Communication Disorders.* Shawnee Mission, KS: AAPC.

Using small talk to get to know someone

Materials

Handout A: Venn Diagram for Finding Common Interests

Handout B: Topics to Get to Know Someone

Goals

To use a Venn diagram as a visual aid for asking questions to get to know someone better.

To apply the Rules for Fluency to conversation.

Procedures

1. **Review the homework from the last lesson.** Give feedback on your student's small-talk questions.

2. **Explain the purpose of the lesson:** To help your student to use small talk to get to know another person better.

3. **Tell the student that he is expected to use the Rules for Fluency throughout the exercises below.** Review how to use the Breath–Pause technique in a stealth way. Tell him you will be giving him reminders.

4. **Learn to use small talk to get to know someone:**

   a. Give the student a copy of Handout A: Venn Diagram for Finding Common Interests. The student will learn to begin by asking a very general, opening question, followed by questions about school/work, interests, family, and friends (S/Wiff), as well as likes, dislikes, goals, other people, and memories.

   b. Have the student begin the conversation with a greeting and then a good, general opening small-talk question such as, "What have you been doing lately?" (Explain that a question like this will give him information about a person's interests and activities, and a scripted opening like this will help him get started easily with anyone.) The student will listen to your response, and then ask two to three follow-up questions. Then he will fill in on the Venn diagram what he learned with regard to your interests and common interests.

   c. Next the student will ask a small-talk question about one of the topics in Handout B and two to three follow-up questions. Then the student will fill in new information about each of you on his Venn diagram.

    d. Finally, you will ask a small-talk question about one of the topics in Handout B and two to three follow-up questions. And the student, again, will fill in new information about each of you on his Venn diagram.

5. **Homework:**

    a. Play the Conversation Game at home with your parents, a family member, or friend during the week. Make sure to use the Breath–Pause technique to improve fluency.

    b. Use small talk to get to know someone better. Make a Venn diagram about your interests and those of a friend or family member. Study and bring back for discussion.

Venn Diagram for Finding Common Interests

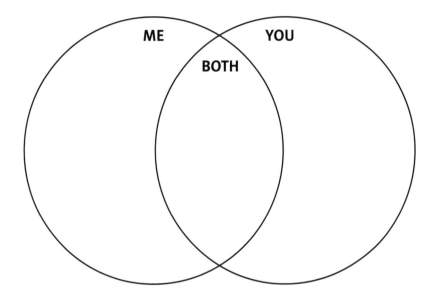

✓

Topics to Get to Know Someone

Ask general and specific questions about:

S/Wiff topics

School/work

Interests

Family

Friends

Other topics

Likes

Dislikes

Goals

Other people

Memories

Learning the red card technique to monitor use of the Rules for Fluency

Materials

Handout C from Lesson 1: Rules for Fluency

A couple of Graphic Organizers from the student's notebook, which were used in earlier lessons

A red laminated piece of oak-tag paper 3" × 5"

Goal

To help the student become more aware of his own dysfluencies or overly rapid rate in spontaneous speech as he is speaking, and then self-correct in the moment by stopping, calming, and beginning again, using the Breath–Pause technique.

Procedures

1. **Explain the purpose of the lesson:** To give the student a nonverbal cue to help him to become more aware of his own false starts, hesitations, and excessive rate of speech, as well as any other dysfluencies in spontaneous speech, while he is speaking; and then to self-correct in the moment by stopping, calming, and beginning again, using the Breath–Pause technique.

2. **Review how to use the Breath–Pause technique in a stealth way.** Tell him that in this lesson, each time he is cued that he is becoming dysfluent or speaking too quickly, he will stop and consciously employ the Rules for Fluency, beginning with a calming breath.

3. **Explain that the red card will be used as a visual cue that tells the student he is currently dysfluent or speaking too quickly.** Show him the card. Explain that up until now you have been verbally stopping him each time he speaks too quickly or becomes dysfluent. When you have done this you have expected him to self-calm and settle himself and then begin speaking again, using Breath–Pause between sentences and at clause boundaries. Tell him that from this lesson forward you will cue him with the red card instead of telling him. The red card is like a "stop" sign. When you hold it up he must just stop speaking and then systematically follow the Rules for Fluency.

4. **Practice cuing with the red card.** Have your student choose two of his past Graphic Organizers from the collection in his notebook. Explain that

as he talks to you based on his Graphic Organizer, you will flash the red card any time he begins to speak too rapidly or if he is dysfluent. When he sees the card he must immediately look at the Rules for Fluency (Handout C from Lesson 1) and follow them as he begins to speak again (i.e., immediately stop, take a calming breath, use "Breath–Pause," formulate his thoughts, and then speak again, fluently, as he continues to use the Breath–Pause technique between sentences and at clause boundaries).

5. **Homework:** Play the Conversation Game at home with your parents, a family member, or friend during the week. Make sure to use the Breath–Pause technique to improve fluency.

Fluently relating information and making a point about something you learned

Materials

Handout C from Lesson 1: Rules for Fluency

Handout A: Soccer Ball–Jump Rope Article

Handout B: Web Graphic Organizer: Soccer Ball–Jump Rope

Handout C: Selfie Accidents Article

Handout D: Web Graphic Organizer: Selfie Accidents

Handout E: How to Shift a Bicycle Uphill Article

Handout F: Web Graphic Organizer: How to Shift a Bicycle Uphill

A red laminated piece of oak-tag paper 3" × 5"

Goal

To learn to fluently summarize and make a point about something the student has learned, using a Web Graphic Organizer to organize spontaneous speech.

Procedures

1. **Explain the purpose of the lesson:** To summarize and make a point about something that the student learns from something he has read or seen on television news, while using the Rules for Fluency.

2. **Read the article in Handout A together.** As you read it the first time, help your student to identify the main topic and subtopics. If he is having any difficulty identifying the subtopics in the article, help him by writing facts from the article on a piece of paper, grouping them according to subtopic. He can then look at each group of facts and label each (with a subtopic label).

3. **Outline his summary of the article with a Web Graphic Organizer.** Once the main topic and subtopics have been identified, have him make a Web Graphic Organizer with the main topic and those subtopics. He should then fill in details that correspond to each subtopic. This is the outline for his summary.

4. **Consider and include the importance of the article in the Web Graphic Organizer.** Now he should add a subtopic called "So what?" (Importance).

He should then fill in the details for why he thinks this information is interesting and important.

5. **Compare his Web Graphic Organizer to the model.** Once his Web Graphic Organizer is complete, have him compare it to the one in Handout B. He should add anything from Handout B which he is missing to his Web Graphic Organizer.

6. **Now he should tell you about the article, including the point he wants to make, using his Web Graphic Organizer.** Tell him to be certain to use the Rules for Fluency as he tells you about his article. You will use the red card to alert him to times when he is speaking too rapidly or is dysfluent. When he sees the red card flashed, he must immediately look at the Rules for Fluency (Handout C from Lesson 1) and follow them as he begins to speak again (i.e., immediately stop, take a calming breath, use "Breath–Pause," formulate his thoughts, and then speak again, fluently, as he continues to use the Breath–Pause technique between sentences and at clause boundaries).

7. **Give the student Handouts C, D, E, and F to look at for homework.**

8. **Homework:**

   a. Play the Conversation Game at home with your parents, a family member, or friend during the week. Make sure to use the Breath–Pause technique to improve fluency.

   b. Choose either the article in Handout C or the one in Handout E, read it, make a Web Graphic Organizer to summarize the article, and make a point about that article. Use the Web Graphic Organizer in Handout D or F for comparison. Practice talking to people you know about the article and your thoughts, using the Breath–Pause technique to aid fluency by reducing false starts and hesitations.

Soccer Ball–Jump Rope Article

Soccer Balls and Jump Ropes Generate Power

A company called Uncharted Play has developed an interesting and important power source for developing countries (including Brazil, Nigeria, Haiti) in the form of toys that generate electricity. Jessica Matthews and Julia Silverman founded the company.

Years before, when Jessica visited her cousins in Nigeria, she identified a significant challenge in that country. Daily life was seriously negatively impacted by inconsistent access to electricity. When Jessica was a junior at Harvard, she was given an assignment in her engineering class to build something that would address a central challenge in developing countries. She teamed up with some fellow students, including Julia and they invented Soccket. Soccket is a normal looking soccer ball that captures kinetic energy as it is being kicked around and can then supply electricity to an LED light for up to 72 hours. The researchers found that they could charge a "shake-to-charge" flashlight by rolling it around in a ball. Their final design is a soccer ball with a pendulum inside which drives a motor as it is being rolled around, which in turn charges a lithium-ion battery. The ball itself has an outlet for plugging in the LED light and with a USB cord the ball can charge mobile phones and even a water filtration machine. The tricky part was to make the ball light enough and bouncy enough to play soccer with, yet tough enough that the energy producing mechanism inside could not be destroyed.

In addition to the Soccket, Jessica developed a jump rope ("the Pulse"), which also captures kinetic energy generated while spinning the rope. This toy generates electricity even faster than the Soccket.

Reference

Li, Z. (2015) These Soccer Balls and Jump Ropes Can Generate Power. Uncharted Play, a New York City-Based Startup, Enables Children in Developing Countries to Build Reserves of Energy Through Play. www.smithsonianmag.com/innovation/ soccer-balls-and- jump-ropes-can-generate-power-180955853/?no-ist

Web Graphic Organizer: Soccer Ball–Jump Rope

- Energy through play movement
- Plug LED lamp into ball
- USB cable

- Harvard students
- Engineering class
- Class project

How the toys work

Inventors

Toys that Generate Usable Electricity

"So what?" (Importance)

Challenges

- For third world villages
- Provides electrical power where there is none or it is erratic
- Charges phones/water filtration
- Could help kids get homework done

- Protecting mechanism
- Protecting generation
- Making the ball light/bouncy enough to actually play soccer with

✓

Selfie Accidents Article

Selfie Accidents Have Killed More People Than Sharks Attacks

In her article in the Huffington Post, Hillary Hanson reported that selfie accidents have killed more people than sharks. In fact, according to Conde Nast Traveler, in one year, 12 people died in Selfie accidents while only 8 had died in shark attacks and only 6 of these were unprovoked. Ms. Hanson seemed most interested in dispelling people's fear of sharks but it is remarkable how many people die due to the distraction associated with taking selfies.

Why do people risk taking selfies in dangerous situations? It seems from the examples in the article that some people, who may be social media junkies, want fame, or they want to show off their courage. They may want to record an event so that they keep a special memory or they may want proof that they were in a special place. Sometimes the selfie takers may be unaware of some impending danger. Sometimes dangerous events are actually created by the Selfie takers themselves.

So who are these people who lost their lives in taking Selfies? Some Selfie-related deaths involved tourists, like the young man who died falling down the stairs when he tried to take a Selfie at the Taj Mahal. Taking the selfie distracted him. Some who died taking selfies were thrill seekers, like the students who were killed when they were taking Selfies on train tracks, and were hit by an oncoming train, or the teen was killed when she tried to take a selfie while on top of a train and she touched live high-voltage wire. Other thrill seekers were killed when they took a Selfie with a live hand grenade. Two people accidentally shot themselves while trying to take Selfies with a gun. In most cases people were overconfident and taking chances. They wanted the rush of energy and ignored the risks.

Reference

Hanson, H. (2015) Selfie Accidents Have Killed More People Than Sharks This Year, But Both Types of Fatalities Are Pretty Rare. www.huffingtonpost.com/entry/selfie-deaths-shark- attacks_us_5602c0c5e4b0fde8b0d09cbe

✓

Web Graphic Organizer: Selfie Accidents

- Proving one's courage
- Showing off
- Fame
- Making special memories
- Recording event for proof

- People taking selfies
- People using cell phone
- Thrill seekers
- Tourists
- Social media junkies

Why take the chance?

Who dies?

Do selfies cause more deaths than shark attacks?

Why people die?

Where it happens

"So what?" (importance)

- Taking chances
- Get distracted
- Overconfident
- Ignoring laws of nature
- Seeking a rush of energy

- Dangerous place
- Dangerous event
- Dangerous action
- Unaware of danger

How to Shift a Bicycle Uphill Article

By Beth Rifkin

Beth Rifkin wrote a helpful article about the most effective way to ride a bicycle up hills. There is no question that climbing steep hills on a bicycle is physically challenging. The article says that conquering hills is made easier by correctly adjusting the bicycle's gears. Lower gears make the bicycle easier to pedal, while higher gears make it harder to pedal. This means that shifting the bicycle into a lower gear will make it easier to get up a hill.

Ms. Rifkin indicates that the first thing to do is to get into a regular pedaling speed (pedal stroke/minute). This is called your cadence. The idea when heading up a hill is to keep the same cadence that you had when on flatter ground. The next thing she says is, do not stand to pedal up hill. If you down shift correctly, you can stay seated. You use less energy this way and it is easier to balance. Sliding back on the bicycle seat and leaning forward as you start up the hill also aids balance. As you head up the hill your cadence will start to slow down. The idea is to always keep it the same. So as soon as it starts to slow, she says shift into a lower gear in the front first and then to a lower gear on the back tire. Any time the resistance becomes enough that your cadence slows again it is time to down shift.

She says that it is important for beginners to practice shifting gears on flat ground first to get used to it and then to start with smaller hills first. Learning an effective way to ride a bicycle up hills means less getting off the bike to walk it up the hills, and a safer more relaxing ride.

Reference

Rifkin, B. (2013) *How to Shift a Bicycle Uphill.* www.livestrong.com/article/480124-how-to-shift-a-bicycle-uphill

✓

Web Graphic Organizer: How to Shift a Bicycle Uphill

• Don't have to get off the bike as much
• Ride up hills easier
• Less tired

• Smooth gear changing
• Best time to shift gears
• The order in which to shift the gears (front first)

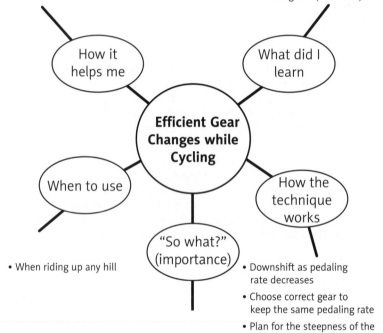

How it helps me

What did I learn

Efficient Gear Changes while Cycling

When to use

How the technique works

"So what?" (importance)

• When riding up any hill

• Downshift as pedaling rate decreases
• Choose correct gear to keep the same pedaling rate
• Plan for the steepness of the hill

Applying the Rules for Fluency to spontaneous conversation

Materials

A red laminated piece of oak-tag paper 3" × 5"

Goals

To practice applying the Rules for Fluency in structured spontaneous conversation.

To obtain an outcome assessment.

Procedures

1. **Explain the purpose of the lesson:** To practice applying the Rules for Fluency. The student will do this in playing the Conversation Game, in telling about something he has learned, and in spontaneous conversation.

2. **Play the Conversation Game (according to the rules for just two players).** Listen to the quality of his topic sentences, questions, comments, and additions to the conversation. Encourage him to use the Rules for Fluency. Use the red card as you play, to alert him to any dysfluencies or overly rapid speech.

3. **Review the homework from the last lesson.** Check his Web Graphic Organizer. Ask him to orally summarize what he learned from the article he read and what he views as the importance of the article. As he talks, you should ask questions, make comments, and add information. Encourage him to use the Rules for Fluency. Use the red card to alert him to any dysfluencies or overly rapid speech.

4. **Now you should orally summarize the remaining article from the last lesson, using the included Web Graphic Organizer.** As you do this, your student should ask questions, make comments, and add information. He should again use the Rules for Fluency. Also use the red card to stop him when there are dysfluencies or he speaks too quickly.

5. **Use the Fluency Assessment at the beginning of this chapter to do an outcome assessment.** Let the student listen to the recordings of the story he told at baseline and the story he tells today. Ask for his observations and comments.

6. **Homework:** Play the Conversation Game at home with your parents, a family member, or friend during the week. Make sure to use the Breath–Pause technique to improve fluency.

CHAPTER 6

Pitch

Introduction: Pitch modulation to convey meaning

This set of lessons is for students who do not use pitch appropriately in speech. Impairment in the use of pitch modulation in speech may involve overall pitch, pitch contour, or stress through the use of pitch. The modal register of the voice is the one used most frequently in spoken language.

Overall pitch in individuals with ASD may be too high (falsetto range) or too low, which may include vocal fry. Vocal fry (creaky voice) is created when the vocal cords are loosely approximated and allowed to flap, releasing small irregular sputs of air and sound. When pitch is too low, it is often associated with low volume. For the student who speaks in an overall low pitch range and/or in too low a volume, the inability to monitor breathing and coordinate breath-support may be the culprits. This must be addressed using lessons in Chapter 4 on Volume in this book.

Some individuals with ASD may produce utterances with an appropriate overall pitch but may not regulate or be able to make changes within overall pitch, appropriately responding to the person with whom they are speaking. Specifically, it is appropriate to use a higher overall pitch when speaking to a young child but not to an adult.

Pitch contour is the rise and fall of pitch in speech over time, which affects the meaning of spoken language. Pitch contour signifies sentence type (e.g., question or statement). Pitch contour can be disrupted in people with ASD in a few ways. Pitch contour can be "sing-song" (exaggerated pitch), flat, and inflexible, with little or no pitch variation.

Stress through pitch is an important tool for expression and effective communication of meaning. When there is a failure to emphasize certain words over others, intended meaning is lost. English is a language of variable stress. This means that any word in a sentence can be stressed over others, modifying the meaning of the sentence. Different syllables within words, again spelled the same, can be stressed, resulting in two versions of the word with completely different meanings. Often one version is a noun and the other a verb (e.g., **pre**sent versus pre**sent**). The lessons in this chapter teach the student how to effectively use pitch change to stress particular words in a sentence, or syllables within words, to communicate the intended message. Incorrect use of stress is one of the major deficits in prosody identified in people with ASD.

The sequence of lessons in this chapter is constructed to teach your student how to vocally modulate pitch in speech, and then how to apply those modulations to his language, in order to communicate more expressively and therefore effectively. As in other chapters of this book, the student is taught a visual notation system. Pitch notation serves to make him aware of pitch modulation and how it is used to convey meaning. It gives the student the opportunity for better control over how he modulates his pitch.

It is essential that your student practices these skills. This practice is accomplished during the lessons themselves, enforced with direction and feedback from the therapist, and through homework assignments (which generalize the skills to the rest of life). Practice serves to automate the newly acquired motor skills, which then allows the student to allocate more of his attentional resources to what he wants to say rather than to how he will produce the sound. The student will keep copies of all handouts, homework, and notes in a three-ring binder, which he can refer to at home to practice and must bring to all lessons. The lessons are developmentally ordered. Later lessons refer back to concepts in earlier ones and make repeated use of materials from earlier lessons to solidify the concepts as the student develops the skills.

LESSON 1

Assessment/learning pitch modulation

Materials

Handout A: Pitch Practice Sentences

Goals

To assess the student's modulation of pitch: pattern and range.

To learn to modulate pitch.

Procedures

1. **Explain how people use pitch in speech.** Begin by explaining the concept of pitch and how it enhances communication. People usually speak at a pitch level which is comfortable for them, including pitch variations for emphasis and to distinguish statements from questions, as well as their emotional state. It is distracting to speak with a pitch that is consistently too high, too low, monotone, or sing-song.

2. **Listen to the student's speech and record a baseline sample.** Have the student tell you about the last time he got a gift from someone, who it was from, what it was, and how he felt about getting that gift. Record this. (You will transcribe this story for use in Lesson 9.) Discuss your observations of your student's use of pitch in speech. Is it consistently too high, too low, monotone, or sing-song? Does the student use an appropriate pitch contour to mark statements as distinct from questions? Does the student use pitch appropriately to stress specific syllables in words or important words in sentences? Ask the student to pretend he is speaking to a baby. Does the student change overall pitch depending on the person to whom he is speaking (e.g., higher for children, lower for adults)?

3. **Explain that in this lesson you will be teaching him to produce a wide range of pitches and then to gain control over those different pitches.** Now you will model/produce sounds which will help him learn this skill.

4. **Have the student imitate the sound of a baby crying.** The purpose of this exercise is to familiarize the student with the sensations associated with vocal pitch change. Begin by making a sound like a baby crying (a series of individual cries, on "Eh"). Begin at a pitch that is comfortable. As you produce each crying sound (a single sustained "Eh" sound, lasting three to four seconds), make sure the pitch falls. Practice these sounds in sets of five.

Note: Glottal inhalation is preferred, but not necessary. A glottal inhalation is how you inhale as if you were recovering from not being able to breathe for a long period of time and then you have to breathe so badly that you gasp for that first breath; or when you are holding your breath under water for a long time until you must come up for air and, as you do, you gasp for that first breath. Glottal inhalation promotes active diaphragmatic breath support and musculature awareness.

5. **Have the student imitate the sound of an excited chimpanzee:**

   a. The purpose of this exercise is to practice pitch changes, while engaging diaphragmatic breath support. This exercise is especially helpful for students who speak consistently in a lower-than-normal pitch range. Begin by making a sound, imitating the sound a chimpanzee makes when it gets excited, anxious, or scared. This is a rapid and repetitive "Eh-Eh-Eh-Eh-Eh-Eh-Eh" sound, beginning at a low pitch and rising to a high pitch. Repeat "Eh" rapidly, 15 times, with glottal inhalations between each "Eh."

   b. Now create your own pattern of rising and falling pitches in your chimpanzee sounds. Have the student imitate. The pattern doesn't have to be consistently the same, and he does not have to imitate you exactly. The student must try to obtain some variance in pitch.

6. **Have the student imitate various forms of pitch glide.** The purpose of this exercise is for the student to learn to produce pitch variation on one sustained breath and to explore the pitch range of his own voice.

   a. *Siren.* The student will imitate a sustained siren sound, beginning at the lowest pitch in the student's natural range, rising four or five seconds to the highest pitch that the student can produce, and then falling four or five seconds back to the approximate original pitch.

   b. *Mooing.* Repeat step (a), but this time mooing like a cow.

   c. *On an open vowel.* Repeat step (a) on the open vowel "Uh."

7. **Have the student produce meaningless "sentences" with pitch variation:**

   a. Repeat seven "Bahs" at a high pitch, on one sustained breath (like a little lamb). Repeat the set three times.

   b. Repeat seven "Bahs" at a low pitch, on one sustained breath (like a big old sheep). Repeat the set three times.

   c. Walk with the student to one side of the room while, in unison, you repeat "Bah," rising from a low pitch to a high pitch over the course of four "Bahs." Reverse direction and, while walking back, repeat "Bah" again four times, falling back to the approximate original pitch. Repeat the set three times.

8. **Have the student produce sentences with pitch variation:**

    a. Repeat the sentence "Someone's been sitting in my chair, said the baby bear" at a high pitch, on one sustained breath. Repeat the set three times.

    b. Repeat the sentence "Someone's been sitting in my chair, said the papa bear" at a low pitch, on one sustained breath. Repeat the set three times.

    c. Have the student walk to one side of the room while repeating the sentence "Mama bear said, I don't know why everyone is talking about chairs," rising from a low pitch to a high pitch. Have the student reverse direction and repeat the same sentence while walking back, beginning at the high pitch and falling back to the approximate original pitch. Repeat the set three times.

9. **Homework:** Practice producing the sentences in Handout A in the following four ways: high pitch, low pitch, rising pitch, and falling pitch.

Pitch Practice Sentences

1. We like chocolate cake.

2. Albert Einstein was an amazing human being.

3. This market has lots of fresh fruit.

4. The men are almost finished putting the roof on the new building.

5. Someday, I'll paint a picture of you.

LESSON 2

Pitch modulation: Tones

Materials

Pitch Cards. (*Create the following six Pitch Cards by drawing each symbol on an index card with its corresponding title. These will be used in future lessons as well.*) See Appendix A for a model:

- a diagonal line ascending to the right, with the title "Pitch Rising"
- a diagonal line descending to the right, with the title "Pitch Falling"
- two monotone pitch lines, a lower one followed by a higher one, with the title "Pitch Lift"
- two monotone pitch lines, a higher one followed by a lower one, with the title "Pitch Drop"
- a horizontal line, staying level, with the title "Same Pitch"
- a curved line starting low, showing a peak at the center of the card, and coming back down, with the title "Pitch Glide"

Goal

To learn notation, associated with change in pitch.

Procedures

1. **Review the homework from the last lesson.**

2. **Explain the purpose of the lesson:** To learn to convey meaning effectively by stressing particular words through changes in pitch.

3. **Demonstrate for the student how changes in pitch change meaning.** Say each of the following phrases, first by ending with a rising intonation, and then again, ending with a falling intonation. Ask the student to listen and identify, by pointing up or down, whether the pitch rises or falls at the end of each of these sentences.

   - You finished your homework.
   - The dog ran around the park.
   - Sally is a nice girl.

   Ask your student to explain how the meaning changed as a result of the change in pitch. The student should tell you that one version was a statement and one was a question.

4. **Show the student the Pitch Cards.** As you hold up each Pitch Card, tell the student the title of that card and, with a neutral vowel ("Uh"), demonstrate the pitch change associated with the notation depicted on that card.

5. **Have the student read the notation.** As you hold each card up, have the student imitate you as you read the notation, as in step 4. Then have the student read the notation without your prompts.

6. **Have the student practice reading pitch change notation.** Write a random sequence of the symbols (from the Pitch Cards) which depict changes in pitch, and teach the student to read the "tone sentences" as written, using a neutral vowel ("Uh"). Demonstrate first and then have the student read. For example:

7. **Have the student practice reading pitch change notation using different vowels.** Write a series of the symbols which depict changes in pitch and teach the student to read the "tone sentences" as written, saying the vowel written beneath each symbol. Demonstrate first and then have the student read. The following are examples. Note that, in the first example, the first two syllables are pronounced with two different flat pitches (the first higher and the second lower) and then the last syllable is pronounced with a rising pitch. Make sure the student fully understands the notation.

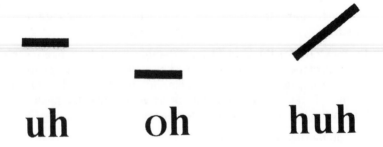

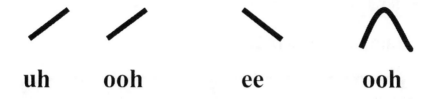

uh   ooh   ee   ooh

8. **Homework:** Create and write five of your own "tone sentences" using these symbols. Practice them at home and bring them to the next lesson, prepared to read them.

Example of Pitch Cards

Pitch Card	Pitch Card
/	\
Pitch Rising	**Pitch Falling**
Pitch Card	Pitch Card
▬ (upper right, lower left)	▬ (upper left, lower right)
Pitch Lift	**Pitch Drop**
Pitch Card	Pitch Card
▬	⌒
Same Pitch	**Pitch Glide**

LESSON 3

Pitch stress and word meaning

Materials

The six Pitch Cards you made for Lesson 2

Goal

To learn how the application of different pitch patterns to the same word changes the meaning of the word.

Procedures

1. **Review the homework from the last lesson.** Have the student show you his "tone sentences" and read them together.

2. **Review the Pitch Card notation.** Show the student the six Pitch Cards and, using a neutral vowel ("Uh"), have him practice the pitch changes signified by the notation on each card.

3. **Explain the purpose of the lesson:** To learn how the application of different pitch patterns to the same word changes the meaning of the word.

4. **Teach the student the concept of grammatical stress.** Write the word "present" twice. Ask the student if he can think of two different ways to say that word. Explain that pitch can be used to stress one syllable over the other. Differences in pitch patterns *completely change* the meaning of the word and often its part of speech. Changing the pitch pattern often changes a word from a noun to verb or verb to a noun. This is called grammatical stress. Give the student the following example:

Now have the student say each of the following words in two different ways, noticing how the change in pitch pattern changes the word from a noun to a verb: *produce, convict, permit, record.*

5. **Demonstrate the concept of how the meaning of any word can change with use of different pitch patterns.** Write the word "important" three times. Say the word three different ways: once with a flat intonation, a

second time with a rising intonation at the end of the word, and a third time with an intonation that first rises and then falls, with the highest pitch occurring on the second syllable. Then say the word "important" in each of the three ways again, having the student write the pitch notation over the word immediately after you say each version of the word (see example below). Then explain to the student that this exercise shows that the same word means something *slightly* different, depending on the pitch(es) with which it was said. Now ask him to tell you what each version means.

Important   Important   Important

6. **Have the student apply at least three different pitch patterns to the same word.** The student will apply the pitch notation symbols to make pitch changes to a particular word so as to modify its meaning. Use the Pitch Cards as a reminder for how to notate pitch change. Have him write his three versions of each of the following words: *nice, exciting, hungry, nutritious, wonderful*. Discuss how the meaning of each word changes, depending on pitch.

7. **Have the student apply different pitch patterns to phrases.** The student will apply the pitch notation symbols to make pitch changes to each phrase so as to modify its meaning. The student will show changing pitches, both ascending and descending, within words and across the following phrases: *I know you, I believe that*. Make sure the student is aware of the change in meaning and feelings which are created with each variation in pitch and discuss. Note that the last example denotes sarcasm.

I believe that   I believe that   I believe that

8. **Homework:** Write each of the following phrases twice, and apply different pitch patterns to each of them. Then practice all your examples.

   a. It's hot.

   b. Pay attention.

   c. You're sure.

   d. You're silly.

Pitch stress in sentences

Materials

Handout A: Pitch Contour Signifying Sentence Type

Handout B: Change in Sentence Meaning Based on the Word that is Stressed

Goal

To learn how pitch is used in sentences to: (1) signify sentence type (statement or question); and (2) emphasize a particular meaning of a sentence.

Procedures

1. **Review the homework from the last lesson.**

2. **Explain the purpose of the lesson:** To learn how pitch is used in sentences to: (1) signify sentence type; and (2) emphasize a particular meaning of a sentence. (*Note:* If the student is having an issue with overall pitch, then this must be addressed in this lesson at the same time as modulation of pitch.)

3. **Explain to the student that one way pitch is used in sentences is to show the difference between a question and a statement.** A question is signified by a rising intonation at the end, while a sentence ends with a falling intonation.

4. **Give the student Handout A: Pitch Contour Signifying Sentence Type to complete.** Have the student read each phrase below, put the correct notation over the final word of the phrase, and then read the phrase with the appropriate corresponding intonation:

   - Hello. I know you.
   - That's exciting.
   - Can your sister swim?
   - I didn't have breakfast.
   - Are you hungry?
   - Apples are nutritious.
   - Please sit down over there.
   - Did you finish the test?

- Are you scared?
- Did you find your key?

5. **Explain that another way pitch is used in sentences is to stress a particular word in order to produce a specific meaning of that sentence.** To illustrate this point, do the following exercise. Write the sentence, "I want chocolate ice-cream." Place the pitch notation symbol over the word "chocolate." Two monotone symbols should be placed over the word, one over each syllable, with the first being higher than the second, signifying that the word "chocolate" is stressed. Have the student read the sentence as notated. Now move these pitch symbols to the word "ice-cream," indicating that now "ice-cream" is the word that is stressed. Then ask specifically what the difference is in the meaning of the sentence, depending on which word is stressed. In the first example, the speaker is indicating that he would prefer to have chocolate ice-cream rather than any other flavor. In the second example, the speaker is indicating that he would prefer to have ice-cream rather than any other dessert.

6. **Now have the student complete Handout B.** In each version of the same sentence, a particular word is stressed over all the others (indicated by bold italic type). The student should write the correct pitch notation above the sentence so that the emphasized word in the sentence is stressed. He should then read each version of the sentence as indicated by the pitch notation. He should then write the meaning of each sentence below.

7. **Homework:** Generate one sentence between five and ten words long, then choose three words in the sentence to stress (in three different versions of the sentence) and write the correct pitch notation above the words in the sentence, using all three versions. Write down the specific meaning of each version of the word.

Pitch Contour Signifying Sentence Type

- Hello. I know you.

- That's exciting.

- Can your sister swim?

- I didn't have breakfast.

- Are you hungry?

- Apples are nutritious.

- Please sit down over there.

- Did you finish the test?

- Are you scared?

- Did you find your key?

Change in Sentence Meaning Based on the Word that is Stressed

I don't think we should buy this new car.

_____

I **don't** think we should buy this new car.

_____

I don't **think** we should buy this new car.

_____

I don't think **we** should buy this new car.

_____

I don't think we **should** buy this new car.

_____

I don't think we should **buy** this new car.

_____

I don't think we should buy **this** new car.

_____

I don't think we should buy this **new** car.

_____

I don't think we should buy this new **car.**

_____

Pitch stress in poetry 1

Materials

Two copies of the poem *Messy Room* by Shel Silverstein (Silverstein, S. (1981) *"Bear in There."* In H. Collins (ed) *A Light in the Attic.* New York, NY: Harper Collins)

Handout A: Example Notation

The six Pitch Cards

Yellow highlighter

Goals

To practice modifying pitch for a given audience (specifically, use a higher pitch when speaking to younger children and a lower pitch when speaking to adults).

To practice the use of pitch change to stress specific words in connected speech in order to convey meaning.

Procedures

1. **Review the homework from the last lesson.** Give any needed clarification and make any needed corrections.

2. **Explain the purpose of the lesson:** (1) To practice using different overall pitches depending on the audience. Specifically, to use a higher pitch when speaking to little children and a lower pitch when speaking to adults. (2) To practice the use of pitch change to stress specific words in connected speech in order to convey meaning and emotion.

3. **Have the student read the poem.** Give the student Handout A and ask him to read out loud the poem *Messy Room* by Shel Silverstein. Allow him to read this in any way that he wants. Do not provide any direction. Record him as he does this.

4. **Discuss the appropriate use of different overall pitches when speaking with little children and with adults.** Model saying "You love chocolate, don't you?" with an appropriate higher pitch for a little child and then with an appropriate lower pitch for speaking to an adult. Now have the student do it.

5. **Read the poem with a higher or lower overall pitch.** Have the student read *Messy Room* with an overall high pitch, as if he is reading to a little child. (*Note:* Be sure he does not increase volume when increasing pitch.)

You might want to use a picture of a child to keep your student focused on the idea. Then have the student read the story at a normal, overall lower pitch to you, an adult. Provide feedback.

6. **Add pitch modulation to overall pitch – review the Pitch Cards with the student.**

7. **Give the student Handout A: Example Notation.** Have him notate the specific words in the first two lines of the poem according to the handout. He should not notate any of the other words in those lines. Discuss how and why this excerpt from the poem is notated for pitch changes in the way that it is. How do the pitch changes enhance conveying the meaning of the poem? Discuss that, as he knows, pitch can be used to stress important words and convey emotion.

8. **Look at the entire poem and with the student, determine which words should be stressed through changes in pitch, and how.** Highlight the words that should be stressed with yellow marker. Write the notation for pitch above the words to be stressed. This includes rising or falling pitch at the end of sentences.

9. **Read the poem out loud, following the notation.** You should read the poem first to the student so as to model the appropriate use of the notation. Then have the student read the poem out loud, employing the notation. Make corrections as needed during the student's first reading. Have the student read the poem a second time, employing the notation. Record this.

10. **Compare the recordings.** Play back and listen to the first recording and then the second. Discuss how stressing specific words through pitch change affected the meaning and feeling of the poem.

11. **Homework:** Practice reading the poem *Messy Room* following the pitch notation, and be ready to speak it.

Example Notation

Messy Room, by Shel Silverstein

Whosever room this is should be ashamed!

His underwear is hanging on the lamp.

Pitch stress in poetry 2

Materials

Handout A: Poem to be Notated by Student
The six Pitch Cards
Yellow highlighter

Goal

To practice the use of pitch change to stress specific words in connected speech in order to convey meaning and emotion.

Procedures

1. **Review the homework from the last lesson.** Listen to the student read the poem *Messy Room* according to the pitch notation. Give feedback as needed.

2. **Explain the purpose of the lesson:** To practice the use of pitch change to stress specific words in connected speech in order to convey meaning and emotion. (*Note:* If the student is having an issue with overall pitch, continue to address that in this lesson at the same time as modulation of pitch.)

3. **Have the student read out loud the poem *The Road Not Taken* by Robert Frost (Handout A).** Allow him to read this in any way that he wants. Do not provide any direction. Record him as he does this.

4. **Look at the poem together and, with the student, determine which words should be stressed through changes in pitch, and how.** Highlight the words that should be stressed with yellow marker. Write the notation for pitch above the words to be stressed.

5. **Read the poem out loud, following the notation.** You should read the poem first to the student so as to model the appropriate use of the notation. Then have the student read the poem out loud, employing the notation. Make corrections as needed during the student's first reading. Have the student read the poem a second time, employing the notation. Record this.

6. **Compare the recordings.** Play back and listen to the first recording and then the second. Discuss how stressing specific words through pitch change affected the meaning of the poem.

7. **Homework:** Practice reading the poem *The Road Not Taken* by Robert Frost, following the pitch notation, and be ready to speak it.

Poem to be Notated by Student

The Road Not Taken, by Robert Frost

Two roads diverged in a yellow wood,
And sorry I could not travel both
And be one traveler, long I stood
And looked down one as far as I could
To where it bent in the undergrowth;

Then took the other, as just as fair,
And having perhaps the better claim,
Because it was grassy and wanted wear;
Though as for that the passing there
Had worn them really about the same,

And both that morning equally lay
In leaves no step had trodden black.
Oh, I kept the first for another day!
Yet knowing how way leads on to way,
I doubted if I should ever come back.

I shall be telling this with a sigh
Somewhere ages and ages hence:
Two roads diverged in a wood, and I—
I took the one less traveled by,
And that has made all the difference.

LESSON 7

Pitch stress in narrative

Materials

Handout A: Story to be Notated by Student

Yellow highlighter

Goal

To practice the use of pitch change to stress specific words in connected speech in order to convey meaning.

Procedures

1. **Explain the purpose of the lesson:** To practice the use of pitch change to stress specific words in connected speech, specifically a story, to convey meaning. (*Note:* If the student is having an issue with overall pitch, continue to address that in this lesson at the same time as modulation of pitch.)

2. **Have the student read the story out loud (Handout A).** Allow him to read this in any way that he wants. Do not provide any direction. Record him as he does this.

3. **Determine with the student which words should be stressed through changes in pitch, and how.** Highlight the words that should be stressed with yellow marker. Write the notation for rising pitch, falling pitch, and pitch glide above the words to be stressed. This includes rising or falling pitch at the end of sentences.

4. **Read the story out loud, following the notation.** You should read the story first to the student, to model the appropriate use of the notation. Then have the student read the story out loud, employing the notation. Make corrections as needed during the student's first reading. Have the student read the story a second time, employing the notation. Record this.

5. **Compare the recordings.** Play back and listen to the first recording and then the second. Discuss how stressing specific words through pitch change affected the meaning of the story.

6. **Have the student tell the story from memory.** Have the student try to tell the story from memory, using all of the pitch stress markings he used.

7. **Homework:** (1) Tell your story to friends and family. (2) Find a new story to tell. You can ask one of your family members or parents to teach you one. Write the story down, highlight important words, and bring it to the next lesson. Memorize it so you can tell it at the next lesson, using pitch to emphasize important words.

Story to be Notated by Student

Diet Story

A guy goes to his doctor for a check-up.

The doctor puts him on a diet.

The doctor says, "Here is the diet. Eat vegetables and fruits for two days, then skip a day, and then repeat this procedure for the next three weeks. Then come back and see me. I expect that you will lose about five pounds in three weeks."

When the guy goes back to see the doctor in three weeks, he has lost 20 pounds!

The doctor can't believe it! And asks, "How did you do that?!? Did you follow the diet I gave you?"

The guy says, "Yes I did. That diet is really tough. I thought I was going to drop dead that third day."

The doctor asks, "From hunger, you mean?"

"No, from skipping."

LESSON 8

Pitch stress in written text

Materials

Handout A: Speech to be Notated by Student
Yellow highlighter

Goal

To practice the use of pitch change to stress specific words in connected speech in order to convey meaning and emotion.

Procedures

1. **Review the homework from the last lesson.** Have the student tell the story that he practiced, using pitch to emphasize important words.

2. **Explain the purpose of this lesson:** To practice the use of pitch change to stress specific words in connected speech in order to convey meaning and emotion. (*Note:* If the student is having an issue with overall pitch, continue to address that in this lesson at the same time as modulation of pitch.)

3. **Have the student read the speech out loud (Handout A).** Allow him to read this in any way that he wants. Do not provide any direction. Record him as he does this.

4. **Determine with the student which words should be stressed in the first two paragraphs of the speech through changes in pitch, and how.** Highlight the words that should be stressed with yellow marker. Write the notation on Handout A above the words to be stressed. This includes rising or falling pitch at the end of sentences.

5. **Read the speech out loud, following the notation.** You should read the speech first to the student, to model the appropriate use of the notation. Then have the student read the speech out loud, employing the notation. Make corrections as needed during the student's first reading. Have the student read the speech a second time, employing the notation. Record this.

6. **Compare the recordings.** Play back and listen to the first recording and then the second. Discuss how stressing specific words through pitch change affected the meaning of the speech.

7. **Homework:** Practice reading the first paragraph of the speech by Hillary Clinton, following the pitch notation. Read it to family and friends and ask for their feedback. Notate the third and fourth paragraphs of the speech, and practice.

Speech to be Notated by Student

Hillary Rodham Clinton
Remarks to the U.N. 4th World Conference
on Women Plenary Session

Delivered 5 September 1995, Beijing, China

What we are learning around the world is that if women are healthy and educated, their families will flourish. If women are free from violence, their families will flourish. If women have a chance to work and earn as full and equal partners in society, their families will flourish. And when families flourish, communities and nations do as well. That is why every woman, every man, every child, every family, and every nation on this planet does have a stake in the discussion that takes place here.

The great challenge...is to give voice to women everywhere whose experiences go unnoticed, whose words go unheard. Women comprise more than half the world's population, 70 percent of the world's poor, and two-thirds of those who are not taught to read and write. [Women] are the primary caretakers for most of the world's children and elderly. Yet much of the work [women] do is not valued – not by economists, not by historians, not by popular culture, not by government leaders.

At this very moment, as we sit here, women around the world are giving birth, raising children, cooking meals, washing clothes, cleaning houses, planting crops, working on assembly lines, running companies, and running countries. Women also are dying from diseases that should have been prevented or treated. They are watching their children succumb to malnutrition caused by poverty and economic deprivation. They are being denied the right to go to school, by their own fathers and brothers.

I believe that now, on the eve of a new millennium, it is time to break the silence. It...is no longer acceptable to discuss women's rights as separate from human rights. If there is one message that echoes forth from this conference, let it be that human rights are women's rights and women's rights are human rights once and for all.

As long as discrimination and inequities remain so commonplace everywhere in the world, as long as girls and women are valued less, fed less, fed last, overworked, underpaid, not schooled, subjected to violence in and outside their homes – the potential of the human family to create a peaceful, prosperous world will not be realized.

Clinton, H.R. (2004) "Remarks to the U.N. 4th World Conference on Women Plenary Session delivered 5 September 1995, Beijing, China." In X.-A. Lu and R. Sullivan (eds) Gems from the Top 100 Speeches, a Handy Source of Inspiration for your Thoughts and Language. Lincoln, NE: iUniverse.

Applying pitch notation to spontaneous speech

Materials

Handout A: Transcribed Spontaneous Language Sample (from Lesson 1)

Yellow highlighter

Goal

To learn to use pitch variation in spontaneous speech to enhance meaning.

Procedures

1. **Review the homework from the last lesson.** Have the student read the Clinton speech. Give direction as needed. Check the notation of the last two paragraphs.

2. **Explain the purpose of the lesson:** To take a written sample of the student's own speech and evaluate it for the important words and concepts and then learn to use pitch modulation to stress those words and concepts and express emotion.

3. **Give your student the transcription of his spontaneous language sample from Lesson 1.** Tell him that this is a written version of what he said in Lesson 1, many weeks ago. With your student identify the important words in the sample. Highlight the words that should be stressed with yellow marker and use pitch notation to mark the words to be stressed in the language sample.

4. **Have your student read the transcribed sample out loud following the pitch notation.** Record him as he does this.

5. **Compare the original recording of the language sample (from Lesson 1) with the recording with the pitch notation.** Discuss the differences with the student and what he feels he expressed more effectively in the second recording.

6. **Explain to the student that pitch change is only one of the ways to stress words in speech.** The others are volume and rhythm. The use of these for stress will be addressed in Chapter 7.

7. **Homework:** Write a paragraph about anything that interests you (at least five sentences in length). Apply the pitch notation to words you would like to emphasize. Practice reading the paragraph according to the notation. Bring the paragraph to the next lesson and be prepared to read it in the lesson.

Talking about a topic using pitch inflection

Materials

Handout A: Web Graphic Organizer

Yellow highlighter

Goal

To generate speech, based on a Web Graphic Organizer, which has an appropriate overall pitch and pitch changes to enhance meaning.

Procedures

1. **Review the homework from the last lesson.** Look at the paragraph written by the student. Have the student read his paragraph according to the pitch notation he used. Assess how the student read the notation and give feedback. Evaluate the choices the student made for pitch modulation. Make additions and corrections if needed. Read the paragraph out loud so the student can hear it. Reach agreement with the student regarding how pitch is used for emphasis and whether what he wants to emphasize is being stressed. He should then read the paragraph out loud.

2. **Explain the purpose of this lesson:** To generate speech, based on a Web Graphic Organizer, which has an appropriate overall pitch and pitch changes to enhance meaning and emotion.

3. **Give the student Handout A: Web Graphic Organizer.** Instruct the student to fill in details for each of the subtopics to outline the story about one of their best days. Help the student to fill in adequate detail. Then have the student tell the story outlined in the Web Graphic Organizer. Make certain the student begins with an overall topic sentence regarding the main topic, and then begins discussion of each subtopic with a topic sentence, followed by the details associated with it, before moving on to the next subtopic.

4. **With the student, identify important words to stress.** As the student tells the story a second time, stop him after each sentence. Ask him to tell you which words in the sentence are most important. Write these words near the details contained in that sentence on the Web Graphic Organizer and highlight them with a yellow highlighter. Have the student tell you how he will use pitch to emphasize those important words. Write the appropriate pitch notation above those words. (Do not

write out the entire sentence.) Have the student say the sentence again, using pitch for emphasis, the way he had planned.

5. **Now have the student tell the entire story.** He should emphasize the important words he chose, with pitch, in the way that he planned. If he has any difficulty doing this, model for him.

6. **Homework:** Make a Web Graphic Organizer about your favorite vacation or holiday. Tell the story from your Web Graphic Organizer. Then choose which specific words in the story you will emphasize, using pitch. Write them near the details on the Web Graphic Organizer as you did during the lesson. Remember that you should emphasize the words that are important. Practice telling the story by yourself. Make certain to emphasize the important words.

   Once you have practiced, tell your story to an adult and then to a little child. Modify your overall pitch for your listener. You should use a higher pitch for little children and a lower pitch for adults.

✓

Web Graphic Organizer

CHAPTER 7

Stress

Introduction: Using stress to convey meaning

Stress, in spoken language, is the emphasis placed on certain syllables in words or words in sentences. Stress is conveyed by volume, pitch, and rhythm (duration). Stress helps convey meaning and engages the listener. There are two types of stress: grammatical and pragmatic. Grammatical stress provides syntactic information in sentences (Warren 1996). Grammatical stress is also the emphasis on one syllable or another, within a particular word, which determines whether that word is a noun or a verb (e.g., **pre**sent *versus* pre**sent**). Pragmatic/affective stress is the emphasis placed on a particular word within a sentence. That word becomes the focus. This type of stress conveys both meaning and emotion. Pragmatic stress placed on a different word in the exact same sentence changes the intent of the sentence: for example, **I** love your brother's cooking (meaning I love it but nobody else does) *versus* I love **your** brother's cooking (meaning I love your brother's cooking but not my brother's cooking). Deficits in the comprehension and use of grammatical and pragmatic stress are addressed in this chapter.

The *sequence of lessons* in this chapter is constructed to first have your student practice modulating volume, pitch, and rhythm of vocal sounds, and then speech. This chapter moves very quickly from nonverbal vocalization to the application of stress to single words and then to words within sentences. The student is taught that, in spoken connected language, meaning is conveyed not only by the words themselves, but also by which words are stressed. The student learns to define the meanings that differ between two versions of the same sentence when different words are stressed. The work then moves on to the use of stress in connected speech by having the student notate written text with symbols denoting the method (volume, pitch, rhythm) he would like to apply in order to stress specific important informational or emotional words within the text. The stress notation (illustrated in Figure 7.1) serves as a visual cue to support his understanding of this concept. Notating the text gives the student an opportunity for better control over how he modulates his volume, pitch, and rhythm in connected speech. He learns to make choices about which words he will stress based on the meaning he wants to convey. Once he can effectively stress words in written text, he moves on to generating more spontaneous speech based on an outline (Web Graphic Organizer), which allows him to plan in advance what he will say and which words he will stress. He even has the opportunity to apply word stress as he gives a PowerPoint presentation. Finally, he applies his knowledge of how to stress important words in connected speech to his completely spontaneous conversational speech. What the student learns in this chapter of lessons not only allows him to communicate meaning more effectively but also enables him to become more expressive and more capable of engaging his listener.

Figure 7.1 Stress notation cards

It is essential that your student practices these skills. This practice is accomplished during the lessons themselves, enforced with direction and feedback from the therapist, and through homework assignments (which generalize the skills to the rest of life). Practice serves to automate the newly acquired skills, which then allows the student to allocate more of his attentional resources to what he wants to communicate rather than to how he will produce the sound. The lessons are developmentally ordered. Later lessons refer back to concepts in earlier ones. The student will keep copies of all handouts, homework, and notes in his three-ring binder, which he can refer to at home for practice. He must bring it to all lessons.

LESSON 1

Introduction to stress in spoken language

Materials

Audio recording device

Goals

To obtain an evaluation of your student's ability to modulate volume, pitch, duration of sounds, and words in connected speech.

To practice modulation of volume, pitch, and duration of sounds.

To introduce the student to the concept of word stress (appropriate and inappropriate) in connected speech.

Procedures

1. **Explain the purpose of the lesson:** To listen to the student's speech to hear how he uses volume, pitch, and duration. You will introduce him to the concept of word stress in connected speech.

2. **Listen to the student's speech.** Have the student tell you about a personal experience (this could be about an important family gathering he attended). Record this. (You will transcribe this story for use in Lesson 10.)

3. **Discuss your observations of your student's use of volume, pitch, and rhythm and his use of them to stress words in his speech.** Listen to the recording you just made. Does he modulate volume, pitch, and rhythm? Does he use volume, pitch, and rhythm to appropriately stress specific syllables in words or important words in sentences?

4. **Explain that in this lesson you will be working on producing a range of volumes, a wide range of pitches, and changes in duration.** It is important for him to gain control over these fundamentals of prosody so they may be used to put stress on the important information in connected speech. Now you will model/produce sounds which will help him learn these skills.

5. **Modulating volume:**

    a. Have your student say a string of "ahs" alternating between a loud *ah* and a soft ah: *ah* ah *ah* ah *ah* ah... If he needs help, you should demonstrate so he can imitate. You may want to have him tap on the table every time he says a loud *ah*.

b. Now have the student follow the same sequence using the word "run."

6. **Modulating pitch:**

a. Teach the student to alternate between a high and a low pitched speaking voice on the vowel "ah." There should be a slight break between each high and low vowel. You will demonstrate and he will imitate. Now produce the same alternating pitch sequence saying "*blue* jeans *blue* jeans..." Again demonstrate and have him imitate.

b. Teach the student how to go from a lower pitch and slide up to a higher pitch on "ah." Then begin at the higher pitch and slide to a lower pitch on "ah." You will produce the sounds and he will imitate. Repeat this sequence using the word "mom."

c. Teach the student how to make a pitch glide. He should first make the sound of a siren, beginning at the lowest pitch in the student's natural range, rising four or five seconds to the highest pitch that the student can produce, and then falling four or five seconds, and then returning back to the approximate original pitch. Now produce a pitch glide on the vowel "ah." Finally produce a pitch glide using the word "mom."

d. Have the student produce the following pitch sequence using the vowel "ah": rising, falling, high, low, glide, rising, falling, high, low, glide. Help him by labeling each sound you want him to make. You produce it first and then have him imitate. Write down the sequence and have the student produce it on his own.

7. **Rhythm (increasing duration):**

a. Have your student say a string of "ahs" alternating between a long ah and a short ah (*aaaaaah* ah *aaaaaah* ah *aaaaaah* ah...), while holding volume and pitch constant. If he needs help, you should demonstrate and he can imitate. You may want to have him press into the table every time he says a long aaaaaah.

b. Now have the student follow the same sequence using the word "run."

8. **Demonstrate how volume, pitch, and rhythm can each be used to stress the words in a sentence.** Stress the word *chocolate* first with increased volume, then with pitch, and finally by increasing the duration of the word: "Sally wants to have *chocolate* cupcakes at her birthday party."

9. **Use the following sentences to illustrate appropriate and inappropriate use of stress.** You will read the sentence pairs to your student, stressing the emphasized word. Ask the student which version sounds better and which version gives more information. Discuss this.

a. Albert Einstein was an *amazing* human being.
   Albert Einstein was *an* amazing human being.

b. The men are almost **finished** putting the roof on the new building.
   The men are almost finished putting **the** roof on the new building.

c. **Someday**, I'll paint a picture of you.
   Someday, I'll paint **a** picture of you.

10. **Homework:** Practice saying a sustained "ah" repeatedly:

a. alternately increasing and decreasing volume

b. alternately increasing and decreasing the duration of the sound

c. following this pitch sequence: rising, falling, high, low, glide, rising, falling, high, low, glide, and so on.

LESSON 2

Grammatical stress in single words

Materials

Handout A: Words that Change in Meaning when a Different Syllable is Stressed

Goals

To learn how certain spoken words change in meaning depending on which syllable is stressed (first syllable stressed = noun; second syllable stressed = verb).

To learn to use increased volume, a change in pitch, and a change in rhythm (increased duration) to stress syllables.

Procedures

1. **Explain the purpose of the lesson:** To learn how certain words change in meaning depending on which syllable is stressed; and to learn three methods for stressing words/syllables in words.

2. **Discuss that words change in meaning depending on which syllable we stress.** Emphasizing the first syllable can make a word a noun, while emphasizing the second syllable in a word of the same spelling can make it a verb:

   a. **Stress syllables using increased volume.** Read each of the words in Handout A, using increased volume to stress the emphasized syllable. Have your student imitate you after you read each word.

   b. **Now take turns reading words which are spelled in the same way, stressing different syllables.** Specifically, you will read **pro**gress and he will read pro**gress**. You will then read **sub**ject and he will read sub**ject**, and so on.

   c. **Ask your student how the meaning changes depending on what syllable is stressed.** For one pair at a time, have him tell what each version of the word means. Make sure he notices that when the first syllable is stressed the word is a thing/noun. When the second syllable is stressed the word is an action/verb.

3. **Stressing syllables in other ways.** Explain that words and syllables can be stressed using pitch and rhythm as well as volume:

   a. **Stress syllables using pitch.** Read each of the words in Handout A, using a higher pitch to stress the emphasized syllable and a lower pitch for the unstressed syllable. Have your student imitate you after you read each word.

b. **Stress syllables using rhythm.** Again, read each of the words in Handout A. This time, increase the duration of the syllable to be stressed (emphasized syllable). Have your student imitate you after you read each word.

c. **Discuss the three different methods for stressing words or syllables.** Which one did your student find the easiest to use? Which method did he find the most difficult to use? Which did he like the best?

4. **Play the Stress Table Tap Game:** Both of you should look at Handout A. Player 1 will choose a word from Handout A and say the word, stressing whichever syllable he wants, using *one* method of his choosing (volume, pitch, rhythm). Player 2 must then tap the table to mirror the stress pattern of the word that was just said. He must tell Player 1 which method he used to stress the syllable and whether or not Player 1's word was said as a noun or an action word (verb). Now Player 2 chooses a word from Handout A and follows the same procedure as Player 1. Player 1 will then tap the table to mirror the stress pattern of the word Player 2 just said, name the method used to stress the syllable, and whether or not the word said was a noun or an action verb. Play continues. If you want to keep score, the listener has a chance to get three points on each turn.

5. **Homework:** Tell a family member or a friend what you learned about how words change in meaning according to which syllable is stressed. Explain how they become nouns or verbs. Demonstrate how you stress words in Handout A, first using volume, followed by pitch, and after that, rhythm (duration).

Words that Change in Meaning when a Different Syllable is Stressed

Progress	Pro**gress**
Subject	Sub**ject**
Increase	In**crease**
Desert	De**sert**
Contract	Con**tract**
Record	Re**cord**
Object	Ob**ject**
Protest	Pro**test**
Content	Con**tent**
Address	Ad**dress**
Combine	Com**bine**
Compact	Com**pact**
Extract	Ex**tract**

Stressing words in sentences

Materials

Handouts A, B, C, D, E, F, and G (Changing the stressed word in sentences changes meaning)

Goal

To learn that placing stress on different words in a sentence changes the meaning of that sentence.

Procedures

1. **Explain the purpose of the lesson:** To learn how the meaning of a sentence is changed depending on which word in the sentence is stressed.

2. **Read a sentence multiple times, stressing a different word each time.** Read the sentence "You shouldn't have done that" in the two following ways (stressing the word that is emphasized): "**You** shouldn't have done that" and "You shouldn't have done **that**." Ask the student if he hears a difference between the two versions and what that difference is. Help him to understand that the sentences sounded different and that they mean different things, even though they are the exact same words. Read each sentence again, stopping after each to talk about its meaning. ("**You** shouldn't have done that" means that someone else should have done that, not you. "You shouldn't have done **that**" means you should have done something else, not that.)

3. **Read sentences to your student, stressing the emphasized word, and have him imitate you.** Look at Handout A with the student. You can use any method or combination of methods to stress the emphasized word. Have the student repeat the sentence after you. Then move on to the next version of the sentence. Again stress the emphasized word and have the student imitate you. Repeat this process until your student has imitated all versions of the sentence.

4. **Discuss how the meaning of the sentence changes when different words are stressed.** As the student saw in the last lesson, words can be completely changed in meaning, depending on which syllable is stressed. Make sure he understands that the same is true for all sentences, depending on which word is stressed. Look at Handout A for how the meaning changes with each version of the sentence.

5. **Have the student read the sentences in Handouts B through D.** Listen to him as he reads each handout out loud, stressing the emphasized words. He may use any stress method he chooses. He may also combine methods when stressing the emphasized words. If he has difficulty in correctly stressing the specified words, read them for him and have him imitate you. As he completes reading each of the handouts he should fill in the meaning for each version of the sentence in that handout.

6. **Homework:** Complete Handouts E through G for homework. Practice stressing the emphasized words in the sentences using any method or combination of methods of your choosing for stressing words. Then write the meaning of each version of each sentence in the space provided, just as you did in the lesson.

✓

Sentence	Meaning
Jack will cycle to the restaurant tonight.	*Jack, and not some other person, will do this.*
Jack **will** cycle to the restaurant tonight.	*He definitely is going to do this!*
Jack will **cycle** to the restaurant tonight.	*He will ride his bike there, not drive or take the bus.*
Jack will cycle to the **restaurant** tonight.	*He will cycle to the restaurant, not some other place.*
Jack will cycle to the restaurant **tonight**.	*He will cycle there tonight, not some other night.*

Sentence	Meaning
I didn't say he stole the money.	
I *didn't* say he stole the money.	
I didn't *say* he stole the money.	
I didn't say *he* stole the money.	
I didn't say he *stole* the money.	
I didn't say he stole the *money*.	

Sentence	Meaning
I bought a blue car on Tuesday.	
I *bought* a blue car on Tuesday.	
I bought a *blue* car on Tuesday.	
I bought a blue *car* on Tuesday.	
I bought a blue car on *Tuesday*.	

Sentence	Meaning
I love your brother's cooking.	
I *love* your brother's cooking.	
I love *your* brother's cooking.	
I love your *brother's* cooking.	
I love your brother's *cooking*.	

Sentence	Meaning
I bought a car on Tuesday.	
I *bought* a car on Tuesday.	
I bought a *car* on Tuesday.	
I bought a car on *Tuesday*.	

She played piano yesterday.	
She *played* piano yesterday.	
She played *piano* yesterday.	
She played piano *yesterday*.	

Sentence	Meaning
I asked you to buy a bunch of red roses.	
I *asked* you to buy a bunch of red roses.	
I asked *you* to buy a bunch of red roses.	
I asked you to *buy* a bunch of red roses.	
I asked you to buy a *bunch* of red roses.	
I asked you to buy a bunch of *red* roses.	
I asked you to buy a bunch of red *roses*.	

✓

Sentence	Meaning
I don't think we should buy this new car.	
I *don't* think we should buy this new car.	
I don't *think* we should buy this new car.	
I don't think *we* should buy this new car.	
I don't think we *should* buy this new car.	
I don't think we should *buy* this new car.	
I don't think we should buy *this* new car.	
I don't think we should buy this *new* car.	
I don't think we should buy this new *car*.	

Stressing words in sentences with a louder volume, using volume stress notation

Materials

Handout A: Practice Sentences with Volume Notation 1

Handout B: Practice Sentences with Volume Notation 2

Handout C: Practice Sentences to Share Information: Volume Notation by Student

Handout D: Practice Sentences to Share Feelings: Volume Notation by Student

Index cards

Goals

To learn written notation indicating that a particular word in a sentence is to be stressed with a louder volume.

To practice speaking words in sentences which are stressed with a louder volume.

Procedures

1. **Explain the purpose of the lesson:** To learn to choose important words in sentences to be stressed; and written notation indicating that a particular word in a sentence is to be stressed with an increase in volume. Notating written communication will help the student to visualize the use of an increased volume to stress words, thereby helping him to more effectively inform and share feelings with others in his communication.

2. **Explain to the student how you will be having him mark a text to notate an increase in volume.** First he will read through the entire text. Then he will choose words that he thinks are particularly important and underline them. Underlining will indicate to him that, when he reads, he is to increase his volume for those words.

   To give him a visual, write "word" in the middle of an index card and underline it. At the bottom of the index card write "Increase Volume." This will be the first of seven stress notation cards to be used in future lessons (see the illustration in the introduction to this chapter).

3. **Have the student imitate sentences which contain words stressed by increased volume.** Give your student Handout A. Read the sentences one at a time, as you follow the volume notation, with your student

imitating you after each one. Make certain that he is correctly imitating your prosody.

4. **Have the student read sentences which contain words stressed by increased volume.** Have him read the sentences in Handout B following the volume notation. Give feedback and correction as needed. (*Note:* If the student stresses the words in other ways, for example pitch or increasing duration, do not comment on this as long as you hear him increase volume in saying the underlined words.)

5. **Discuss the change in meaning of each sentence depending on which word was stressed.** The student should notice that the sentences in Handouts A and B were the same. Look at both handouts, one sentence at a time, and compare the meaning of the sentence based on how it was said in Handout A compared with how it was said in Handout B. How was the meaning of each sentence changed?

6. **Have the student decide which words in sentences he wants to stress so as to convey his intended meaning.** Have the student select the words he wants to stress in each of the sentences in Handout C, and underline them. He will then read the sentences to you, stressing the words that are underlined by using an increase in volume. Give feedback and correction as needed.

7. **Homework:** Select the words you want to stress in each sentence in Handout D and underline them. Practice reading the sentences stressing the words that are underlined, increasing their volume.

Practice Sentences with Volume Notation 1

1. The <u>red</u> car is much faster.

2. My <u>milk</u> spilled on the carpet.

3. <u>Sam's</u> horse came in second.

4. <u>That</u> house is haunted.

5. The <u>best</u> cereal is oatmeal.

6. Your dirty <u>shoes</u> are tracking mud into the house.

7. <u>My</u> chicken lays more eggs.

8. The <u>Bronx</u> zoo is the best on the east coast.

9. <u>I</u> prefer science fiction movies.

10. Snow <u>always</u> causes terrible automobile accidents.

Practice Sentences with Volume Notation 2

1. The red car is <u>much</u> faster.

2. My milk spilled on the <u>carpet</u>.

3. Sam's horse came in <u>second</u>.

4. That house is <u>haunted</u>.

5. The best cereal is <u>oatmeal</u>.

6. Your dirty shoes are tracking <u>mud</u> into the house.

7. My chicken lays <u>more</u> eggs.

8. The Bronx zoo is the <u>best</u> on the east coast.

9. I prefer science <u>fiction</u> movies.

10. Snow always causes <u>terrible</u> automobile accidents.

Practice Sentences to Share Information: Volume Notation by Student

1. Mars is so far away.

2. That dog looks so hungry.

3. Brown is my favorite color.

4. In the summer I love to swim.

5. Jimmy can jump over that stump.

6. The air smells so sweet.

7. Sue will never eat tomatoes.

8. John fell out of his boat.

9. That meatloaf is delicious.

10. Halloween is my favorite holiday.

Practice Sentences to Share Feelings: Volume Notation by Student

1. My brother's jokes make me feel so silly.

2. That picture embarrasses me.

3. This puppy makes me feel happy.

4. I really like my close friends.

5. Riding in this car makes me feel scared.

6. That chicken makes me feel sick.

7. I hate this computer.

8. Hurry! I feel alone out here.

9. My smart phone frustrates me.

10. I can't go with you because I am so angry with you.

LESSON 5

Stressing words in sentences with a change in pitch

Materials

Handout A: Practice Sentences with Pitch Notation 1 (to be written in advance)

Handout B: Practice Sentences for Pitch Notation 2

Handout C: Practice Sentences to Share Information: Pitch Notation by Student

Handout D: Practice Sentences to Share Feelings: Pitch Notation by Student

Index cards

Yellow highlighter

Goals

To learn written notation indicating that a particular word in a sentence is to be stressed with a change in pitch.

To practice stressing words through changes in pitch.

Procedures

1. **Explain the purpose of the lesson:** To practice choosing words in sentences that are important. The student will learn to stress them through various changes in pitch. He will also learn notation indicating that a particular word in a sentence is to be stressed by changing its pitch in a specific way. Notating written communication will help the student to visualize pitch change to stress words, thereby helping him to more effectively inform and share feelings with others in his communication.

2. **Explain to the student how you will be having him notate text to indicate a change in pitch to stress a word.** First he will read through an entire text. Then he will choose words that he thinks are particularly important, and highlight them with a yellow highlighter. He will then choose how he will use pitch to stress those particular highlighted words in the sentences. Explain that using pitch for stressing words is complicated because there are a number of ways to use it.

    To give him a visual for all of the ways pitch can be used to stress words in sentences, write "word **word**" in the middle of five index cards (see the illustration in the introduction to this chapter). Make the second "word" bold to show that it is the one being stressed. You will then draw each of the following sets of symbols on one of the index cards as instructed below. On the back of each card write the associated example provided. Read the example, apply the pitch stress notation, and have the student imitate you:

- A flat line over the first "word" and a diagonal line over the second (stressed) "word" that starts higher than the line over the first word and descends to the right. Write the title "High Pitch Falling" on the bottom of the card. (For example, I felt **really** good.)

- Two flat pitch lines, a lower one over the first "word" followed by a higher one over the second (stressed) "word," with the title "Pitch Lift" on the bottom. (For example, It was a **big** dog.)

- A flat line over the first "word" and a curved line starting low, showing a peak at the center of the card, and coming back down over the second (stressed) "word." Title the card "Pitch Glide." (For example, When I drink **milk** I get sick.)

- A flat line over the first "word" and diagonal line ascending from the level of the line over the first "word" to the right over the second (stressed) "word," with the title "Pitch Rising." (For example, These aren't your **glasses**.)

- Two flat pitch lines, a higher one over the first "word" followed by a lower one over the second (stressed) "word," with the title "Pitch Drop" on the bottom. (For example, He had a **rough** morning.)

These will become part of your set of stress notation cards to be used in future lessons. Keep these cards out on the table in front of the student as you work.

3. **Read each "word" on the cards, demonstrating how to apply the pitch notation.** Have the student imitate you after you read each one.

4. **Have the student imitate sentences containing words stressed by changing pitch.** Give your student Handout A. The bold words are those to be stressed. (*Note:* You must write specific pitch notation over the words to be stressed in advance.) Read the sentences following the volume notation, one at a time, with your student imitating you after each one. Make certain that he is correctly imitating your prosody.

5. **Have the student read the sentences containing words to be stressed by changing pitch.** On Handout B you will see that the words to be stressed are in bold. Have the student highlight the bolded words in yellow. Now together you will decide which type of pitch change to use to stress each of the highlighted words. You should then write in the notation above the highlighted words. Now have your student read the

sentences in Handout B according to the pitch notation. Give feedback and correction as needed. (*Note:* If the student stresses the words in other ways, for example volume or increasing duration, do not comment on this as long as you hear him change pitch to stress the highlighted words.)

6. **Discuss the change in meaning of each sentence depending on which word was stressed.** The student should notice that the sentences in Handouts A and B were the same. Look at both handouts together, one sentence at a time, and compare the meaning of the sentence based on how it was said in Handout A compared with how it was said in Handout B. How was the meaning of each sentence changed? Have the student explain the meaning of each version of each sentence.

7. **Have the student decide which words in sentences he wants to stress to convey his intended meaning.** Have the student select the words he wants to stress in each of the sentences in Handout C, and highlight them in yellow. He should write the pitch notation that he wants to use above each highlighted word. Then he will read the sentences to you, stressing the words according to the pitch notation. Give feedback and correction as needed.

8. **Homework:** Select the words you want to stress in each sentence in Handout D and highlight them in yellow. You will then write the pitch notation you want to use above each of the highlighted words. Then practice reading the sentences, stressing the words according to the pitch notation.

Practice Sentences with Pitch Notation 1 (to be written in advance)

1. I said the bus was **late**.

2. It's too long to have to **wait** for her.

3. Please let me get a drink of **water**.

4. I'm so excited about my mom's new **car**.

5. No, this December was not so **cold**.

6. I have to clean all the dirt off **my** bike.

7. You are so out of breath from all that **running**.

8. Our team had a **rough** year.

9. Orange has always been a **favorite** color of mine.

10. To me it looks like your **knee** is swollen.

Practice Sentences for Pitch Notation 2

1. I **said** the bus was late.

2. It's too **long** to have to wait for her.

3. **Please** let me get a drink of water.

4. I'm **so** excited about my mom's new car.

5. No, **this** December was not so cold.

6. I **have** to clean all the dirt off my bike.

7. You are **so** out of breath from all that running.

8. **Our** team had a rough year.

9. Orange has **always** been a favorite color of mine.

10. To **me** it looks like your knee is swollen.

Practice Sentences to Share Information: Pitch Notation by Student

1. All this grass makes me sneeze.

2. Star Wars is my all-time favorite.

3. The train is very slow this morning because of the weather.

4. The weather is perfect for hiking today.

5. Your dog can jump so high.

6. I like eating chicken noodle soup when it is cold outside.

7. Your typing speed is much better than mine.

8. This cheese smells awful.

9. My family always sleeps late on Saturday mornings.

10. The construction workers installed the windows today.

Practice Sentences to Share Feelings: Pitch Notation by Student

1. I'm so mad at Jimmy.

2. Jazz makes me feel so good.

3. The sound of a stream really relaxes me.

4. I am so upset because you are always looking at your phone instead of talking to me.

5. When she sings, I just feel so warm inside.

6. I love geometry, but I hate linear algebra.

7. My frustration is because of this slow bus.

8. My cat really makes me happy when she snuggles up to me.

9. This food makes me smile because it reminds me of when I was little.

10. I will never forget about my wonderful summer.

Stressing words in sentences with a change in rhythm, specifically an increase in duration

Materials

Handout A: Practice Sentences with Rhythm Notation 1

Handout B: Practice Sentences with Rhythm Notation 2

Handout C: Practice Sentences to Share Information: Rhythm Notation by Student

Handout D: Practice Sentences to Share Feelings: Rhythm Notation by Student

Index cards

Yellow highlighter

Goals

To learn written notation indicating that a particular word in a sentence is to be stressed with a change in rhythm, specifically increased duration of a word.

To practice stressing words by increasing the duration of those words.

Procedures

1. **Explain the purpose of the lesson:** To learn to choose words in sentences that are important to the student, and stress them by increasing their duration. The student will also learn the notation indicating that a particular word in a sentence will be stressed by increasing its duration.

2. **Explain to the student how you will be having him notate words to stress them by changing their rhythm.** First he will read through an entire text. Then he will choose words that he thinks are particularly important. He will highlight these words with a yellow highlighter. He will then put a → (the symbol for increasing duration) over the word to indicate that its duration when spoken should increase relative to the other words.

   To give him a visual cue, write "word" in the middle of an index card and draw the symbol for increased duration (an arrow pointing to the right) over it. At the bottom of the index card write "Change Rhythm: Increase Duration." This will complete the set of seven stress notation cards (see the illustration in the introduction to this chapter). These stress notation cards will be used in all subsequent lessons. You should keep them for your student. Keep the duration card out on the table in front of the student, helping to remind him as he works today.

3. **Have the student imitate sentences containing words which are to be stressed by increasing their duration.** Give your student Handout A. Read the sentences out loud, as indicated by the rhythm notation, one at a time, and your student will imitate you after each sentence. Make certain that he is correctly imitating your prosody.

4. **Have the student read sentences containing words to be stressed by increasing rhythm.** Have him read the sentences in Handout B following the rhythm notation. Give feedback and correction as needed. (*Note:* If the student also stresses the bolded words in other ways, for example pitch or volume, do not comment on this as long as you hear him increase duration as he speaks the bolded words, as his main focus needs to be on duration.)

5. **Discuss the change in meaning of each sentence depending on which word was stressed.** The student should notice that the sentences in Handouts A and B were the same. Look at both handouts, one sentence at a time, and compare the meaning of each form of the sentence based on which word was stressed (how it was said in Handout A compared with how it was said in Handout B). How was the meaning of the sentence changed?

6. **Have the student decide which words in sentences he wants to stress to convey his intended meaning.** Have the student select the words he wants to stress in each of the sentences in Handout C, and highlight them in yellow. He should put the symbol for increased duration over each of the highlighted words. Then he will read the sentences to you, stressing the words he highlighted by using an increase in duration. Give feedback and correction as needed.

7. **Homework:** Select the words you want to stress in each of the sentences in Handout D. Highlight them and put the symbol for increased duration over them. Practice reading the sentences stressing the words that are bolded by using an increase in duration.

Practice Sentences with Rhythm Notation 1

(Make sure the student focuses on duration)

1. I'm **aware** of that sort of big mistake.

2. I could **smell** the odor of the huge fire.

3. **Our** team wins first place every year.

4. Primates **sometimes** prefer to eat the entire banana.

5. The weather **today** will be clear but very hot.

6. After **that** the wasp just flew away.

7. My **keyboard** has been repaired over and over.

8. The plane engine almost **stopped** and then we were just expecting the worst.

9. Our garden **was** about to bloom when this dog rolled around right in the middle of it.

10. The farmer rode in and **seemed** upset but then he started laughing.

Practice Sentences with Rhythm Notation 2

(Make sure the student focuses on duration)

1. I'm aware of that sort **of** big mistake.

2. I could smell the odor of the **huge** fire.

3. Our team wins first place **every** year.

4. Primates sometimes prefer to eat the **entire** banana.

5. The weather today will be clear but **very** hot.

6. After that the wasp just **flew** away.

7. My keyboard has been repaired over and **over**.

8. The plane engine almost stopped and then we were just **expecting** the worst.

9. Our garden was about to bloom when this dog rolled around **right** in the middle of it.

10. The farmer rode in and seemed upset but **then** he started laughing.

Practice Sentences to Share Information: Rhythm Notation by Student

(Make sure the student focuses on duration)

1. He drank seven soft drinks at dinner and seemed very full.

2. The white poodle sitting on that table won the grand prize at the dog show.

3. At our family's dinner some of the eggs were spoiled.

4. When I see blue bonnets, I always think of Texas, because it is the state flower.

5. California is the home of the oldest living organisms, giant redwood trees.

6. It's always most dangerous at the moment when ice begins to melt.

7. When I found your notebook I was happy to return it to you.

8. This literature professor is always very interesting.

9. We wanted to stay longer and share the sunset because it was our last day of vacation.

10. My walls are completely covered with pictures of my family.

Practice Sentences to Share Feelings: Rhythm Notation by Student

(Make sure the student focuses on duration)

1. The man at the front door scares me more than I expected.

2. Yesterday I felt exhausted all day because my dog ran away and I was looking for her.

3. It's true, I always get alarmed when I eat strawberries and get a rash all over my face.

4. I was so excited to see you Tuesday night and share that beautiful moon with you.

5. Your ancestors must have been so scared when they arrived in Brooklyn.

6. This is the most exhausted I've ever been in my life, so I am going to bed.

7. After we lost our soccer game I felt very sad, so I called my best friend.

8. I was really mad when I fell into the mud when I was cycling this morning.

9. I felt so peaceful as I imagined how beautiful the sunset was over the ocean.

10. We were all alarmed when he arrived on his Harley-Davidson motorcycle.

LESSON 7

Stressing words in poetry to inform and share feelings

Materials

Two copies of the poem *Bear in There* by Shel Silverstein (Silverstein, S. (1981) *"Bear in There."* In H. Collins (ed.) *A Light in the Attic*. New York, NY: Harper Collins.)

Stress notation cards

Audio recording device

Yellow highlighter

Goal

To practice the use of stress (volume, pitch, rhythm) on specific words (through the use of stress notation) in connected speech in order to convey meaning.

Procedures

1. **Explain the purpose of the lesson:** To practice using all stress forms (volume, pitch, rhythm) on specific words, through the use of stress notation, in connected speech to convey meaning within the poem. Put the stress notation cards out on the table in front of your student for reference. Remind the student of what each symbol means. Have him pronounce "word," applying each method for stressing a word. Tell him that he will be using all of the symbols in this lesson.

2. **Have the student read the poem out loud.** Allow him to read the poem any way that he wants. Do not provide any other direction. Record him as he does this.

3. **Determine with the student which words should be stressed.** You will go line by line and highlight the important words. Discuss why you and your student think that each of the words you choose is important. The student will then mark words using stress notation for volume, pitch, and rhythm.

4. **Read the poem out loud, following the notation as you read it.** You will be modeling the appropriate use of the notation for your student. Exaggerate the stress that you place on each word emphasized.

5. **Then have the student read the poem out loud, employing the notation.** This is a silly, comic poem, and so the student should be encouraged

to be quite emphatic in his use of stress. Placing exaggerated stress on words in this humorous way will help him solidify the concepts. Make corrections as needed during the student's first reading. Have the student read the poem a second time, employing the notation. Record this second reading.

6. **Compare the recordings.** Play back and listen to the recording of his reading of the poem before he made a plan to stress particular words, and then listen to the recording you just made. Talk about how stressing words in his reading affected the listener. Discuss how stressing specific words affected the meaning of the poem. Look in particular at lines 12 through 15.

    Try saying these lines stressing different words than the ones your student chose and see how the meaning changes. Try saying these four lines in two different ways.

    In the first reading, have the student stress the words *roar, open, scare* and *know*. Then, in a second reading have him stress *roar, you, me*, and *he's*.

    Discuss the meaning of these lines of the poem when the stressed words are different. In the first, the speaker hears a roar only when the door opens and that's scary because it is proof the bear is in there. In the second, the bear roars at you, not me, but it scares me, not you, because he, a bear, is in there.

7. **Homework:** (1) Practice reading the poem *Bear in There* by Shel Silverstein according to your stress notation. (2) Find another, more emotional, poem (for example, *If You Forget Me* by Pablo Neruda). Read it through. Identify and highlight the important words and apply stress notation. Practice reading the poem according to your stress notation.

Stress notation on a famous speech to inform and share feelings

Materials

Handout A: Copy of the Martin Luther King speech (get online) for Instructor

Handout B: Copy of the same speech to be notated by student

Handout C: Homework: The Frog Story

Stress notation cards

Audio recording device

Yellow highlighter

Goal

To practice the use of stresses on specific words in connected speech in order to convey meaning.

Procedures

1. **Review the homework from the last lesson.** Listen to your student read *Bear in There* by Shel Silverstein. Give feedback. Look at how he notated the "more emotional" poem he chose. Query him about his choices. Listen to him read the poem.

2. **Explain the purpose of the lesson:** To practice all methods for stressing words in connected speech (volume, pitch, rhythm (duration)), to convey meaning. Put the seven stress notation cards out on the table. Remind the student of what each symbol means and tell him that he will be using them in this lesson.

3. **Have the student read the speech out loud.** Allow him to read the speech any way that he wants. Do not provide any other direction. Record him.

4. **Determine with the student which words should be stressed to convey meaning in the most effective way.** Highlight the important words. Write in, using stress notation, the main method by which he will stress each of the highlighted words.

5. **Read the speech out loud, according to the notation which you and the student decided on together.** Have the student imitate each sentence immediately after you read it.

6. **Now the student will read the speech out loud, employing the notation**. This first reading is to practice, so make corrections as needed.

7. **Have the student read the speech out loud a second time, employing the notation.** Record this.

8. **Compare the recordings.** Play back and listen to the recordings. Discuss how stressing words through pitch change affected the meaning of the speech.

9. **Homework:** Practice the Martin Luther King speech. Memorize The Frog Story for next time.

✓

Homework: The Frog Story

Once a guy named Charlie went hiking with his buddies. They loved to explore places no one had gone before. One day while they were out exploring, Charlie found a large river frog. He picked up the frog and put it on his head, under his cap. On his way back he heard someone talking. He quickly turned around and found no one in sight. He kept walking and heard the voice again, but this time he knew where it came from. It came from under the cap on his head. He couldn't believe it. He quickly but carefully took off his cap. The frog then started to talk again. The frog said, "Hi there. My name is Fiona." Charlie gasped and asked, "Are you real?" Fiona said, "I sure am, and if you give me a kiss I will give you a million dollars." Charlie said, "No way," and put Fiona and his cap back on his head. Fiona again began to speak, and this time said, "If you give me a kiss I will give you the largest yacht in the world." Again Charlie said, "No way," and put the frog and cap back on his head. Once more the frog spoke, but this time said, "If you kiss me I will become the most beautiful girl in the world and will be your girlfriend." Again Charlie said, "No way." The frog asked him, "Why not?" Charlie said, "Look Fiona, lots of people have girlfriends, but nobody has a talking frog!"

Telling a story from memory, applying all types of stress: Volume, pitch, rhythm (duration)

Materials

Handout A: The Frog Story (for Notation)

Stress notation cards

Audio recording device

Yellow highlighter

Goal

To practice the use of all methods of stress (volume, pitch, rhythm) on specific important words in order to convey meaning and emotion when telling a story.

Procedures

1. **Review the homework from the last lesson.** Have the student read out loud the Martin Luther King speech with his notation. Provide feedback and correction as needed.

2. **Explain the purpose of the lesson:** To practice the use of all stress forms (volume, pitch, rhythm) in connected speech in order to convey meaning and emotion when telling a story. Put the stress notation cards out on the table in front of your student for reference. Remind the student of what each symbol means. Have him pronounce "word," applying each method for stressing a word. Tell him that he will be using all of the symbols in this lesson.

3. **Have the student tell The Frog Story out loud, from memory.** Allow him to tell The Frog Story the way he practiced it. Do not provide any specific direction with regard to how he should tell it. Record him.

4. **With your student, highlight important words in the printed version of The Frog Story (Handout A).** After you have discussed and determined which words are important, have your student decide which type of stress he wants to focus on (volume, pitch, rhythm) and apply to each of his highlighted words. Then have him write in the correct stress notation. (*Note:* Your student may, in reality, apply more than one method to stress a word as he speaks. That's OK. Just make certain he focuses on and uses the one that he marked on the page (along with the others).)

5. **Now read The Frog Story with the stress notation.** You will read the story first, modeling the stressed words according to the notation. Then have the student read the story. Record this.

6. **Listen to the recording and discuss.** Make any additional changes to the notation you believe are needed.

7. **Now have the student tell The Frog Story from memory again, trying to remember the words he wants to stress and how he wants to do it.** Record this.

8. **Compare the recording of his retelling of the story from memory, done at the beginning of the lesson, to the one you just made.** Have the student discuss the differences between the recordings.

9. **Homework:** (1) Practice telling The Frog Story from memory, employing as much of the stress notation as you can recall. (2) Ask someone you know to teach you a short joke you can tell at the next lesson. Memorize the joke, trying to stress important words.

The Frog Story (for Notation)

Once a guy named Charlie went hiking with his buddies. They loved to explore places no one had gone before. One day while they were out exploring, Charlie found a large river frog. He picked up the frog and put it on his head, under his cap. On his way back he heard someone talking. He quickly turned around and found no one in sight. He kept walking and heard the voice again, but this time he knew where it came from. It came from under the cap on his head. He couldn't believe it. He quickly but carefully took off his cap. The frog then started to talk again. The frog said, "Hi there. My name is Fiona." Charlie gasped and asked, "Are you real?" Fiona said, "I sure am, and if you give me a kiss I will give you a million dollars." Charlie said, "No way," and put Fiona and his cap back on his head. Fiona again began to speak, and this time said, "If you give me a kiss I will give you the largest yacht in the world." Again Charlie said, "No way," and put the frog and cap back on his head. Once more the frog spoke, but this time said, "If you kiss me I will become the most beautiful girl in the world and will be your girlfriend." Again Charlie said, "No way." The frog asked him, "Why not?" Charlie said, "Look Fiona, lots of people have girlfriends, but nobody has a talking frog!"

LESSON 10

Telling a personal experience story, placing stress on important words

Materials

> Handout A: Sentences for Notation
>
> Handout B: Homework Sentences
>
> Transcription of student's personal experience story from Lesson 1
>
> Audio recording from Lesson 1
>
> Stress notation cards
>
> Audio recording device

Goal

> *To use stress on specific words in a personal experience story to convey meaning, to inform, share emotions, and increase the listener's interest.*

Procedures

1. **Review the homework from the last lesson.** Ask your student to tell you the joke that he learned from his family or a friend. Listen for how he uses stress and what types of stress he seems to use most. Discuss your observations.

2. **Explain the purpose of the lesson:** To use stress in relating a personal experience story to inform, share emotions, and engage the listener's interest. Put the stress notation cards out on the table in front of your student for reference. Remind the student of what each symbol means. Have him pronounce "word," applying each method for stressing a word. Tell him that he will be using all of the symbols in this lesson.

3. **Now give the student your transcription of the personal experience story he told you in Lesson 1.** Have the student read this story out loud. Record this.

4. **Discuss how feelings are emphasized mostly through pitch and volume.** Write the following sentences. You will first speak the sentences with even pitch and volume. Have the student imitate you. Then highlight the important words and apply pitch and volume notation. Speak the sentences, stressing those highlighted words using pitch and volume to express emotion:

    a. I tripped over my own feet and fell in a puddle of mud.

    b. I spent the entire day hiking with my best friend.

5. **Discuss how important information is stressed largely through rhythm (increases in duration).** Write the following sentences. You will first speak the sentences with even rhythm. Then highlight important informational words. Mark the sentences with notation for increased word duration. Then speak the sentences again, according to the notation, to stress important information.

   a. All living creatures must breathe to relax and to thrive.

   b. In order to become good at anything, a person needs to practice.

6. **Have the student notate the sentences in Handout A.** Stress emotion in the first set by focusing on and using pitch and volume. In the second set, stress the main point using rhythm.

7. **Now talk about the emotions and information communicated in the student's personal experience story.** Have the student write down the main point of his story, the most important information he wants people to know, and the feeling he wants to convey. Make sure he understands that his use of stress must emphasize each of these things. Now together highlight in pink important words that convey emotions. Decide together the best way to stress those words. Notate them. Now highlight in yellow the main topic and important information words to be stressed. Decide the best way to stress these and notate.

8. **Now read the student's story to him, making sure to emphasize the main point, important information, and feelings through the use of appropriate stress as you and your student notated.** Talk about how the changes in stress in telling his story help to convey meaning, inform, increase interest, and share feelings.

9. **Have the student tell his personal experience story again.** First have him read the transcription, applying stress notation. Then have him tell his personal experience story, from memory. Record this.

10. **Play the recordings.** Play back the original recording from Lesson 1. Then play back the recording you just made and ask the student to compare them. Discuss his observations and your own. Make necessary corrections and recommendations.

11. **Homework:** Notate the sentences in Handout B. Employ all appropriate notation types for words in the sentences you want to stress. Stress emotion in the first set by focusing on and using pitch and volume. In the second set, stress the main point or most important information using rhythm.

Sentences for Notation

Add stress notation to the following four sentences, stressing emotions:

1. When I'm at the train terminal all the noises really make me feel anxious.

2. When my cousin and I play with my dog it makes me feel so happy.

3. At lunch I got really sick and my mom was scared, so she took me to the hospital.

4. Yesterday while picking apples I noticed so much love from my family.

Add stress notation to the following four sentences, stressing the main point:

1. While watching the kids fly kites I noticed that there were no clouds in the sky.

2. My cousin runs so fast at track meets that he nearly always wins gold.

3. The policeman rescued the family before the car fire was extinguished.

4. I watched the big crane lift a huge tractor up onto the deck of the ship.

Homework Sentences

Add stress notation to the following four sentences, stressing emotions:

1. The little monkey stared at me and made me feel so connected to him.

2. The policeman was so relieved when the car fire was extinguished.

3. This game excited me so much that I feel like jumping and screaming.

4. The farmer was very concerned when his rooster ran away.

Add stress notation to the following four sentences, stressing the main point:

1. When the man dropped his phone it broke into a million pieces.

2. While I was in Egypt I went to the great pyramids but didn't climb them.

3. After the brown grass was pulled some flowers were put in its place.

4. Before the singer began he took a big breath, but I didn't see him do it.

LESSON 11

Talking about a topic, using appropriate stress

Materials

Handout A: Web Graphic Organizer (make copies of this)

Stress notation cards

Recording device

Yellow highlighter

Goal

To use appropriate stress when talking about a topic from a Web Graphic Organizer outline.

Procedures

1. **Review the homework from the last lesson.** Check the student's application of stress notation to the sentences. Have your student read the sentences out loud. Provide feedback.

2. **Explain the purpose of the lesson:** To learn to use appropriate stress to emphasize important words when talking about a topic from a Graphic Organizer outline. Put the stress notation cards out on the table in front of your student for reference. Remind the student of what each symbol means. Have him pronounce "word," applying each method for stressing a word. Tell him that he will be using all of the symbols in this lesson.

3. **Remind the student how to use a Web Graphic Organizer to support an oral discussion of a topic.** A Web Graphic Organizer is a visual aid which is used to outline information about a topic. This type of outline can be used to support an oral discussion of that topic. In construction of a Web Graphic Organizer the label for the main topic goes in the largest oval in the center. Labels for subtopics which are related to the main topic go into the smaller ovals surrounding the main topic. Details associated with each subtopic are written next to, and linked to, the subtopic oval.

4. **Give the student Handout A: Web Graphic Organizer.** Help the student to make a Web Graphic Organizer to describe his favorite vacation. Help him determine the main topic and subtopic labels and to fill in adequate details if necessary.

5. **Instruct the student to use the Web Graphic Organizer to share his information as he speaks.** Have the student tell the story he has outlined

with his Web Graphic Organizer. Make certain the student begins with a main topic sentence, followed by a subtopic sentence and the detail sentences associated with that subtopic, before he moves on to the next subtopic. Record this.

6. **With the student, identify words that are important in the story.** Have him highlight those words in his Web Graphic Organizer or add them next to the appropriate subtopic if they are not included already.

7. **Notate each of the highlighted words with the stress notation symbol he would like to use to emphasize that word.** Discuss his choices of notation. Tell him that he should choose just one type of stress to focus on for each word (acknowledging that he may naturally combine different types of stress on the same word as he is speaking, and that's fine, but he should try to focus mostly on his preference).

8. **Now have the student tell the story again, using his stress notation and his Web Graphic Organizer to cue him.** Record this.

9. **Compare the recordings of his story based on the Web Graphic Organizer with and without stress notation.** Ask for his observations and give him yours.

10. **Homework:** Fill in another Web Graphic Organizer to outline a description of an event that made you feel a strong emotion (e.g., happy, proud, frustrated). After you decide on your main topic, decide on subtopics (these can include "who" you were with, "what" happened, and "why" you felt the way you did). Include at least three details for each subtopic. Make sure you fill in your Web Graphic Organizer with notes and not full sentences. Highlight important words in your description that are in your Web Graphic Organizer and add others and highlight them. Mark each highlighted word with the stress notation of your choice. At home, practice telling your story out loud to yourself, in front of a mirror, using your Web Graphic Organizer. Make sure to apply your stress notation. Memorize the ideas in your story and your use of stress. Be prepared to talk about your topic from memory at the next lesson, employing the appropriate word stress.

✓

Web Graphic Organizer

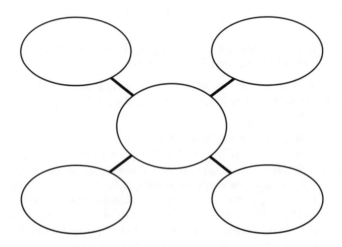

LESSON 12

Planned discussion of a topic from memory, using all stress forms to inform and share feelings

Materials

Stress notation cards

Yellow highlighter

Goal

To practice the use of stresses on specific words in connected speech in order to convey meaning.

Procedures

1. **Review the homework from the last lesson.** Look at the Web Graphic Organizer your student filled in for homework about an event that made him feel a strong emotion (e.g., happy, proud, frustrated). Recall that he was to include subtopics such as "who" he was with, "what" happened, and "why" he felt the way he did and at least three details for each subtopic. Be sure he filled in his Web Graphic Organizer with notes and not full sentences. Look to see that he highlighted important words and marked them with stress notation. Discuss his choices regarding the method he used to stress certain words. Give feedback and correction.

2. **Have your student speak, spontaneously and from memory, on his topic (about his event that made him feel a strong emotion).** Record this.

3. **Listen to the recording with your student and compare the stressed words to those marked in the Web Graphic Organizer from his homework to see if they match.**

4. **Have your student speak, spontaneously and from memory, once again on the same topic (emotional event) as he tries to stress more of the words he intended to.** Ask him questions about his topic. Record this.

5. **Listen to both recordings and compare.** Discuss the differences with the student and what he feels he expressed more effectively in the second recording.

6. **Homework:** Plan a story, a joke, or information you would like to share, using a Web Graphic Organizer and stress notation in the way you did to prepare for this lesson. Practice your story and then tell your family or your friends.

PowerPoint presentation to inform: Part 1 – Deciding what to include

Materials

Handout A: Instructions for PowerPoint Presentation

Computer

Goal

To create a PowerPoint presentation which you will give at the next lesson to practice using word stress in connected speech.

Procedures

1. **Explain the purpose of the lesson:** To create an informational PowerPoint presentation, which will later be used to practice stressing important words and concepts in connected speech.

2. **Give the student the outline for a PowerPoint presentation about considering a career (Handout A).** Explain that he will make six slides according to this outline.

3. **Help the student with the logistics of generating the PowerPoint presentation.**

4. **With your student discuss important concepts, in addition to the ones in the outline, to include on each slide.** The outline lists general considerations involved in thinking about a career. The student can add to these general considerations if he wants. He must also include information specific to himself on each slide for each subtopic.

5. **Work with the student on his PowerPoint presentation.**

6. **Homework:** If you were unable to complete making your PowerPoint presentation during your lesson, finish it for homework and bring it next week. Remember that you should write in bullet form, not in full sentences.

Instructions for PowerPoint Presentation

You will make a PowerPoint presentation called Thinking About Careers. You must include six slides, according to the outline below. Each slide covers an important subtopic about finding a career. There is some specific information provided which you must include in your presentation. You may add to this if you have other important ideas. On each slide you must add personal information about the subtopic which answers the question provided.

1. Title slide: Thinking About Careers

    a. Your name

2. Important considerations

    a. Interests

    b. Abilities

    c. Meaningfulness

3. Interests

    a. Creative, social, academic, investigation, business, athletic

    b. What are your interests?

4. Skills

    a. Academics

        i. English, language, history

        ii. Math, science

        iii. Problem solving

    b. Personal qualities

        i. Organized

        ii. Leadership

    c. People skills

    d. What are your skills?

5. Values

    a. High income

    b. Gain respect

    c. Help others

      d. Flexible hours

      e. Interacting with others

      f. What do you value?

6. Work experience

      a. Volunteer

      b. Internships

      c. Try different jobs

      d. Shadow a professional

      e. Sit in on a college class

      f. What will you try?

PowerPoint presentation to inform:
Part 2 – Deciding which words to stress

Materials

Computer with projector, if possible

Video recording device

Stress notation cards

Yellow highlighter

Goal

To use a PowerPoint presentation which you created, in order to practice using word stress (volume, pitch, rhythm (duration)) in connected speech.

Procedures

1. **Explain the purpose of the lesson:** To practice stressing important words in connected speech based on a PowerPoint presentation.

    Put the stress notation cards out on the table in front of your student for reference. Remind the student of what each symbol means. Have him pronounce "word word," applying each method for stressing a word. Tell him that he will be using all of the symbols in this lesson.

2. **Print out the student's PowerPoint presentation and identify important words on the printout.** Highlight those words with a yellow highlighter. Apply stress notation to those words. Discuss decisions regarding what method of stress to apply (volume, pitch, rhythm). The student may combine methods.

3. **Have the student practice giving the presentation, stressing words as notated.** Make certain the student begins with an overall topic sentence for his introductory slide regarding the main topic, and then begins discussion of each subtopic (on the subsequent slides) with a topic sentence. Give feedback on his presentation and use of stress. Also help him to insert strategic pauses into his presentation so that his audience has time to process what he is telling them.

4. **Now have your student give the presentation stressing the words he decided are important.** Help him to use nonverbal, gestural prosody by having him look at his audience and not just at his slides. Videotape him.

5. **Review the videotape together.** Ask the student what he thinks of his presentation and give feedback.

6. **Homework:** Try to give your PowerPoint presentation to family members or friends, for practice.

LESSON 15

Spontaneous speech in conversation, employing word stress to inform and share feelings

Materials

Stress notation cards

Goal

To practice generating spontaneous speech in a conversation, employing word stress to share information and to share feelings.

Procedures

1. **Explain the purpose of the lesson:** To generate spontaneous speech in conversation, employing word stress to communicate information, express emotions, and to engage the listener with interesting prosody.

2. **Have your student begin a conversation with a greeting and then with the story, joke, or information he outlined for homework in lesson 12.** Listen to how he stresses specific important emotion or content words with volume, pitch, and rhythm (duration of words).

3. **Continue on to have a conversation about his topic.** Ask him questions, make comments, and add information, continuing the conversation. Encourage your student to continue to contribute to this conversation by doing the same. Record the entire conversation.

4. **Listen to the recording.** Point out how your student stressed particular words to emphasize emotion and important information. Also point out how you used stress during the conversation. Choose particular sentences as examples of the strong use of stress. Choose other sentences where the use of stress could be improved by either choosing different words to stress or a different method by which to stress them.

5. **Homework:** Continue to practice using stress any time you talk to others, whether it be telling a story or a joke, or providing information, whether in an informal conversation or in a formal presentation. Stressing particular words emphasizes emotion and the importance of information and better engages the listener.

Conclusion

In this book we have presented a comprehensive prosody intervention program for high-functioning adolescents and adults with Autism Spectrum Disorders. Predominant expressive prosody deficits in this population are hyper-nasality, dysfluent rhythm, and impaired use and understanding of contrastive stress. Other prosodic issues identified in people with ASD include large pitch excursions, monotone speech, stretched syllables, dropped syllables, rapid rate, low volume, and creaky voice. Unusual vocal quality and impaired prosody compromise communication and social acceptance, presenting significant obstacles for the development of relationships and the ability to obtain employment. Though the generation of models to drive the development of intervention is hampered by the paucity of empirical data regarding prosody development and neural underpinnings, we must still endeavor to intervene.

We have provided a comprehensive set of lessons for addressing hyper-nasality, low or inappropriate volume, and difficulties with the rhythm of speech (including dysfluency, excessively rapid rate, and misarticulation caused by muscle tension associated with each of these), as well as impaired pitch modulation and the use and understanding of stress in speech. We have made the case that emotional and behavioral regulation are a necessary foundation for the development of voice and prosody, since dysregulation interferes significantly with the ability to learn and implement the strategies taught. It disrupts both cognitive processing and muscle relaxation. In doing so, formulation of expressive language and comprehension are negatively impacted. Dysregulation creates tension in the body that can interfere with timbre and volume.

Prosody deficits are resistant to therapeutic intervention and tend to persist into adulthood even when other language issues have abated. Imitation of prosody alone is not a particularly effective intervention technique. Our lessons employ a technique which alerts the individual to bodily sensations, which cue: (1) the anatomic position of the vocal anatomy for creating a particular timbre; (2) effective expansion of the ribcage and release of breath; (3) balanced phonation; and (4) pausing to formulate expressive language. We have taken an approach which makes use of the visual and rote memory strengths possessed by the majority of people with ASD. We have built skills beginning with nonverbal sounds, then single words, followed by sentences, written text, preplanned connected speech, and finally spontaneous speech. The techniques make logical sense given the processing style of high-functioning individuals on the autism spectrum. We have preliminary evidence that fluency and hyper-nasality are significantly improved by these techniques (Dunn and Harris, in preparation). We are encouraged by a promising start, but only time and further investigation will tell.

Very little has been published regarding the efficacy of intervention methods for deficient prosody in individuals with ASD (Lim 2010). This is because there are few intervention methods for prosody in this population. Evidence-based prosody intervention is an essential goal. This curriculum represents an effort to create a comprehensive prosody intervention program based on the current state of the art, such as it is, and will be refined as evidence regarding its efficacy becomes available.

Building a more complete model of prosody will lead the way to better assessment and intervention practices for those with ASD. This will require further investigation into the development and characteristics of typical and impaired prosody in ASD. However, the development of a model is not exclusively dependent on empirical findings concerning the typical development of prosody, neurologic underpinnings, and subtypes of prosody. Model development must be an iterative process. Empirical evaluation of the response to intervention methods is an important part of that process.

References

American Psychiatric Association (2013) *Diagnostic and Statistical Manual of Mental Disorders* (5th edition). Washington, DC: APA.

Baltaxe, C., and Simmons, J. (1992) *High-Functioning Individuals with Autism.* New York: Plenum Press.

Bates, E., and MacWhinney, B. (1979) "A Functionalist Approach to the Acquisition of Grammar." In E. Ochs and B. Schieffelin (eds) *Developmental Pragmatics.* New York: Academic Press.

Bowers, D., Blonder, L.X., and Heilman, K.M. (1999) *The Florida Affect Battery.* Gainesville, FL: University of Florida Brain Institute.

Centers for Disease Control and Prevention (2014, March 14) *Press Release: CDC Estimates 1 in 68 Children has been Identified with Autism Spectrum Disorder.* Available at www.cdc.gov/media/releases/2014/p0327-autism-spectrum-disorder.html, accessed on 17 May 2016.

DePape, A.M.R., Chen, A., Hall, G.B.C., and Trainor, L.J. (2012) "Use of prosody and information structure in high functioning adults with autism in relation to language ability." *Frontiers in Psychology 3,* 72.

Diehl, J.J., and Paul, R. (2009) "The assessment and treatment of prosodic disorders and neurological theories of prosody." *International Journal of Speech and Language Pathology 11,* 4, 287–292.

Diehl, J.J., and Paul, R. (2012) "Acoustic differences in the imitation of prosodic patterns in children with autism spectrum disorders." *Research in Autism Spectrum Disorders 6,* 123–134.

Diehl, J.J., Bennetto, L., Watson, D., Gunlogson, C., and McDonough, J. (2008) "Resolving ambiguity: A psycholinguistic approach to understanding prosody processing in high-functioning autism." *Brain and Language 106,* 2, 144–152.

Diehl, R.L. (2008) "Acoustic and auditory phonetics: The adaptive design of speech sound systems." *Philosophical Transactions of the Royal Society B 63,* 965–978.

Dr. Seuss (Theodor Geisel) (1960) *Green Eggs and Ham.* New York: Random House.

Dr. Seuss (Theodor Geisel) (1965) *Fox in Socks.* New York: Random House.

Dr. Seuss (Theodor Geisel) (1970) *Mr. Brown can Moo! Can You?: Dr. Seuss's Book of Wonderful Noises!* New York: Random House.

Dunn, M., and Harris, L. (in preparation) *When Opera meets Autism: Efficacy of a Prosody Intervention Method for Adolescents and Adults with ASD.*

Dunn, M., Gomes, H., and Gravel, J. (2008) "Mismatch negativity in children with autism and typical controls." *Journal of Autism and Development Disorders* *38*, 1, 52–71.

Dunn, M., Vaughan, H.G. Jr, Kreuzer, J., and Kurtzberg, D. (1999) "Electrophysiologic correlates of semantic classification in autistic and normal children." *Developmental Neuropsychology 16*, 1, 79–99.

Fay, W., and Schuler, A. (1980) *Emerging Language in Autistic Children*. Baltimore, MD: University Park Press.

Gerken, L., and McGregor, K.K. (1998) "An overview of prosody and its role in normal and disordered child language." *American Journal of Speech-Language Pathology 7*, 38–48.

Ghaziuddin, M., and Gerstein, L. (1996) "Pedantic speaking style differentiates Asperger syndrome from high-functioning autism." *Journal of Autism Development and Disorders 26*, 585–595.

Kalathottukaren, R.T., Purdy, S.C., and Ballard, E. (2015) "Behavioral measures to evaluate prosodic skills: A review of assessment tools for children and adults." *Contemporary Issues in Communication Science and Disorders 42*, 138–154.

Kanner, L. (1971) "Follow-up study of eleven autistic children originally reported in 1943." *Journal of Autism and Childhood Schizophrenia 1*, 119–145.

Lim, H.A. (2010) "The effect of 'developmental speech-language training through music' on speech production in children with autism spectrum disorders." *Journal of Music Therapy 47*, 1, 2–28.

Lord, C., Risi, S., Lambrecht, L., Cook, E.H., *et al.* (2000) "The Autism Diagnostic Observation Schedule – Generic: A standard measure of social and communication deficits associated with the spectrum of autism." *Journal of Autism and Developmental Disorders 30*, 3, 205–223.

McCann, J., and Peppé, S. (2003) "Prosody in autism spectrum disorders: A critical review." *International Journal of Language and Communication Disorders 38*, 325–350.

McCann, J., Peppé, S., Gibbon, F.E., O'Hare, A., and Rutherford, M. (2007) "Prosody and its relationship to language in school-aged children with high-functioning autism." *International Journal of Language and Communication Disorders 42*, 6, 682–702.

McPartland, J., and Klin, A. (2006) "Asperger's syndrome." *Adolescent Medical Clinicians 17*, 771–788.

Mesibov, G. (1992) "Treatment Issues with High-Functioning Adolescents and Adults with Autism." In E. Schopler and G. Mesibov (eds) *High-Functioning Individuals with Autism*. New York: Plenum Press.

Minshew, N.J., Johnson, C., and Luna, B. (2001) "The cognitive and neural basis of autism: A disorder of complex information-processing and dysfunction of neocortical systems." *International Review of Research in Mental Retardation 223*, 111–138.

Paul, R., Augustyn, A., Klin, A., and Volkmar, F.R. (2005) "Perception and production of prosody by speakers with autism spectrum disorders." *Journal of Autism and Developmental Disorders 35*, 205–220.

Paul, R., Bianchi, N., Augustyn, A., Klin, A., and Volkmar, F.R. (2008) "Production of syllable stress in speakers with autism spectrum disorders." *Research in Autism Spectrum Disorders 2*, 1, 110–124.

Paul, R., Shriberg, L., McSweeney, J., Cicchetti, D., Klin, A., and Volkmar, F.R. (2005) "Brief report: Relations between prosodic performance and communication and socialization ratings in high functioning speakers with autism spectrum disorders." *Journal of Autism and Developmental Disorders 35*, 861–869.

Pearson (2009) *Advanced Clinical Solutions for WAIS–IV and WMS–IV.* San Antonio, TX: Pearson.

Peppé, S., and McCann, J. (2003) "Assessing intonation and prosody in children with atypical language development: The PEPS–C test and the revised version." *Clinical Linguistics and Phonetics 17*, 345–354.

Peppé, S., McCann, J., Gibbon, F., O'Hare, A., and Rutherford, M. (2006) "Assessing prosodic and pragmatic ability in children with high-functioning autism." *Journal of Pragmatics 38*, 1776–1792.

Peppé, S., McCann, J., Gibbon, F., O'Hare, A., and Rutherford, M. (2007) "Receptive and expressive prosodic ability in children with high-functioning autism." *Journal of Speech, Language and Hearing Research 50*, 4, 1015–1028.

Provonost, W., Wakstein, M., and Wakstein, D. (1966) "A longitudinal study of speech behavior and language comprehension in fourteen children diagnosed as atypical or autistic." *Exceptional Children 33*, 19–26.

Rapin, I., and Dunn, M. (2003) "Update on the language disorders of individuals on the autistic spectrum." *Brain and Development 25*, 3, 166–172.

Rothstein, J.A. (2013) *Prosody Treatment Program.* Austin, TX: Pro-Ed.

Scott, D.W. (1985) "Asperger's syndrome and non-verbal communication: A pilot study." *Psychological Medicine 15*, 683–687.

Shriberg, L., and Widder, C.J. (1990) "Speech and prosody characteristics of adults with mental retardation." *Journal of Speech and Hearing Research 33*, 627–653.

Shriberg, L., Kwiatkowski, J., and Rasmussen, C. (1990) *The Prosody-Voice Screening Profile.* Tucson, AZ: Communication Skill Builders.

Shriberg, L., Paul, R., McSweeney, J., Klin, A., Cohen, D., and Volkmar, F.R. (2001) "Speech and prosody characteristics of adolescents and adults with high functioning autism and Asperger syndrome." *Journal of Speech, Language and Hearing Research 44*, 1097–1115.

Simmons, J., and Baltaxe, C. (1975) "Language patterns in adolescent autistics." *Journal of Autism and Childhood Schizophrenia 5*, 333–351.

Sparrow, S., Balla, D., and Cicchetti, D. (1984) *The Vineland Adaptive Behavior Scales (Survey Form).* Circle Pines, MN: American Guidance Service.

Strand, E.A., Stoeckel, R., and Baas, B. (2006) "Treatment of severe childhood apraxia of speech: A treatment efficacy study." *Journal of Medical Speech – Language Pathology 14*, 297–307.

Tager-Flusberg, H. (1981) "On the nature of linguistic functioning in early infantile autism." *Journal of Autism Development and Disorders 11*, 45–56.

Tager-Flusberg, H. (2001) "Understanding the language and communicative impairments in autism." *International Review of Research on Mental Retardation* *23*, 185–205.

Van Bourgondien, M.E., and Woods, A. (1992) "Vocational Possibilities for High-Functioning Adults with Autism." In E. Schopler and G. Mesibov (eds) *High-Functioning Individuals with Autism.* New York: Plenum Press.

Warren, P. (1996) "Prosody and parsing: An introduction." *Language and Cognitive Processes* 11, 1–16.

Wiklund, M. (2016) "Interactional challenges in conversations with autistic preadolescents: The role of prosody and non-verbal communication in other-initiated repairs." *Journal of Pragmatics 94*, 76–97.

Subject Index

Achieving fluency in spontaneously
  generated small talk (lesson) 333–6
Advanced Clinical Solutions (ACS) 28
anatomic gate 78–9, 81
Applying pitch notation to spontaneous
  speech (lesson) 379
Applying the Rules for Fluency to
  spontaneous conversation (lesson)
  351–2
assessment
  availability of tools for 26–9
  checklist for 29–33
  of fluency 261–3
  future of 29
  of pitch 32, 355–8
  of volume 153–61
Assessment/learning pitch modulation
  (lesson) 355–8
Autism Diagnostic Observational Scale –
  G (ADOS-G) 17
Autism Spectrum Disorder (ASD)
  forms of deficits in prosody 14–16
  prevalence of impaired prosody 13

B (letter)
  oral timbre lessons for 106–14
behavioral modulation
  goals of 35
  importance of 34–5
  lessons for 36–62
Breath control associated with the Breath–
  Pause technique (lesson) 274–5
Breath-Pause technique 22–3, 149, 193
  lessons for volume 210–35, 245–57
  lessons for rhythm 264–92, 293–350
  and rhythm 258–9

breath release
  lessons for 204–35
breath support
  for increasing volume 149, 193
  lessons for 194–203
Breath support: Optimal expansion and
  maintaining expansion (lesson)
  198–203
Breath support: Posture and expansion
  (lesson) 194–7

calmness
  importance of 34–5
  lessons for 36–57
ch (consonant)
  oral timbre lessons for 123–31
Communicating emotions and the need
  for help
communication
  links with prosody deficits 16–17
connected speech
  oral timbre lessons for 144–6
  rhythm lessons for 276–9
consonants
  nasal timbre lessons for 183–4
  oral timbre lessons for 89–91, 95–140

D (letter)
  oral timbre lessons for 106–14
dynamic temporal and tactile cuing
  (DTTC) 18

emotional modulation
  goals of 35
  importance of 34–5
  lessons for 36–62

Florida Affect Battery (FAB) 28–9
fluency
    assessment of 261–3
    lessons for 264–352
    and rhythm 258–60
Fluently relating information and making
a point about something you learned
(lesson) 343–50
Fox in Socks (Dr. Seuss) 92, 93

G (letter)
    oral timbre lessons for 106–14
grammatical stress 15, 17, 23–4, 383
    lessons for 363–4, 389–90
Grammatical stress in single words (lesson)
    389–91
Graphic Organizer: Formulating a
    description of a person (lesson)
    297–301
Graphic Organizer: Using a book,
    periodical, or article (lesson) 302–6
Green Eggs and Ham (Dr. Seuss) 141

Having a calm baseline: Mindfulness
    of breathing and internal triggers
    (lesson) 42–6
How calming positively influences fluency
    and rate of speech (lesson) 280–1

Importance of being calm, The:
    Understanding the consequences for
    your thinking (lesson) 54–6
interventions in prosody 17–18
Introducing the Breath–Pause technique
    for improving fluency and rate
    (lesson) 264–73
Introduction to stress in spoken language
    (lesson) 386–8

J (letter)
    oral timbre lessons for 123–31

K (letter)
    oral timbre lessons for 97–105

L (letter)
    oral timbre lessons for 132–40
Learning about timbre (lesson) 68–76
Learning to play the Conversation Game
    to develop fluency in conversation
    (lesson) 330–2
Learning the red card technique to
    monitor use of the Rules for Fluency
    (lesson) 341–2
lessons
    behavioral modulation 36–62
    calmness 36–57
    emotional modulation 36–62
    fleuncy 264–352
    mindfulness 47–53
    pitch 355–82
    rhythm 264–352
    stress 386–441
    structure of 24–5
    timbre 68–146
    volume 163–257
loudness
    assessment for 31

M (letter)
    oral timbre lessons for 115–22
Maintaining calm through mindfulness of
    emotions, thoughts, and behaviors
    (lesson) 47–53
mindfulness
    lessons for 42–6, 47–53
Modulating breath release: Learn the
    Breath–Pause notation to practice
    management of breath release (lesson)
    227–32
Modulating breath release: Learning the
    relationship between the speed of
    airflow and volume (lesson) 204–6
Modulating breath release: Maintaining an
    expanded chest (lesson) 207–9
Modulating breath release: Regulating the
    volume of sustained sounds (lesson)
    213–18
Modulating breath release: Using the
    Breath–Pause technique and arc
    phrasing to increase volume in
    spontaneous connected speech
    (lesson) 233–5

Modulating breath release: Using the vocal cords as a valve (lesson) 210–12

Modulating release and increasing volume: Combining the Breath–Pause technique with nasal timbre (lesson) 219–23

Modulation of volume: Adjusting to situation (lesson) 253–7

Mr. Brown can Moo! Can You? (Dr. Seuss) 92, 93

N (letter)
  oral timbre lessons for 115–222
nasal timbre
  to increase volume 148, 162
  lessons for 68–76, 163–93
Nasal timbre: Introduction to discrimination, production, and anatomy (lesson) 163–71
Nasal timbre: Learning the sensations associated with directing airflow and sound through the nasal pharynx: "ah," "uh," and "awh" (lesson) 185–8
Nasal timbre: Learning the sensations associated with directing airflow and sound through the nasal pharynx: "oh," "ow," and "ooh" (lesson) 189–92
Nasal timbre: Tongue position – nasal and oral vowels (lesson) 177–82
Nasal timbre: Tongue position for vowels (lesson) 172–6
Nasal timbre: Tongue position for vowels, consonants, and words (lesson) 183–4
nasality
  assessment for 31

Open passage: Releasing tension in the jaw (lesson) 236–8
Open passage: Releasing tension in the jaw and tongue (lesson) 239–43
oral timbre
  lessons for 68–76, 77–146
Oral timbre: Connected speech 1 (lesson) 144–5
Oral timbre: Connected speech 2 (lesson) 146

Oral timbre: Consonants B, D, and G in consonant–vowel syllables and words (lesson) 106–8
Oral timbre: Consonants B, D, and G in pre-formulated sentences (lesson) 109–13
Oral timbre: Consonants B, D, and G in spontaneously formulated sentences (lesson) 114
Oral timbre: Consonants J and ch in consonant–vowel syllables and words (lesson) 123–5
Oral timbre: Consonants J and ch in pre-formulated sentences (lesson) 126–30
Oral timbre: Consonants M and N in consonant–vowel syllables and words (lesson) 115–17
Oral timbre: Consonants M and N in pre-formulated sentences (lesson) 118–21
Oral timbre: Consonants M and N in spontaneously formulated sentences (lesson) 122
Oral timbre: Consonants P, T, and K in consonant–vowel syllables and words (lesson) 97–9
Oral timbre: Consonants P, T, and K in spontaneously formulated sentences (lesson) 105
Oral timbre: Consonants W, L, and R in consonant–vowel syllables and words (lesson) 132–4
Oral timbre: Consonants W, L, and R in pre-formulated sentences (lesson) 135–9
Oral timbre: Consonants W, L, and R in spontaneously formulated sentences (lesson) 140
Oral timbre: Consonants in spontaneous speech (lesson) 95–6
Oral timbre: Persistent problems (lesson) 141–3
Oral timbre: Tongue position – vowels 1 (lesson) 77–82
Oral timbre: Tongue position – vowels 2 (lesson) 83–8
Oral timbre: Tongue position, vowels, consonants, and words (lesson) 89–91
Oral timbre: Words and pre-formulated sentences (lesson) 92–4

P (letter)
  oral timbre lessons for 97–105
Personal Story Graphic Organizer
  in emotional and behavioral modulation
    lessons 37
phrasing
  impairments in 15
pitch
  assessment for 32, 355–8
  as category of prosody 14
  lessons for 355–82
  and meaning 353–4
Pitch modulation: Tones (lesson) 359–62
Pitch stress in poetry 1 (lesson) 369–71
Pitch stress in poetry 2 (lesson) 372–3
Pitch stress in narrative (lesson) 374–6
Pitch stress in sentences (lesson) 365–8
Pitch stress and word meaning (lesson)
    363–4
Pitch stress in written text (lesson) 377–8
Planned discussion of a topic from
    memory, using all stress forms to
    inform and share feelings (lesson)
    435
Plot Contour Graphic Organizer: Telling a
    good story (lesson) 319–21
PowerPoint presentation to inform: Part
    1 – Deciding what to include (lesson)
    436–8
PowerPoint presentation to inform: Part
    2 – Deciding what to stress (lesson)
    439–40
pragmatic stress 15, 17, 19, 23–4, 383
Profiling Elements of Prosodic Systems –
    Children (PEPS–C) 27–8
prosody
  categories of 13–14
  checklist for deficit 29–33
  deficit link to communication and
    socialization 16–17
  deficits in people with ASD 14–16
  description of 13
  interventions in 17–18
  prevalence of impaired 13
Prosody Treatment Program (Rothstein)
    18
Prosody Voice Screening Profile (PVSP)
    16, 27–8

Putting it all together: Sound production
    with an open passage, in combination
    with nasal timbre and appropriate
    breath support 1 (lesson) 245–8
Putting it all together: Sound production
    with an open passage, in combination
    with nasal timbre and appropriate
    breath support 2 (lesson) 249–52

R (letter)
  oral timbre lessons for 132–40
rate of speech
  lessons for 264–352
  and rhythm 258–0
Regulating breath release: Mindfulness of
    sensations associated with Breath–
    Pause (lesson) 224–6
resonance
  impairments in 14
rhythm
  assessment for 32
  as category of prosody 14
  and fluency 258–60
  lessons for 264–352
  stress lessons for 414–19
Rules for answering others' questions
    about you (lesson) 293–6

Self-calming (lesson) 36–41
sentences, pre-formulated
  oral timbre lessons for 92–4, 100–4,
    109–13, 118–21, 126–30, 135–9
  stress lessons for 392–419
sentences, spontaneously formulated
  fluency lessons for 286–8
  oral timbre lessons for 105, 114, 122,
    131, 140
  stress lessons for 392–419
Sequential Graphic Organizer: Giving
    step-by-step instructions 1 (lesson)
    307–9
Sequential Graphic Organizer: Giving
    step-by-step instructions 2 (lesson)
    310–12
Shadow Vowel technique: Addressing
    misarticulation produced by muscle
    tension resulting from overly rapid
    speech or anxiety/overexcitement
    (lesson) 289–92

socialization
    links with prosody deficits 16–17
source-filter model 65, 147
speech, spontaneous
    oral timbre lessons for 95–6
    pitch lessons for 379
    rhythm lessons for 351–2
    stress lessons for 441
Spontaneous speech in conversation,
    employing word stress to inform and
    share feelings (lesson) 441
Staying calm and mindful to promote
    effective fluency through the Breath–
    Pause technique (lesson) 282–3
stress
    assessment for 33
    grammatical 15, 17, 23–4, 363–4, 383,
        389–90
    impairments in 14
    lessons for 386–441
    and meaning 383–5
    pitch lessons for 363–78
    pragmatic 15, 17, 19, 23–4, 383
Stress notation on a famous speech to
    inform and share feelings (lesson)
    422–4
Stressing words in poetry to inform and
    share feelings (lesson) 420–1
Stressing words in sentences (lesson)
    392–400
Stressing words in sentences with a change
    in pitch (lesson) 407–13
Stressing words in sentences with a change
    in rhythm, specifically an increase in
    duration (lesson) 414–19
Stressing words in sentences with a louder
    volume, using volume stress notation
    (lesson) 401–6
syllables, consonant-vowel
    oral timbre lessons for 97–9, 106–8,
        115–17, 123–5, 132–4

T (letter)
    oral timbre lessons for 97–105
Talking about a topic, using appropriate
    stress (lesson) 432–4
Talking about a topic using pitch
    inflection (lesson) 380–2

Telling a personal experience story,
    placing stress on important words
    (lesson) 428–31
Telling a story from memory, applying all
    types of stress: Volume, pitch, rhythm
    (duration) (lesson) 425–7
timbre
    balanced-mix 63–7
    as category of prosody 13–14
    exercises for 66–7
    hyper-nasal voice 64–7
    lessons for 68–146
    source-filter model 65
tongue position
    nasal timbre lessons for 172–84

Using the Breath–Pause technique to
    speak spontaneous sentences fluently
    and at an appropriate rate (lesson)
    286–8
Using the Breath–Pause technique with
    spontaneous questions and sentences
    (lesson) 284–5
Using the Breath–Pause technique with
    spontaneous single words and pre-
    formulated connected speech (lesson)
    276–9
Using small talk to get to know someone
    (lesson) 337–40

Vineland Socialization score 16, 17
volume
    assessment for 153–61
    breath support for 149, 193
    as category of prosody 14
    introduction to increasing 147–8
    lessons for 163–257
    nasal timbre for 148, 162
    open passage for 150
    rules for increasing 150–2
    stress lessons for 401–6
vowel-consonant combinations
    oral timbre lessons for 141–3
vowels
    nasal timbre lessons for 172–84
    oral timbre lessons for 77–91, 106–8,
        115–17

W (letter)
oral timbre lessons for 132–40
Web Graphic Organizer: Description of a
vacation (lesson) 316–18
Web Graphic Organizer: My best day ever
(lesson) 313–15
Web Graphic Organizer: Recounting a
fable and its significance (lesson)
326–9

Web Graphic Organizer: Recounting what
I learned from an article (lesson)
322–5
words
nasal timbre lessons for 183–4
oral timbre lessons for 89–94, 97–9,
115–17, 123–5, 132–4
rhythm lessons for 276–9
stress lessons for 389–91, 428–31

Author Index

Aesop 328
American Psychiatric Association 13
Augustyn, A. 15, 16

Baas, B. 18
Balla, D. 17
Ballard, E. 27
Baltaxe, C. 13
Bates, E. 15
Begg, C. 304
Begg, K. 304
Blonder, L.X. 28
Bowers, D. 28

Cartright, M. 305
Centers for Disease Control and
     Prevention (CDC) 13
Cicchetti, D. 17
Clinton, H.R. 378

DePape, A.M.R. 17
Diehl, J.J. 13, 15, 17, 65, 147
Dr. Suess 92, 93, 141
Dunn, M. 18

Fay, W. 13

Gates, S. 324
Gerken, L. 15
Gerstein, L. 13
Ghaziuddin, M. 13
Gomes, H. 18
Gravel, J. 18

Hanson, H. 347
Harris, L. 18
Heilman, K.M. 28

Johnson, C. 18

Luna, B. 18

Kalathottukaren, R.T. 27
Kanner, L. 13
Klin, A. 13
Kwiatkowski, J. 16

Li, Z. 345
Lord, C. 17

MacWhinney, B. 15
McCann, J. 13, 16, 24, 27
McGregor, K.K. 15
McPartland, J. 13
Mesibov, G. 13
Minshew, N.J. 18

Paul, R. 15, 16, 17
Pearson 28
Peppé, S. 13, 24, 27
Provonost, W. 13
Purdy, S.C. 27

Rapin, I. 18
Rasmussen, C. 16
Rothstein, J.A. 18

Schuler, A. 13
Scott, D.W. 13
Shriberg, L. 13, 14, 15, 16, 17, 27
Simmons, J. 13
Sparrow, S. 17
Stoeckel, R. 18
Strand, E.A. 18

Tager-Flusberg, H. 13

Van Bourgondien, M.E. 13

Wakstein, D. 13
Wakstein, M. 13
Warren, P. 15, 383
Widder, C.J. 17
Wiklund, M. 14
Woods, A. 13

Building Language Using LEGO® Bricks
A Practical Guide
Dawn Ralph and Jacqui Rochester

Paperback: £16.99 / $27.95
ISBN: 978 1 78592 0 615
eISBN: 978 1 78450 317 8
152 pages

Building Language using LEGO® Bricks is a flexible and powerful intervention tool designed to aid children with severe receptive and expressive language disorders, often related to autism and other special educational needs.

This practical manual equips you for setting up and adapting your own successful sessions. Downloadable resources enable you to chart progress in the following key areas:

- The use of receptive and expressive language
- The use and understanding of challenging concepts
- Joint attention
- Social communication

Help children with complex needs to communicate with this unique tool, derived from the highly effective LEGO®-Based Therapy.

Dawn Ralph gained her Speech Pathology & Therapy degree from Queen Margaret University, Edinburgh in 1985 and has worked as a paediatric speech and language therapist ever since. She has worked in a variety of settings from a paediatric brain injury unit to both specialist and mainstream schools. **Jacqui Rochester** has been working with SEN children for over sixteen years. In 2014 she gained her Bachelor of Philosophy in Special Education: Autism (Children) from the University of Birmingham's Autism Centre for Education and Research. Both Dawn and Jacqui run Building Language using LEGO® Bricks workshops for schools and training for professionals.

Developmental Speech-Language Training through Music for Children with Autism Spectrum Disorders
Theory and Clinical Application
Hayoung A. Lim

Paperback: £23.99 / $36.95
ISBN: 978 1 84905 849 0
eISBN: 978 0 85700 415 4
208 pages

Speech and language impairments are one of the most challenging features of Autism Spectrum Disorders (ASD). Children with ASD are also known to be particularly responsive to music. This book makes a valuable connection between the two traits to showcase music as an effective way of enhancing the speech and language skills of children with ASD.

This is a comprehensive guide to Dr. Hayoung Lim's highly effective approach of using music in speech-language training for children ASD. Part I provides a sound theoretical foundation and employs the most up-to-date research, including the author's own extensive study, to validate the use of music in speech and language training for children with ASD. Part II analyzes the clinical implications of "Developmental Speech- Language Training through Music" (DSLM) protocols and explains in detail specific interventions that can be used with the approach. The practical application of DSLM to Applied Behavior Analysis (ABA) Verbal Behavior (VB) approaches is also explored.

This is essential reading for music therapists, speech and language pathologists and other professionals working with children with autism, as well as researchers and academics in the field.

Dr. Hayoung Lim is Assistant Professor of Music Therapy and Director of Graduate Studies in Music Therapy at Sam Houston State University, Texas. She has a PhD in music education with an emphasis on music therapy, from the University of Miami, Florida. She has worked as a music therapist in a number of hospitals, schools and organizations with a diverse range of clients including individuals with mental illnesses, developmental disorders, medical problems, neurologic impairments and dementia. Her research focuses on the effect of music on children with ASD and the effect of musical experiences on cognition, speech and language, and physical rehabilitation. She is also a concert cellist and lives in The Woodlands, Texas with her husband and son.

Speech in Action
Interactive Activities Combining Speech Language Pathology and Adaptive Physical Education
America X Gonzalez, Lois Jean Brady and Jim Elliott

Paperback: £21.99 / $36.95
ISBN: 978 1 84905 846 9
eISBN: 978 0 85700 500 7
160 pages

Children, particularly those on the autism spectrum, are able to acquire communication skills much more easily when their learning incorporates movement. Even very simple actions such as tapping and hand clapping can have a noticeable impact on their speech and language development.

Speech in Action is an innovative approach to learning that combines simple techniques from speech and language pathology with physical exercises that have been carefully designed to meet the individual child's particular needs and abilities. This practical workbook describes the approach, and how it works, and contains 90 fully-photocopiable lesson plans packed with fun and creative ideas for getting both mouth and body moving. Suitable for use either at school or at home, the activities can be dipped into in any order, and are organised by level of ability, with something for everyone. The final chapter contains the success stories of children the authors have used the activities with, demonstrating how the approach can be used in practice.

This will be a useful resource for teachers, occupational therapists, and other professionals who work with children with delayed communication skills, as well as parents and carers who would like to support their child's speech and language development at home.

America X. Gonzalez is a Speech Language Pathologist Assistant who works at various institutions in the San Francisco Bay Area. She has an Associate Teacher degree and a Bachelor's degree in Psychology. She lives in Benicia, California. **Lois Jean Brady** is a Speech Language Pathologist with 20 years' experience. She has a Master's degree in Speech Language Pathology, a Certificate in Assistive Technology and has completed an Animal Assisted Therapy program. **Jim Elliott** is an Adapted Physical Educator. For the past five years, America, Lois and Jim have worked together at Spectrum Center San Paolo, a private school for children with autism, Asperger Syndrome and severe emotional distress in Sao Paolo, California.

Helping Adults with Asperger's Syndrome Get & Stay Hired

Career Coaching Strategies for Professionals and Parents of Adults on the Autism Spectrum
Barbara Bissonnette

Paperback: £15.99 / $24.95
ISBN: 978 1 84905 754 7
eISBN: 978 1 78450 052 8
232 pages

Employment expert Barbara Bissonnette provides strategies that professionals and parents need to guide individuals with Asperger's Syndrome (Autism Spectrum Disorder) to manageable jobs, and keep them employed.

Career counselors and coaches, vocational rehabilitation specialists, other professionals, and parents are often unsure of how to assist people with Asperger's Syndrome. Traditional career assessments and protocols do not match their unique needs. In this practical book, readers will gain insight into how people with Asperger's Syndrome think and the common employment challenges they face. It explains how to build rapport and trust, facilitate better job matches, improve interpersonal communication and executive function skills, and encourage flexible-thinking and problem-solving.

With tried-and-tested advice, assessment tools, and in-depth profiles of actual coaching clients and innovative companies that are utilizing the specialized skills of people with Asperger's, this book shows the way to a brighter employment future for those on the autism spectrum.

Barbara Bissonnette is a certified coach and the Principal of Forward Motion Coaching. She specializes in career development coaching for adults with Asperger's Syndrome and Non-Verbal Learning Disorder. She also provides training and consultation to employers. Prior to this, Barbara spent more than 20 years in business, most recently as Vice President of Marketing and Sales for an information services firm. She holds a graduate certificate in executive coaching from the Massachusetts School of Professional Psychology and is certified by the Institute for Professional Excellence in Coaching (iPEC). Barbara is the author of The Complete Guide to Getting a Job for People with Asperger's Syndrome and Asperger's Syndrome Workplace Survival Guide, also published by Jessica Kingsley Publishers. She lives in Stow, Massachusetts.

Michelle Dunn, Ph.D. is Director of the Montefiore Autism Center for Autism and Communication Disorders and Professor of Clinical Neurology at the Albert Einstein College of Medicine. Michelle is the author of *S.O.S.: Social Skills in our Schools: A Social Skills program for children with Pervasive Developmental Disorders and their typical peers.*

Larry Harris, M.S. is a former NFL American Football player turned opera singer. He is a psychologist, vocal coach and research assistant at the Montefiore Einstein Center for Autism and Communication Disorders. Larry uses his experience in both sport and music to help young people understand the mechanics of their voices.